# THE HISTORY OF
# CENTRAL AND
# EASTERN AFRICA

# THE HISTORY OF
# CENTRAL AND
# EASTERN AFRICA

EDITED BY AMY McKENNA, SENIOR EDITOR, GEOGRAPHY AND HISTORY

Britannica®
Educational Publishing

IN ASSOCIATION WITH

ROSEN
EDUCATIONAL SERVICES

Published in 2011 by Britannica Educational Publishing
(a trademark of Encyclopædia Britannica, Inc.)
in association with Rosen Educational Services, LLC
29 East 21st Street, New York, NY 10010.

Distributed exclusively by Rosen Educational Services.
For a listing of additional Britannica Educational Publishing titles, call toll free (800) 237-9932.

First Edition

Britannica Educational Publishing
**Michael I. Levy: Executive Editor**
Marilyn L. Barton: Senior Coordinator, Production Control
Steven Bosco: Director, Editorial Technologies
Lisa S. Braucher: Senior Producer and Data Editor
Yvette Charboneau: Senior Copy Editor
Kathy Nakamura: Manager, Media Acquisition
Amy McKenna, Senior Editor, Geography and History

Rosen Educational Services
Heather M. Moore Niver: Editor
Nelson Sá: Art Director
Cindy Reiman: Photography Manager
Matthew Cauli: Designer, Cover Design
Introduction by Sean Price

**Library of Congress Cataloging-in-Publication Data**

The history of Central and Eastern Africa / edited by Amy McKenna. — 1st ed.
    p. cm. — (The Britannica guide to Africa)
"In association with Britannica Educational Publishing, Rosen Educational Services."
Includes bibliographical references and index.
ISBN 978-1-61530-322-9 (library binding)
1. Africa, Central—History. 2. Africa, Eastern—History. I. McKenna, Amy, 1969-
DT351.H57 2011
967—dc22

                                                                          2010024034

*Manufactured in the United States of America*

**On the cover:** A Tanzanian Maasai warrior. Many multiethnic Africans blend sundry
traditions and customs that create a fertile cultural legacy. © *www.istockphoto.com/Brian
Raisbeck*

**On pages 1, 24, 31, 39, 53, 59, 65, 72, 76, 105, 110, 119, 140, 154, 167, 181:** Acacia trees heavily
pepper eastern Africa's savannas. *Martin Harvey/Getty Images*

# CONTENTS

3

29

33

117

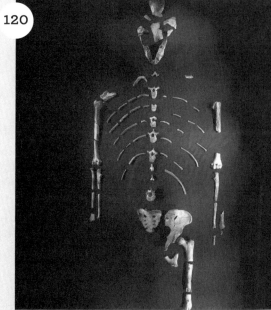

120

123

169

180

189

INTRODUCTION

The story of Central Africa begins with the Congo River. This mighty waterway originates in the highlands of northeastern Zambia between Lakes Tanganyika and Nyasa and snakes through dense equatorial rainforest surrounded by other forests and patches of savanna. Mangrove thickets line the banks of the estuaries, lagoons, and deltas in the region.

To the east of the Congo basin is East Africa's Olduvai Gorge in modern Tanzania, also known as the "Cradle of Mankind" for the fossil remains of more than 60 hominins (members of human lineage) discovered there. The longest uninterrupted known record of human evolution, it spans more than 2 million years. The Olduvai Gorge area has also yielded the longest known archaeological record of the development of stone-tool industries.

The oldest population of Central Africa is known primarily through tools, such as hand axes, which gradually became more sophisticated. Early humans of Central Africa were probably never organized into more than small, scattered bands of nomadic hunters and gatherers. But about 10,000 years ago, as hunters began to settle beside the rivers and hone their fishing skills and gatherers discovered they could sow wild grains in the fertile lakeside soils, the northern border of Central Africa emerged as one of the first food-producing regions of the world. This agricultural revolution created a more settled lifestyle, which in turn led to trade and intermarriage among different peoples. New languages, known as Bantu, spread throughout the region.

Around 3,000 years ago, about when Europe began using iron tools and weapons, so, too, did the Iron Age begin in Central Africa. The new iron implements were so superior to the previously used wood and stone objects that iron masters were bestowed a nearly religious reverence. Although iron was highly valued, copper was treasured. The shiny metal could be turned into jewelry, the inlays of knife handles, and other beautiful objects. The three main zones of copper working in Central Africa were the Nile watershed, the eastern savanna, and the southwestern forest. These sites were thousands of miles from one another, and demand for the metal stimulated trade in the region. The regional demand for copper remained especially strong through the 1st millennium CE and beyond. By the end of the 16th century, trade had extended into Europe. In addition to copper, Central African trade was also stimulated by production and exchange of huge amounts of salt, textiles, and dried fish.

Another type of trade—that of human beings—deeply scarred the region. In the 15th century, Central Africa was exposed to Islamic traders via the Mediterranean Sea and Christian traders via the Atlantic

*Ruins of Husuni Kubwa, a palace built c. 13th century on the island of Kilwa, off the coast of what is now southern Tanzania.* Ariadne Van Zandbergen/Lonely Planet Images/Getty Images

Ocean, the latter having the most impact on the region. Portuguese traders from the Atlantic were experimenting with colonial plantations that needed slaves, and the island of São Tomé became the first centre for the great Atlantic slave trade. Slaves originally from Central Africa went to three main destinations: some worked locally, others went to the gold mines of Africa's Gold Coast, and still others were shipped to Europe—and later to the Americas. Portuguese slavers were later joined by the Dutch and then the French. This hemorrhaging of people was so extreme that the population of Central Africa did not recover until the about the mid-20th century.

The arrival of the Dutch had created new trading opportunities for elephant ivory. The scramble for ivory intensified by the mid-19th century thanks to the growing prosperity in both North America and Europe. People wanted ivory for everything from piano keys to billiard balls. As with the slave trade, the ivory trade disrupted life for people in Central Africa. Traders like the Swahili merchant-prince Tippu Tib used brutal methods such as kidnapping and murder to obtain ivory, and European overlords soon mimicked these cruel practices.

It was rubber that financed the complete takeover of Central Africa by European powers, however, launching the era of colonialism. The pioneer colonizer was Belgian King Leopold II, who established the Congo Free State in the heart of Central Africa during the 1880s. His reign was vicious. Adults and children alike experienced beatings, lashings, and even amputations when they did not meet their rubber-gathering quotas. Leopold was soon joined by the French in the northern and western parts of the region, and by the Germans in the east. Like the Belgians, these European powers were after African's known natural resources, which also included timber, copper, gold, and diamonds. Although other colonial powers were critical of Leopold's brutal rule, they allowed similar methods of forced labour to make their colonies profitable.

Naturally, European powers left their religious mark as well. Missionary churches provided services previously ignored by colonizing governments, such as health care. Albert Schweitzer, a physician and theologian, established a hospital in a French colony. British Baptists brought Protestantism to the region as they set up a bare-bones system of human services, including education, communications, and health care, and Roman Catholics established a university. These services and institutions would remain the region's primary welfare options, particularly in remote areas, until well after the colonial era ended abruptly in 1960.

Rising black nationalism in western Africa during the 1950s convinced France and Belgium to give up their Central African colonies in the early 1960s, but Portugal did not grant independence to São Tomé and Principe until 1975. Although independence was welcomed, it did not necessarily bring peace or prosperity to the countries whose borders and societies were shaped by colonial rule.

Eastern Africa, comprising the areas of East Africa and the Horn of Africa, is a region in sub-Saharan Africa along the Indian Ocean and stretches from modern Eritrea in the north to Tanzania in the south (and includes landlocked Uganda and Ethiopia). More than 160 different ethnic groups inhabit this mostly tropical region. Rainfall and temperatures vary, however, particularly by elevation: the higher areas of Uganda, Tanzania, and western Kenya receive plentiful rainfall, while the lower areas of Somalia, eastern Ethiopia, and northeastern Kenya receive far less. The Oromo are largest of the ethnic groups, occupying much of southern Ethiopia and part of Kenya. Further south, the ethnic picture is much more elusive with ethnic groups that are much smaller, intermingled, and split among different territories.

As previously mentioned, the region, home to the "Cradle of Mankind," has a long history. More recent history begins around 700 CE, when Muslim Arabs began trading along the East African coast, part of which they called Azania, and its offshore islands. Africans exported rhinoceros horns, tortoiseshell, ivory, and coconut oil to the Arabs in exchange for such items as metal weapons and iron tools. Later, they also imported Islamic pottery and Chinese porcelain. Ruins along the Tanzanian coast suggest some extensive pre-Muslim settlements in the area.

Mogadishu, on the Horn of Africa in modern Somalia, was the most important coastal city during much of the 13th century. New migrants arrived there, including those known as the Shirazi, who had set up an empire that eventually took over Mogadishu and its profitable gold trade. They also created settlements up and down the East African coast. During the 15th century, the Shirazi ruled at cities like Malindi and Mombasa, and islands like Kilwa, Zanzibar, and Pemba. Most city-states were intensely independent.

In 1498 vast changes occurred with the arrival of Portuguese ships led by Vasco da Gama. Portuguese military power quickly overwhelmed the divided and poorly defended coastal city-states. Within eight years, the Portuguese dominated the East African coast and its lucrative trade routes to India, cementing its power in 1589 with the sack of Mombasa. Far more interested in trade than building empires, the Portuguese used their control of Mombasa to export African ivory, gold, ambergris, and coral for ironware, weapons, beads, jewelry, cotton, and silks. Individual Portuguese traders fostered strong bonds with Swahili-speaking people on the coast.

Portuguese rule in East Africa eventually came to an end. Although they were not threatened by local rebellions, they were by foreign invaders. Persian and then Omani forces had launched attacks on Portuguese holdings elsewhere, and in the 1650s, the Omanis turned their attention to East Africa. By the early 1700s, the Portuguese were driven from the region, and their attempts to regain power were either unsuccessful or short-lived.

The slave trade began to flourish in East Africa from about 1776 on, spurred by demand from the French. The demand for slaves became more widespread with the discovery that cloves could be grown on expanding plantations on the islands of Zanzibar and Pemba. British pressure closed down some of the slave trade, but it made little difference. By 1856 Zanzibar was firmly established as the East African coast's main trading centre.

Meanwhile, the interior of East Africa developed much differently than the coastal areas. Without written records before 200 years ago, most of the region's history has been deduced from linguistic, cultural, and anthropological clues as well as oral histories and archaeological findings. As in Central Africa, early East Africans were hunter-gatherers who settled into fishing and farming communities during the agricultural revolution. Much is unclear, however, such as when iron smelting spread to East Africa.

Sometime before 1500 CE, the Chwezi dynasty established a short-lived rule over part of the area, which is associated with several great earthwork sites in modern western Uganda, including a religious centre in Mubende. Although the 1500s saw the Chwezi dynasty supplanted by other rulers and kingdoms—some of which persisted into the 20th century— their religious movements lived on. Meanwhile, slaving activity in the East African interior began, fueled by the

trade along the coastal areas. By the 1860s at least 7,000 slaves were being sold each year at Zanzibar's slave market. Although a treaty with the British in 1873 ceased this commerce, there was a final period of slave trading on the mainland, where the demand for porters and the ivory trade sustained the sale of slaves.

By this time interest in East Africa grew among Europeans thanks in part to the efforts of explorers like David Livingstone, Richard Burton, and John Hanning Speke to find the source of the Nile. As in other parts of Africa, ambitious Christian missionaries also arrived, and by 1885 there were almost 300 in the region. Eager evangelists were soon joined by businessmen and imperial rulers as well. Also in 1885 Germany granted the German East Africa Company a charter to do business in Africa, part of the "scramble for Africa," in which European colonial powers sought to stake their claims across the vast continent. Soon, most of East Africa was divided between the British and Germans. The Germans would lose control of their colonies after their defeat in World War I, but the British maintained control of the region until the early 1960s, when the countries of Tanganyika and Zanzibar (both now part of modern Tanzania), Kenya, and Uganda gained independence.

Much of the recorded history of the Horn of Africa is essentially that of Ethiopia, one of the world's oldest countries. Inhabited from earliest antiquity and once under ancient Egyptian rule, the area was home to the powerful state of Aksum that flourished in the 1st millennium CE. Aksum was succeeded by the Zagwe and Solomonic ruling dynasties and the development of smaller states, and it was the consolidation of these formerly separate states in the late 19th century that established the modern Ethiopian country.

Given its geographical location, the Horn of Africa has long been an important centre for trade. Early states such as Aksum were active in the Mediterranean trading arena. The coastal areas saw much trading activity with Arabs, Persians, people from the hinterland of the Horn, and, beginning in the late 15th century, with Europeans, which eventually led to the era of European colonization.

The French, British, and Italians were all active in the coastal areas of the Horn of Africa, and by the late 19th century, their colonial holdings corresponded to the modern countries of Djibouti, Somalia, and Eritrea, the first two gaining independence in 1960, while Eritrea eventually found itself joined with Ethiopia and only gained independence from that country in 1993, after nearly three decades of violent struggle. With the exception of the short-lived Italian occupation in the 20th century (1936–41), Ethiopia avoided being colonized by a European power. Ethiopia and Eritrea have not been the only centre of conflict on the Horn: Somalia, the amalgamation of an Italian colony and a British protectorate, has been in the grips of civil war since 1991.

Despite progress made in many sectors, postcolonial Central and eastern Africa both continue to experience some amount of upheaval and conflict rooted in such factors as religious and ethnic differences, economics, and politics. This book provides a comprehensive overview of the history that will help readers put current events in perspective.

# CHAPTER 1

## CENTRAL AFRICA

Central Africa is the region of Africa that straddles the Equator and is drained largely by the Congo River system. It contains, according to common definitions, the Republic of the Congo, the Central African Republic, and the Democratic Republic of the Congo; Gabon is usually included along with the Central African Republic because of their common historical ties, both of these countries having once been part of French Equatorial Africa. Rwanda and Burundi, although they are located east of the East African Rift System, which forms the eastern divide of the Congo basin, are also often considered part of the region because of their long administrative connections with the former Belgian Congo (now the Democratic Republic of the Congo). The island republic of Sao Tome and Principe, off the Atlantic coast of Gabon, is also included in the region.

### EARLY SOCIETY AND ECONOMY

The population of Central Africa has evolved in three broad time zones. During the earliest, which covered a million years, early humans sought food and shelter throughout the savanna regions and probably in the forest as well, though the forest may have been much thinner in the great dry phases of Africa's climatic history. In the second phase *Homo sapiens*, modern man and woman, appeared in the region and absorbed or eclipsed the thinly scattered original inhabitants

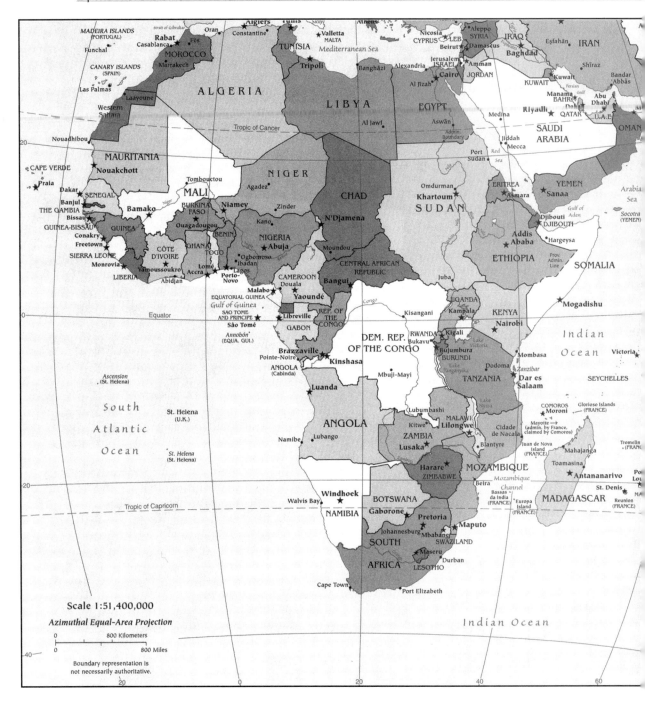

*Central Africa overlaps the Equator and meanders down with the Congo River System.* Courtesy of the University of Texas Libraries, The University of Texas at Austin

over a 100,000-year stretch. The third phase covered less than 10,000 years and brought the development of the societies that have become familiar to modern history. These societies arose from a blend of old populations familiar with the environment and new immigrants with fresh skills to impart.

## EARLY TOOLMAKERS

The oldest population of Central Africa is known almost exclusively from the evidence of its tools. Humankind had made a great intellectual step beyond its fellow primates by learning how to fashion and use tools of a regular form for a specific purpose. The most famous of the Paleolithic tools are the Acheulian knives, oddly known to scientists as "hand axes," used to skin animals and cut meat into chunks that could be chewed raw. Those used in Central Africa bear an uncanny resemblance to those used in many other parts of the Old World, which suggests that learning was an intercontinental phenomenon, however slow the transfer of technology may have

*Hand axes were used for skinning animals and chopping meat.* Kenneth Garrett/National Geographic Image Collection/Getty Images

been. Some of the tools used in Central Africa bear marks of local specialization and adaptation, but Central Africa was broadly integrated into the culture of the Paleolithic Period.

The middle phase of Central Africa's prehistory saw significant changes, but again the changes suggest that the region was linked to development in other parts of the world. The use of fire to roast vegetable foods as well as meats increased the range of diet and probably resulted in greater human health and fertility. The expanding population may have benefited from new skills in communication. The first use of language enabled societies to become more organized and efficient in their command of natural resources. Mobility in search of food was still the norm, but speech allowed the coordination of effort on a scale that animals could not achieve despite their powers of instinct. Tools became ever more varied, though most were probably made of wood or vegetable and animal fibre and so have not survived in the archaeological record. The stone weapons have survived, however, and show a growing inventiveness among the scattered small bands of Central African peoples who survived for millennia in competition with their much fiercer and stronger animal neighbours.

## The Agricultural Revolution

About 10,000 years ago Central Africa began to undergo an economic revolution. It started in the north, where a new dry phase in the Earth's history forced people to make better use of a more limited part of their environment as the desert spread southward once more. Hunters who had roamed the savanna settled beside the rivers and perfected their skills as fishermen. Gatherers who had harvested wild grain on the plains settled beside lakes, where they could sow some of their gleanings as seed in the moist and fertile soils left by the waters that withdrew at the end of each wet season. The northern border of Central Africa became one of the cradles of the world's food-producing revolution.

The first features of the new way of life in northern Central Africa were vegeculture and agriculture. Vegeculture enabled people to collect wild plants on a more systematic basis and to protect the regions where wild tubers grew most plentifully. The regular harvesting of wild roots led to the perfection of specialized digging tools. Stone hoes were ground to a finer polish than the chipped cutting tools of an earlier age. Gradually, women and men learned how to clear plots of fertile land and deliberately plant a piece of each root or tuber they ate to allow it to regenerate. They began to select the plant types that most readily lent themselves to domestication, to the ennoblement of regular crops, and to the development of agriculture. The white Guinea yam, *Dioscorea rotundata*, was the basis of the new root farming, which enabled the population to grow in the northern savanna from about 5000 BCE.

The second phase of the local agricultural revolution was even more important and had an impact over a wide area of the tropical world. A type of cereal farming based on wild seed of the millet and sorghum families was first developed in the northern savanna. Millet farming became particularly successful in the tropics because, unlike wheat and barley, it did not require the long daylight hours of summer that occur in the temperate climes. Tropical cereals spread from Central Africa not only into western Africa but also eastward to India and eventually southward to Southern Africa.

The third phase of the food-producing revolution brought an increase in the scale of food production and in its quality. The tending of trees and the gathering of fruit were probably as old as any other form of vegeculture. One of the most valuable of the tree crops was the oil palm, *Elaeis guineensis*. The preparation of palm fruits to make cooking oil enhanced the nutritional quality of the diet with both proteins and vitamins, further enhancing health and leading to population growth and the search for new land to be colonized and cultivated. The tending of trees also enhanced the quality of life in another dimension: some palm trees could be tapped for their sap, and the juice became the basis of a widespread wine industry, adding a festivity to communal life.

A fourth and last aspect of early farming in Central Africa was the arrival of a new family of plants. This was the banana family (Musaceae), originally domesticated in the islands of Southeast Asia. Banana plants, like yam tubers, were propagated by cuttings and roots rather than by seeds, but they gradually spread from neighbour to neighbour until the crop had become a dominant one in many parts of Central Africa. Banana plants supplied edible roots and textile fibres, but the two fundamental contributions were vegetable bananas (plantains) for cooking and sweet bananas for brewing. The banana flourished particularly well in the wetter areas—in the forests, along the rivers, and in the mountains—and in many societies it became the essential crop. Steamed, baked, fried, or boiled, the banana became the staple carbohydrate of many Central African peoples, and they washed it down with a nutrient-rich banana beer.

The agricultural revolution in Central Africa was paralleled by another nutritional change as people became more skilled at catching fish. Fishermen—like farmers but unlike hunters—could settle in more permanent village communities. Their diet was richer and more varied. They could own more possessions than simply the weapons and clothes they carried with them. They could make rafts and canoes to transport people and goods on the numerous rivers and lakes. The most important technical innovation was the use of clay for making pots for cooking, brewing, and storing food or drink. A whole "fish-stew revolution" occurred when cooking could be done in earthenware vessels. Pottery also gives the earliest clues about the artistic styles of Central Africa with patterns of dots and waves drawn on pot rims.

The growth of settled communities of hamlets and villages to which food was taken by carriers and canoes led to changes in architecture, social organization, land law and property rights, and warfare and the defense of territory. Although most families probably remained self-sufficient and did their own building, thatching, net making, and pot throwing, some skills may have been concentrated in the hands of a few people of authority or experience. Little evidence survives of Neolithic religion and ritual, but societies surely would have had priests to mediate between the gods and the mortals and to assist with the search for security in an age when the natural forces of fire or flood, plague or famine, were subject only to the most limited human control.

One important change that entered into the Neolithic world of Central Africa in the last millennium BCE was the spread of new languages. These were spoken in the relatively prosperous and thickly peopled savanna and plateau regions of the Cameroon-Nigeria borderland and came to be known as the Bantu languages, meaning simply the languages of the people, the *bantu*. Languages spread along lines of communication: they followed trade as specialists offered their finest pots or their best axes for sale to their neighbours. They became the vernacular of the clustered villages. They were picked up by country folk who came to market. They were carried into new frontier lands by pioneers seeking less-crowded spaces. Within 1,000 to 2,000 years the eastern Bantu languages had spread across the northern border of Central Africa to reach the highlands of East Africa. Meanwhile, the speakers of the western Bantu languages had found new niches in the great forest and established rapport with the old hunting and foraging communities of both the coast and the river basins.

Not all the peoples of Central Africa were converted to Bantu speech and to the economic way of life of their new neighbours in the first flush of contact. Some hunting societies, commonly known as Twa (Pygmies), retained much of their own culture and lifestyle for another 2,000 years. Some intermarriage occurred with the Bantu speakers of the new villages, and the exchange of hunted meat for grown produce fostered a fairly close symbiotic relationship. Eventually, even the Twa groups spoke the language of the new majority, which came to outnumber them in nearly all parts of the region. In the deepest forest, however, the hunting societies were able to protect traditional values to a marked degree. Even the great social and political upheavals that accompanied the advent of the Iron Age did not unduly disturb their long-standing and highly specialized relationship with the tropical environment.

## THE IRON AGE

The Iron Age reached Central Africa more or less at the same time it reached western Europe, some 3,000 years ago. The hallmark of the new era was

# BANTU LANGUAGES

The Bantu languages are a group of some 500 languages belonging to the Bantoid subgroup of the Benue-Congo branch of the Niger-Congo language family. The Bantu languages are spoken in a very large area, including most of Africa from southern Cameroon eastward to Kenya and southward to the southernmost tip of the continent. Twelve Bantu languages are spoken by more than 5 million people, including Rundi, Rwanda, Shona, Xhosa, and Zulu. Swahili, which is spoken by 5 million people as a mother tongue and some 30 million as a second language, is a Bantu lingua franca important in both commerce and literature.

Much scholarly work has been done since the late 19th century to describe and classify the Bantu languages. Special mention may be made of Carl Meinhof's work in the 1890s, in which he sought to reconstruct what he called ur-Bantu (the words underlying contemporary Bantu forms), and the descriptive work carried out by Clement Doke and the Department of Bantu Studies at the University of Witwatersrand, South Africa, in the period 1923–53. A monumental four-volume classification of Bantu languages, *Comparative Bantu* (1967–71), which was written by Malcolm Guthrie, has become the standard reference book used by most scholars—including those who disagree with Guthrie's proposed classification, which sets up a basic western and eastern division in Bantu languages with a further 13 subdivisions.

A variety of tonal systems are found in Bantu languages; tone may carry a lexical or grammatical function. In Zulu, for instance, the lexical function is shown in the contrast between *íyàngà* 'doctor' and *íyāngá* 'moon' or *yālá* 'refuse' and *yàlà* 'begin.' The grammatical function is illustrated in *ūmúntù* 'person' and *ùmúntù* 'it is a person' or *ngīhlānzā* 'I wash' and *ngīhlánzà* 'I washing' (the participial form).

The Bantu verb consists of a root that can be accompanied by affixes with various lexical and grammatical functions. In Zulu the passive form is marked by the suffix -wa, as in *thanda* 'love' and *thandawa* 'be loved'; the reciprocal by -ana (e.g., *thandana* 'love one another'); the causative by -isa (e.g., *thandisa*); the applied form ('for,' 'on behalf of') by -ela (e.g., *thandela*); the intensive by -isisa (e.g., *thandisisa* 'love exceedingly'); and the diminutive by reduplication. The verb also carries the subject and object prefixes.

Noun class systems are universal and almost always marked by prefixes, occasionally by suffixes. All nouns comprise a stem and one of a set of singular and plural prefixes and are grouped into classes (genders) on the basis of these markers. Zulu, for example, has nine pairs of singular and plural prefixes. Most words in a Bantu sentence are marked by a prefix indicating the category to which the noun used as the subject of the sentence belongs, and, if there is an object, the words in that noun phrase and the verb are also marked by a prefix determined by the noun class of the object.

technological innovation, but the social and economic changes that metalworking brought about were fundamental to the agricultural communities—if not to the hunting communities—of the tropics. Ironworking, unlike agriculture, was not a local invention but a skill that spread from community to community as the superiority of metal tools and weapons came to be recognized. Iron smelting came into Central Africa from two directions. In the northwest the oldest source of the new knowledge was on the Nigerian plateau. The skill necessary to dig pit furnaces and surround them with ranks of bellows spread among the Bantu-speaking peoples of the western forest. Gradually the polished stone tools that they had perfected were replaced by much more expensive but effective iron ones. Initially iron was probably used mainly for small and valuable objects such as razors, needles, and knives; later, as the smelting technique became more commonplace, iron came to be used for cutlasses, axes, and, eventually, hoes, which replaced the old wooden digging sticks.

The second source of technical information in Central Africa was probably the middle valley of the Nile, where the city of Meroe had been an early industrial site with a huge charcoal industry and great piles of iron slag surrounding its furnaces. The eastern tradition of smelting used furnaces as well as bellows to create the necessary draft with which to turn charcoal and ironstone into wrought iron and molten waste. The iron masters became revered craftsmen and were accorded a quasi-religious status. They lived in some seclusion and often commanded a degree of political authority over their neighbours. Legends of blacksmith-princes became commonplace in the historical folklore of Central Africa. Iron became important not only in the immediate locality but also in a developing interregional trade. Although ironstone and wood for charcoal were relatively common in most areas, the best smiths could nevertheless command a premium for their wares. And in some regions of deep blown sand or wide alluvial soils, where ores were unavailable, iron tools and weapons had to be bought from itinerant tinkers.

Iron was a valuable commodity, both raw in wrought bars and worked into spears or machetes. Even more valuable, however, was copper. Central Africa had no Copper or Bronze Age in the last millennium BCE, and it was in the Iron Age that the value of copper came to be recognized. Copper was particularly appreciated for its colour and lustre and was used for personal jewelry, rings, bangles, chains, necklaces, and hair ornaments—all made with great craftsmanship and given to persons loved or revered. Copper was also used in the ornamenting of personal belongings, the inlaying of decorations on knife handles, the binding of spear hafts with fine copper wire, and the embellishing of shields with burnished copper nails. Much of the copper mined in Central Africa was used to furnish the graves of important people with beautiful objects. The demand for fresh copper rose with each new generation. In particular, the development of new political authorities in the Iron Age led to the need for court regalia for chiefs and kings. Copper was used not only for its visual brilliance but also for the musical quality of the copper instruments that accompanied the nobility on their progress around their domains.

The three main zones of copper working in Central Africa were the Nile watershed, the eastern savanna, and the southwestern forest. Each industrial complex was a thousand miles from the next, and trade intensified as the demand for copper increased. The oldest and largest mines were those of the east. By the end of the 1st millennium CE, the mines of what is now the Katanga (Shaba ["Copper"]) area of the Democratic Republic of the Congo were casting copper ingots into molds of standard sizes for the international traffic. The region remained one of the world's greatest copper-mining areas for the next thousand years. In the north the copper was used to enhance the wealth and prestige of the local population, but it also fed into the long-distance trade networks of the southern Sahara, particularly after these had been strengthened and organized by Muslim merchants and entrepreneurs in the 14th and 15th centuries. The third copper complex, on the lower Congo River, remained an important but localized industry until a later date. At the end of the 16th century, however, the miners discovered a new outlet for their copper in Europe and sold large quantities to sea merchants from the Netherlands in exchange for Indian textiles, Chinese porcelain, South American tobacco, and stone jars of Dutch gin.

## GROWTH OF TRADE

The development of the copper industry caused many of the peoples of Central Africa to look to their own resources for produce that could be sold in order to buy the prestigious new metal and other exotic goods. The salt industry developed out of the needs of long-distance trade. The salt lagoons of the west coast became particularly important, and salt tracks ran far into the interior to agricultural communities without salt of their own to season the cereal dishes that were their staple food. Away from the coast, communities that had access to salt mines, or to dried salt lakes, organized exploitation and marketing, sometimes going far afield to the salt mines of East Africa. Where salt was not available, or where the costs of transport made it prohibitively expensive, people had to make do with salt substitutes such as the ash of marsh plants. Where real salt was produced, however, the industry became a focus for political power, and early states were formed, as on the Loango coast of the modern Republic of the Congo.

Of comparable importance to copper and salt was the textile industry. This also led to long-distance trade as specialized cloths were made for export to neighbouring regions. Like the salt industry, the textile industry sometimes was controlled by princes who dominated the markets and supplied protection to the caravanners who carried the bales of cloth. In western Central Africa the textile industry was based on fibre drawn from the raffia palm. The quality of the finished product, which sometimes had a velvetlike pile and a rich range of natural colours, was much admired by the first foreign visitors to the region. Indeed, raffia squares became the basis of colonial currency in the 17th century. Before that, raffia trading to and from the forest palm groves had become one of the sources of wealth among kings in the Kongo kingdom.

Textile weaving in Central Africa was important not only to kings and colonial governors but also to the regulation of social relations. Cloth provided one of the more durable and valuable possessions in every household. It therefore became the preferred item for social payments. In particular, bride wealth—which in other societies might be paid in gold or cattle—was commonly paid in cloth. The control of weaving was in the hands of old men. They no longer had the strength of young men to go hunting or to raid their neighbours, but they did control social wealth by monopolizing the weaving of raffia cloth. Without access to cloth, young men could not get married and set up a household, thus remaining dependent on the elders. With their regulation of cloth, and thus marriage, older men could in the last years of their lives marry several young wives and

ensure that their own line would be dominant in the next generation. In small and scattered societies across Central Africa, marriage was an important link between communities. Marrying within one's own clan or lineage was not always desirable, and maintaining contacts with neighbours to exchange brides was necessary. Permanent overarching political systems were not common, but the regular patterns of social communication went beyond merely commercial ones.

Another source of wealth that became important throughout the history of Central Africa was the trade in dried fish. The management of fish ponds became one way in which the scale of political power increased from village size to state size. The lakes of the eastern savanna provide one example of early state formation. The ancestors of the Luba became wealthy and powerful by controlling the fishing industry, building canoes and drying ovens, and setting up networks of trade paths along which porters carried tightly packed headloads of dried fish. In tropical conditions many foods were perishable, but dried fish could be preserved for months and carried to regions deficient in protein, where it was sold for high prices. The fish trade of the great rivers remained important, and fishermen were among the wealthier of the river dwellers. In the 20th century they were able to motorize their canoes, refrigerate their catches, and use steamers for long-distance transport.

In most of Central Africa the scale of political management remained small. Power brokers were men who gained influence in local communities. Kingdoms were not the norm. In a few places, however, administration was organized on a scale that went beyond a single day's march from the central homestead. The most striking of the early kingdoms was that of the Kuba peoples, at the heart of the southern forest. Kuba kings controlled the resources of a diverse ecological environment. They built up trade networks that enabled them to obtain copper from far afield and, later, even to buy such valuable ornamental assets as cowrie shells from the Indian Ocean, which were traded from community to community across Africa. The kings of the Kuba based their claim to power on a mystical exotic origin, far away down the rivers to the west, though such an alien pedigree bore no historical justification. Power had more to do with membership in influential local groups than with migration. Wealth, the ownership of livestock, the control of land, the mobilization of militias—these were the features of state formation in those rare areas where kingship could flourish. The Kuba knew government on a scale comparable to the early fish-trading states of the Luba and the raffia-weaving principalities of the Kongo kings.

## CENTRAL AFRICA AND THE OUTER WORLD

In the 15th century Central Africa came into regular contact with the non-African world for the first time. Hitherto all external contact had been indirect and slow. Language, technology, and precious objects had spread to affect people's lives, but no regular contact was maintained.

## DEVELOPMENT OF THE SLAVE TRADE

In the 15th century Central Africa opened direct relations both with the Mediterranean world of Islam and with the Atlantic world of Christendom. The Islamic contacts remained limited until the 19th century, though the Moor traveler and geographer Leo Africanus visited the northern states of Central Africa in the early 16th century and described them in Latin for the benefit of the Vatican, where he worked for a time.

The Atlantic opening had an earlier and more direct impact on Central Africa than the Mediterranean opening. In the 1470s a colony of Portuguese was settled on the offshore island of São Tomé. The Portuguese had been experimenting with colonial plantations for more than a century and already had settlements on Cape Verde and the Canary and Madeira islands. On São Tomé they established fields of sugarcane and built sugar mills. This prototype industry, which was later taken to Brazil and the Caribbean, became the richest branch of Europe's colonial enterprise and had a lasting impact on the history of the African mainland. Settlers were unable to build plantations unaided and so recruited local support. European immigrants—predominantly, if not exclusively, male—sought out African consorts from the adjacent communities and established Creole families of plantation owners and managers. They also bought mainland slaves to work the estates. São Tomé became the first bridgehead for the great Atlantic slave trade, which was to have a deep and scarring influence on most of Central Africa.

Central African slaves taken to the island slave market were sold to three destinations. The strongest were sold to the Akan miners of the Gold Coast in western Africa, where royal Portuguese agents were able to buy up to half a ton of gold a year in exchange for imported commodities and slave workers from other parts of the continent. A second category of Central African slave was shipped to Europe and used both for domestic service in the town and for farm labour on the sparsely peopled estates that Portuguese Christians had conquered from Portuguese Muslims in the late Middle Ages. The third class of slave was put to work locally on the island.

The fortunes of the São Tomé plantations fluctuated over the next five centuries. Sugar gave way to coffee as the

*A coffee plant in bloom displays its distinct white flower. Coffee, harvested by slaves, once sustained many São Tomé plantations, but in the 19th century cocoa became more predominant.* © John Warburton-Lee Photography/Alamy

mainstay, and coffee in turn was replaced by cocoa in the 19th century. In the 20th century the island was at the centre of a humanitarian furor over the continued use of slaves on the plantations. Cocoa manufacturers boycotted the island, and the planters tried to improve the working conditions of their employees. In the meantime, however, Central Africa's premier colony had been eclipsed by other European ventures on the mainland.

The second attempt to build a European colony in Central Africa occurred in the kingdom of Kongo surrounding the mouth of the Congo River. Portuguese traders exploited a division in the ruling class to gain a foothold at the court and the support of a royal claimant, who adopted Christianity and assumed the title of Afonso I. The Portuguese had hoped to find precious metals, as they had done in western Africa and were later to do in southeastern Africa, but the only source of profit they could realize was the buying of slaves for the São Tomé market. The king was under increasing pressure to use his army to raid his neighbours for captives. Even the Roman Catholic priests attached to the colonial mission found that they had to finance their activities by trading in slaves. The increasing profitability of slaving, and the lack of alternative sources of exportable wealth, placed growing pressures on the kingdom. Eventually, after the death of Afonso, popular rebellion broke out on a virulent scale. In order to preserve their foothold, the Portuguese equipped the governor of São Tomé with an army of 600 musketeers with which to reconquer their mainland base and install a pliant king in the Kongo capital. The Latin American tradition of the Iberian conquistador was thus introduced into Central Africa.

The great slaving campaigns of the conquistadores began in the 1570s after the Kongo wars had been quelled. The Portuguese harbour of Luanda was taken over by the Spanish Habsburgs in 1580, when the two crowns were united, and a series of armed assaults were launched on the states of the Mbundu peoples of the interior. The basis of the invasion was the rising demand for slaves to colonize the huge but sparsely peopled provinces of Brazil. Many slaves were captured directly or obtained as ransom for important chiefs. Many more were obtained from long-distance trade networks that penetrated ever deeper into the heart of Central Africa both by river and by footpath. The primary imports of the traders were textiles from India, England, northern Africa, or Portugal itself. But Portugal, even with the backing of Spain, was not economically strong enough to maintain its monopoly over the foreign trade in Central Africa. By the end of the 16th century, competitors were frequenting the coast.

The Dutch were the second colonial power to influence the history of Central Africa. Their impact was felt in ways rather different from that of the Portuguese. They were more interested in commodities than in slaves and so opened up the market for ivory. The old hunting skills gained a new value as the market for tusks blossomed and commercial entrepreneurs organized caravans over long distances. Even the Twa forest dwellers were able to benefit from the hunting of elephants. By the mid-17th century, however, the Dutch had established their own American colonies and so joined in the scramble for slaves. They began to sell guns to their trading partners to facilitate the destruction of old communities and the capture of fugitives. The supply and sale of powder, lead, and muskets became profitable to the coastal brokers but devastating to the inland victims.

The geographic scale of the Central African slave trade was enormous. By the 18th century the supply routes to the Atlantic reached the middle of the continent and had begun to intersect with the long-distance trade to the Indian Ocean. As the trade spread, so did the search for political systems that could manage the traffic. The largest and most successful of the new merchant empires was the empire of the Lunda at the heart of the southern savanna. The Lunda people seem to have become aware of the slave trade as early as the 16th century. Wandering Lunda hunters and salt prospectors, known as Imbangala (or Jaga), entered Angola and recruited local followers into heavily armed bands that raided the countryside, sold their captives to European sailors, and eventually formed an alliance with the Portuguese conquistadores, who allowed them to set up their own kingdom in the Kasanje plain on the borders

between Lunda and the European coastal enclaves. At first the kingdom of Kasanje acted solely as merchant brokers to the Portuguese, but, with the rise of rival European buyers on the northern Congo coast, its network spread farther afield. As the market expanded, so did the sources of supply. In the Lunda hinterland a powerful ruler adopting the title of Mwata Yamvo became chief supplier to the Kasanje intermediaries. The Lunda empire spread its commercial network not only to the west but also eastward until it had outlets to the lower Zambezi River and the Indian Ocean. The Mwata Yamvo of the west and his viceroy, the Mwata Kazembe of the east, effectively monopolized the slave trade of the heartland. As the Atlantic market grew, Lunda influence spread both north toward the forest and south into the dry plain of the upper Zambezi. In the early 19th century the court began to receive ambassadorial visits from representatives of the king of Portugal, and some years later echoes of the Mwata's greatness reached the Protestant explorer-missionaries of the far south, such as David Livingstone.

In the 18th century the Dutch were replaced by the French as the leading slave merchants on the north coast of the Congo region as the scale of the trade grew rapidly. Congo captives became the dominant population in Saint-Domingue, later called Haiti, which rose to be the richest of all the world's colonies and before 1791 the largest supplier of sugar. The slaves carried with them some of their cultural values and tried to reconstruct their communities under the shadow of the great plantation houses. Bantu vocabulary and personal names were added to the Creole speech of the Caribbean. Kongo religious practices were preserved in a nominally Christian colonial society when attempts were made to minimize the insecurity and suffering by worship and ritual. But, however much the slaves tried to reconstruct Central African society in the New World, their departure left a serious mark on the Old World. The scale of the French trade rose to about 10,000 men, women, and children each year. The demographic hemorrhage was felt in spreading ripples, and the already frail population of Central Africa was further weakened. Not until the outbreak of revolution in France, and later in Haiti, did the French trade begin to decline.

Although the Central African population had declined and did not begin to recover until the beginning of the 20th century, two new crops introduced to the region from the Americas enhanced the productive capacity of the land and helped Central Africans recover from the ravages of slaving. The first was corn (maize), which required the same agricultural skills as millet and so could be easily adopted. Corn had the advantage over millet that its grain was wrapped in an envelope of leaves that protected the crop from predatory birds. Corn also had higher yields than millet where soil and water were sufficient, which increased food production and partly compensated for the loss of field hands to the slavers. The second new crop was cassava, or manioc,

a root crop easily adopted by tuber farmers but more difficult for grain farmers to accept. It too was better protected from rodents—and even from marauders—than traditional crops. Cassava could be left in the ground when farmers had to flee in war and then recovered whole and edible on their return. To those unfamiliar with cassava, however, it could be dangerous, because the protective poisons in the plant, which made it inedible to vermin, had to be washed out before it was cooked for human consumption.

New crops from outside brought some small benefit to the region, but new diseases had the opposite effect. The growth of long-distance communication led to the spread of smallpox along the slave trails. It was a disease much feared both in the villages and on the slave ships. During serious periods of warfare and raiding, populations were weakened by famine and so easily fell prey to measles and pneumonia. Central Africa was also a malarial zone, although the disease was most deadly for Europeans. Equally dangerous to Africans, especially in the 20th century, were epidemics of sleeping sickness, which periodically spread through the region. As though this were not enough, Central Africa was attacked in the early 20th century by the world influenza pandemic. The already weakened population became thinner still and did not recover until well into the middle of the century.

The Central African slave trade continued into the 19th century, however. The Portuguese moved back into northern

Central Africa when the French trade declined, and Brazil bought more slaves than ever before from Central Africa in the first half of the century, continuing to use slaves until the 1880s. Spain also entered the market to buy slaves for its surviving American colony in Cuba, where the tobacco industry combined the modernization of the railway age with the old plantation use of slaves.

The abolition movement helped to end the slave trade by the late 19th century, although slavery continued in Africa into the 20th century. While the end of four centuries of international slaving might have been expected to lead to a new era of freedom and opportunity in Central Africa, this did not happen. Instead, a whole new set of foreign forces began to penetrate the area. The first of these came from the long-delayed growth of international commerce on the northern border of the region.

## EXPLOITATION OF IVORY

In the second half of the 19th century, the northern border of Central Africa was suddenly opened up to the impact of an intense new trade in ivory. Rapid prosperity in both Europe and North America had led to an increase in demand for ivory to make piano keys, billiard balls, knife handles, and ornamental carvings. Traders from Egypt and the old Ottoman Empire of northern Africa went across the Sahara and up the Nile to cross into the upper reaches of the Congo basin, where elephants were still plentiful. In so doing,

they severely disrupted local societies as they kidnapped local peoples to serve as bearers, servants, and concubines. The victims of the trading and hunting raids not only were used in the heavily armed and fortified ivory camps but also were taken away to be sold as slave girls in the harems of Constantinople or as water carriers in the streets of Cairo.

The second mobile frontier to intrude on Central Africa in the 19th century was in the east, and eventually it became as disruptive as the northern incursion. The first immigrants were long-distance traders from the Nyamwezi kingdom founded by Mirambo, who arrived in search of copper. They set up their own trading kingdom under Msiri and developed a large army of followers equipped with lances and bows. Msiri also trained a military elite of 2,000 men, whom he armed with guns bought on the east coast in exchange for ivory. Msiri's kingdom became one of the largest conquest states to be carved out in Central Africa. He adopted the administrative methods of the old Lunda kings, whose provinces he captured and whose governors he reappointed as his own agents and consuls. He also gained control of the old empire's eastern slave trade. In this field, however, Msiri had a powerful rival in the Swahili trade community, which had reached Central Africa from Zanzibar.

The Swahili traders and their Arab allies were involved with both the slave trade and the ivory trade. Their slaves were put to work on the spice plantations of Zanzibar or sold as pearl divers and domestic servants in the Arabian and Persian gulfs. The ivory went to the United States to buy calico, which was in great demand in the eastern Congo basin. One of the traders took the nickname "Americani" because his American calico was so famed. An even better-known Swahili merchant prince was Tippu Tib, who became the effective ruler of the Swahili towns on the upper reaches of the Congo River. His methods of trade were brutal. Villagers were forcibly rounded up into camps, often with great loss of life—as witnessed by Livingstone on his visit—and then ransomed by their relatives, who were sent out on hazardous elephant-trapping expeditions. The ivory trade thus disrupted the east as effectively as it disrupted the north. Worse still, the pattern of exploitation was one that was soon adopted by the first Europeans to enter the region. They also used capture and ransom to extract wealth from their victims. The first European ruler of the Congo, the Belgian king Leopold, appointed Tippu Tib his governor and gave him command of the east in recognition of his military and commercial achievements.

The great 19th-century scramble for ivory also brought disruption to Central Africa from the south in the years immediately preceding the colonial partition. The agents in the south were Chokwe hunters from Angola. They had been successful collectors of beeswax, and their trade had enabled them to build up armories of guns, which they eventually turned on their neighbours. They penetrated the heartland of the Lunda empire in the 1880s and destroyed the court. Their victims were sold on the Atlantic coast and were the last European-owned slaves on the old plantations of São Tomé. Their ivory went to the Portuguese after the crown had abandoned its restrictive monopoly on tusks and allowed private entrepreneurs to benefit from market forces. But when ivory became scarce and slaves were frowned upon, the Chokwe pioneered a new branch of trade that was to bring even greater horrors to the peoples of Central Africa. This was the search for red rubber, the sap of the wild rubber vine that grew throughout the forest and savanna galleries of the Congo basin. As the price of rubber rose with the development of the electrical and motor industries, so the rubber traders penetrated further into the communities of refugees who had sought to escape the disruptions of the last phase of the slave trade.

## COLONIALISM

It was the rubber trade that financed the first stage of formal colonial rule in Central Africa, and the pioneer colonizer was Leopold II, king of the Belgians. The early attempts of his father, Leopold I, to found colonies in remnants of the Spanish empire in the Pacific or America had failed, and he therefore turned his attention to Central Africa, which was still little known to European geographers and therefore less intensely coveted than Western or Southern Africa.

## ESTABLISHMENT OF EUROPEAN COLONIES

Leopold set up his colony (the Congo Free State) as a private, ostensibly humanitarian venture aimed at limiting the devastation of slaving and the liquor trade. To finance the venture, however, he rented out nation-size fiefs to commercial companies that were licensed to make a profit and pay tax and tribute to the colonizer-king. Companies such as the Anglo-Belgian India Rubber Company, the Antwerp Company, and the king's own Crown Domain took over the extraction of rubber from the Chokwe. Since the profits on rubber were low compared with ivory or slaves, great pressure had to be brought to bear to encourage newly subjected villagers to forsake their agricultural livelihoods and risk their lives in the forest to gather the vine sap. Military force was used, rubber collecting became compulsory, and defaulters were barbarically punished by having their limbs amputated. The rubber regime in the western Congo basin was no more benign than the ivory regime that Leopold adopted from the Swahili in the east.

The humanitarian protest against the rule of Leopold was led by traders who had lost access to their former sphere of interest, by missionaries who deplored the denial of human rights, and by a British diplomat who believed in political freedom. Roger (later Sir Roger) Casement publicized the atrocities in the Congo Free State to such good effect that in 1908 the Belgian government confiscated the colony from its own king in an attempt to put an end to the misrule of exploitation. However much other countries might have condemned Leopold's rule, rival colonizers were also keen to make their colonies profitable and did so by farming out concessions to private enterprise and turning a blind eye to the large-scale use of forced labour.

The most immediate rival to Leopold in creating instant new colonies was Otto von Bismarck, chancellor of the new German Empire. Most of the colonies he created were outside Central Africa, but he did succeed in laying claim to one tiny but richly populated corner on the mountainous border of East Africa. The old kingdoms of Rwanda and Burundi had thrived for centuries. The ruling class grew tall on the milk of its cattle and governed its farming subjects with imperious superiority. In the forest the old inhabitants continued to maintain their hunting lifestyle and, where possible, to escape the attentions of their neighbours. In the late 19th century Burundi underwent severe dislocation, with conflicts over the monarchy and rivalry between chiefs and kings. The Germans moved in from Tanganyika and tried to impose order. They also took over the more stable kingdom of Rwanda.

Although the German intrusion into Central Africa from the east was slight and short-lived, a comparable French intrusion in the west led to the creation of a much bigger and more lasting equatorial empire. It was the work of the explorer-turned-governor Pierre

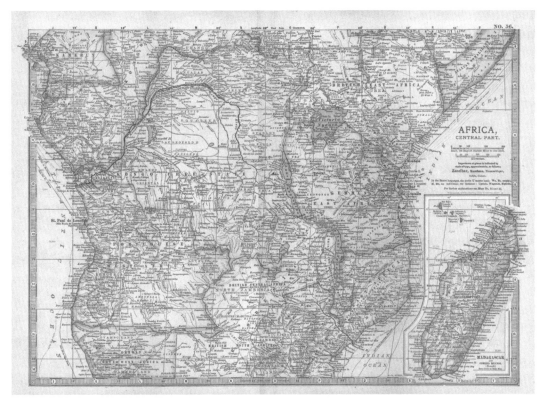

*Map of Central Africa, from the 10th edition of Encyclopædia Britannica, published in 1902.*

Savorgnan de Brazza. The French presence was confined at first to former slaving beaches on the Congo coast and Libreville, a haven for freed slaves on the Gabon Estuary. Brazza aspired to join these coastal enclaves to the middle stretch of the Congo River, where the colonial capital was named Brazzaville in his honour. He also aspired to claim territory for France as far east as the upper regions of the Nile. Such an enterprise brought France into competition not only with Leopold, on the far bank of the river, but also with Britain, which had laid claim to the lower Nile in Egypt and wanted to protect the headwaters by conquering the upper Nile as well. The French were narrowly defeated in the race to the Nile (the Fashoda incident) but nevertheless gained imperial dominion over a huge stretch of northern Central Africa, which they called Ubangi-Shari and which later became the diamond-rich Central African Republic.

The problems that France faced in Central Africa were not materially different from those faced by Leopold. The territories were huge, thinly peopled,

## CONGO FREE STATE

The Congo Free State (French: État Indépendant du Congo) was a former state in Africa that occupied almost all the Congo River basin, coextensive with the modern Democratic Republic of the Congo. It was created in the 1880s as the private holding of a group of European investors headed by Leopold II, king of the Belgians. The king's attention was drawn to the region during Henry (later Sir Henry) Morton Stanley's exploration of the Congo River in 1874–77. In November of 1878 Leopold formed the Committee for Studies of the Upper Congo (Comité d'Études du Haut Congo, later renamed Association Internationale du Congo) to open up the African interior to European trade along the Congo River. Between 1879 and 1882, under the committee's auspices, Stanley established stations on the upper Congo and opened negotiations with local rulers. By 1884 the Association Internationale du Congo had signed treaties with 450 independent African entities and, on that basis, asserted its right to govern all the territory concerned as an independent state. At the Berlin West Africa Conference of 1884–85, its name became the Congo Free State, and European powers recognized Leopold as its sovereign.

Leopold extended his military control over the interior in the early 1890s. The Arab slave traders of the Lualaba River region succumbed in 1890, when their leader Tippu Tib left for Zanzibar. Katanga, rich in copper and other minerals, fell in 1891 after Leopold's troops shot the ruler, Msiri. Later rebellions were repressed. Transportation links to the interior were established with the construction (1890–98) of a railway to bypass the Congo River rapids below Stanley (now Malebo) Pool; the upper course of the river and its tributaries were all navigable by steamboat.

Under Leopold's unrestrained personal control, the regime became notorious for its treatment of the Congolese. Forced labour was used to gather wild rubber, palm oil, and ivory. Beatings and lashings were used to force villages to meet their rubber-gathering quotas, as was the taking of hostages: Leopold's agents sometimes kidnapped the families of Congolese men, who were then coerced into trying to meet often unattainable work quotas to secure the release of their families. Congolese Rebellion elicited swift and harsh responses from Leopold's private army, the Force Publique (a band of African soldiers led by European officers), who burned the villages and slaughtered the families of rebels. Force Publique troops were also known for cutting off the hands of the Congolese, including children. This mutilation was a punishment and a method to further terrorize the Congolese into submission, and the collection of severed hands provided a measure by which the soldiers could prove to their commanding officers that they were actively crushing rebellious activity. Brutality was widespread in mines and on plantations. The population of the entire state is said to have declined from some 20 million to 8 million.

The truth about Leopold's brutal regime eventually spread, largely owing to the efforts of the Congo Reform Association, an organization founded by British citizens in the early 20th century. Finally, indignation among people in Britain and other parts of Europe grew so great that Leopold was forced to transfer his authority in the Congo to the Belgian government. In 1908 the Congo Free State was abolished and replaced by the Belgian Congo, a colony controlled by the Belgian parliament.

and poorly endowed with resources that could finance colonial administration and make a profit for the colonizing power. Transport was the greatest difficulty. Leopold went so far as to claim that the essence of colonization was the creation of a transport system. Both France and Leopold were handicapped by the rapids on the lower Congo River and so each had, at huge cost in money and men, to build a railway to reach the navigable middle river. Leopold used the famous British-American explorer Henry (later Sir Henry) Morton Stanley, the "Breaker of Rocks" (Bula Mutari), to mobilize the necessary forced labour to gain access to his territory. The French tried importing Chinese workers, who could be hired in Asia even more cheaply than local labour could be conscripted in Africa.

The French imitated Leopold, and also the British and Portuguese, by awarding concessions to colonial companies on the condition that they take responsibility for their own administration and infrastructure in return for the right to extract profits from subject peoples and conquered lands. The most notorious of the French colonial entrepreneurs made their money out of timber concessions. Only toward the end of the colonial period and after did French Equatorial Africa discover that it was rich in iron ore, petroleum, and uranium.

## ECONOMIC ORGANIZATION

The violent phase of Central African colonialism, involving the forced extraction of rubber, ivory, and timber, was followed by a more systematic phase of economic organization. One facet was the establishment of formal plantations on which to grow oil palms and rubber trees. These plantations required capital, machinery, and expensive foreign management. As a result, there was little margin left for adequate wages for workers. The recruitment of labour became the duty of the colonial state or its licensed agents. Some workers accepted the incentive of a cash wage to buy material goods or to accumulate the necessary social payments for marriage. Others were driven into the wage sector by the imposition of cash taxes, which could be met only by working for colonial enterprises. But some were recruited on a compulsory basis—not as convicts deserving of punishment but as subjects who needed to be "civilized" by submitting to a work regime imposed by the state.

Where plantations did not develop, the colonial state found a means of extracting wealth from free peasants. They introduced compulsory crops, most notably cotton—"le coton du gouverneur." Forced cotton imposed severe hardships on farmers, who could not grow food for their families but instead had to clear land to sow cotton for the state. When the crop succeeded, they received a small payment. But much of the cotton regime was applied to marginal lands, where it often failed. The risk was borne by the victim, and famine resulted. The planting of cotton led to frequent protests and to harsh repression in Central Africa, as it did in German East Africa and Portuguese West Africa.

The largest industrial complex to develop in Central Africa was the mining industry of the copper belt in what is now the far southeastern Democratic Republic of the Congo. Leopold had won a race with the British South African empire builder Cecil Rhodes to reach the copper mines and had conquered the kingdom of Msiri, killing the king in the process. The next challenge was to build a transport system that could carry machinery into the mining zone and export finished ingots. The politics of transport were the key to development in the high colonial period, as they had been in the early phase. Two railway lines ran to the Indian Ocean coast: one was built across German East Africa to the port of Dar es Salaam and another through British Zambesia to the Portuguese port of Beira; a third railroad crossed Angola to the harbour of Lobito on the Atlantic. None of these, however, was under the control of the Belgians, who planned to create a national route to their own port of Matadi on the Congo estuary. To do so they had to use an expensive and complex mixture of rail and river steamers, and so the copper mines remained integrated in an international network of finance and transport. They also depended on neighbouring regions for their supply of coal and electricity. The industry was dominated by a concession company, the Union Minière du Haut-Katanga, which became almost as powerful as the colonial state itself.

The two were interlocked in rivalry and mutual dependence, and the Belgian Congo was described as the "portfolio state" for its reliance on copper shares.

Two other mining zones added to the wealth of the colonial Congo: diamonds in the west and gold in the east. Between them the three mining zones were large-scale employers of unskilled labour. Some workers were temporary migrants who worked on contract and whose families subsisted on peasants' incomes during their absence. Much of the burden of colonialism fell on women, who became heads of households and managers of family farms when the men were taken to the mines. Part of the mine labour was supplied by migrants who moved permanently to the towns and became proletarian workers exclusively dependent on their wages. Among the townsmen, education and technical training became the road to economic advancement. The Belgian colonial system maintained a rigorous paternal structure, however, and, although more subjects became literate in Congo than in other colonies, few could aspire to higher skills or managerial posts. These positions were reserved for the white expatriate population.

One distinctive feature of the colonial era in Central Africa was the role of the church. The state provided so few services that missions moved in to make up the deficit. The most famous of all missionaries was Albert Schweitzer, the Alsatian musician and theologian who became a physician and set up a hospital in the heart of French Equatorial Africa. British Baptists also played a major role in converting the people of the lower Congo area to Protestantism and providing them with basic education and minimal welfare services. When turmoil again hit the region at the end of the colonial period, it was the Baptists who brought services to the mass refugee camps. In the Belgian sphere the Roman Catholic church took a high profile and eventually established a Catholic university through which to train not only colonial whites but also a small elite of black Africans. The rival to the state church was an independent black church, built in honour of the martyred preacher Simon Kimbangu, who spent most of his life in a Belgian colonial prison. Later still, Central Africa became a prime zone of evangelism for the fundamentalist groups that sprang up in the United States in the last decades of the 20th century. When the postcolonial state withered, the churches took on greater formal and informal responsibilities for health and education and for communications and financial services in remote areas.

## THE END OF THE COLONIAL PERIOD

The colonial period in Central Africa came to an abrupt end in 1960. At a constitutional level, dramatic changes occurred. Both France and Belgium decided that they could not resist the winds of change with armed force. Once the black nationalists of western Africa had won the right to self-determination from Britain, it was not deemed possible to deny the same rights in Central Africa. New constitutions were therefore accepted, parliaments were elected, and flags were flown and anthems played. Gen. Charles de Gaulle of France, whose path to power had led him to Brazzaville during World War II, became the hero of the new equatorial republics to which he granted independence. King Baudouin of the Belgians participated in the independence celebrations of the Democratic Republic of the Congo at Léopoldville (now Kinshasa) but managed to orchestrate his reception with less finesse. "Flag independence" in Central Africa, however, did not bring any real transformation to satisfy the high aspirations of former colonial subjects.

# CHAPTER 2

# BURUNDI

Burundi is a landlocked country in east-central Africa, south of the Equator. The former historical kingdom fell under colonial rule—first by the Germans, then by the Belgians—before it regained its independence in 1962. The capital is Bujumbura.

## PRECOLONIAL BURUNDI

Unlike most countries in sub-Saharan Africa, the boundaries of Burundi were not drawn by European powers. Rather, they reflect a state that was developed by the Burundian monarchy. The country was originally populated by the Twa, a Pygmy hunter-gatherer population. Beginning around 1000 CE, Hutu farmers, who now constitute the largest proportion of the population, arrived in the region. Sometime later the Tutsi entered the country, and a Tutsi monarchy developed in the 16th century, founded by Ntare Rushatsi (Ntare I). According to one tradition, Ntare I came from Rwanda; according to other sources, he came from Buha in the southeast, from which he laid the foundation of the original kingdom in the neighbouring Nkoma region. The relationship between the different groups in the state was complex. The king (*mwami*) was Tutsi, but a princely class (*ganwa*), which consisted of the potential heirs to the throne, interceded between the king and the Tutsi and Hutu masses.

Identification as either a Tutsi or Hutu was fluid. While physical appearance did correspond somewhat to one's identification (the Tutsi were generally presumed to be light-skinned and tall; the Hutu, dark-skinned and short), the difference between the two groups was not always immediately apparent, owing to intermarriage and the use of a common language (Rundi) by both groups. Tutsis were traditionally cattle owners (cattle were a symbol of wealth in precolonial Burundi), while the Hutu were agriculturalists. However, by societal standards a rich Hutu could be identified as a Tutsi, and a poor Tutsi could be identified as a Hutu.

## BURUNDI UNDER COLONIAL RULE

Europeans did not enter Burundi until the second half of the 19th century. The terrain that had made it difficult for slave traders to exploit the country also created problems for European colonizers. English explorers Richard Burton and John Hanning Speke, generally credited as the first Europeans to visit Burundi, entered the country in 1858. They explored Lake Tanganyika as they searched for the source of the Nile. In 1871 two more Britons, Henry Morton Stanley and David Livingstone, also explored the lake.

Burundi, along with Rwanda and Tanganyika, became part of the German Protectorate of East Africa in 1890.

Burundi and Rwanda (as the mandate of Ruanda-Urundi) were awarded to Belgium after World War I, when Germany lost its colonies. Under the Belgian colonial administrators, Burundi was reorganized in the late 1920s, with the result that most chiefs and subchiefs were eliminated.

It would be overly simplistic to blame all of Burundi's postcolonial ethnic troubles on European ignorance of African culture, but such ignorance did significantly contribute to these problems. Assuming that ethnicity could be clearly distinguished by physical characteristics and then using the ethnic differences found in their own countries as models, Germany and especially Belgium created a system whereby the categories of Hutu and Tutsi were no longer fluid. The Tutsi—because of their generally lighter skin and greater height and as a result of European bias toward those physical characteristics—were considered superior to Hutu and given preference in local administration. Thus, power continued to be concentrated in the Tutsi minority.

After World War II, Burundians began to press for independence. Although the traditional leaders of Burundi and Rwanda were denied legal status for a political party they formed in 1955, three years later Unity for National Progress (Unité pour le Progrès National; UPRONA) was established in Burundi. In 1959 the *mwami* was made a constitutional monarch in Burundi.

Legislative elections were held in 1961 and resulted in victory for UPRONA.

Of the 64 legislative seats, the ethnically mixed party won 58, of which 22 were held by Hutu members of UPRONA. The party leader was Prince Rwagasore, a Tutsi and the eldest son of Mwami Mwambutsa. Rwagasore represented populist aspirations and was the strongest supporter of the monarchy. He became prime minister and formed a new government. His assassination on Oct. 13, 1961, ushered in a crisis from which the country has struggled to recover ever since. Despite this crisis, Burundi became independent on July 1, 1962.

## THE FIRST AND SECOND REPUBLICS

Discord and violence have marked Burundi since independence. Although bloodshed has not occurred on the scale seen in Rwanda, ethnic conflict has resulted in hundreds of thousands of deaths and hundreds of thousands of people being displaced from their homes. The first incident did not occur until January 1965, when Pierre Ngendandumwe, a Hutu, took office as prime minister for the second time, at the request of the constitutional monarch, Mwami Mwambutsa. Ngendandumwe was assassinated by a Tutsi gunman on January 15, before he had a chance to establish a government. Joseph Bamina, another Hutu, then served as prime minister until elections could be held later that year. Although elections gave the Hutu a clear majority of seats in the National

Assembly, Mwambutsa ignored the results and appointed a Tutsi—Léopold Biha, his private secretary—prime minister. Mwambutsa insisted that power would continue to rest with the crown Even when he chose to leave the country after an unsuccessful coup led by a group of Hutu officers in October, he decreed that his son, Prince Charles Ndizeyeto, was to rule in his absence.

Control of Burundi fell completely into the hands of the Tutsi before the end of the next year. After the abortive coup, some 34 Hutu officers were executed, and Tutsi control was further strengthened when Michel Micombero was appointed prime minister in July 1966. A Tutsi-Bahima from Bururi province, Micombero had played a key role in thwarting the 1965 coup and in organizing anti-Hutu riots in the countryside. Also in July 1966, Mwambutsa was deposed by his son, who began what was to be an extremely short reign, as he himself was deposed by Tutsi politicians in November. With the formal overthrow of the monarchy and the formal proclamation of the First Republic (with Micombero as president), the last obstacle in the path of Tutsi domination was removed.

No other event cast greater discredit on the First Republic than the genocidal killings perpetrated against the Hutu community in April and May 1972. Although Hutu initially killed some 2,000 Tutsi, ultimately an estimated 100,000 to 200,000 Hutu were killed, as well as another 10,000 Tutsi. The carnage took the lives of approximately 5 percent of the population and virtually eliminated all educated Hutu, as well as causing more than 100,000 Hutu to flee the country. Besides creating deep and lasting hatred on both sides of the ethnic divide, the events of 1972 became the source of considerable tension within the Tutsi minority, thus paving the way for the overthrow of Micombero in 1976 and the advent of the Second Republic under the presidency of Jean-Baptiste Bagaza. Though himself a Tutsi-Bahima from Bururi (like Micombero), Bagaza set out to reinvigorate the UPRONA on an unprecedented scale. At the same time, every effort was made to bring the Roman Catholic Church firmly under the control of the state, as the Tutsi-controlled government thought the church's policies favoured the Hutu. As a result of the government's efforts, the activities of the church were repressed.

## THE THIRD REPUBLIC

The crisis in church-state relations was the critical factor behind Maj. Pierre Buyoya's decision to overthrow the Second Republic in September 1987 and proclaim a Third Republic. Buyoya, also a Tutsi-Bahima from Bururi, took the title of president and presided over a country that was ruled by a 30-member military junta, the Military Committee for National Salvation.

The 1987 coup signaled an important shift of policy on the issue of church-state relations, and, by implication, on the Hutu-Tutsi problem. Buyoya repealed many of the restrictions placed upon the church and released political prisoners he felt had been improperly detained by the previous administration. Ironically, Buyoya's call for liberalization, while significantly raising the expectations of the Hutu masses, did little to alter the rigidly discriminatory practices of Tutsi civil servants in the provinces. The gap between Hutu expectations and the realities of Tutsi control lay at the root of the killings that erupted again in August 1988.

More than 20,000 people were killed in the northern parts of Burundi, the overwhelming majority of Hutu origin. As in 1972, the initial outburst of violence—in the wake of countless provocations by local Tutsi officials—came from Hutu elements. Unlike his predecessor in 1972, however, President Buyoya's response to the crisis was surprisingly conciliatory. For one thing, the existence of a Hutu-Tutsi problem was explicitly recognized by the government, along with the need for appropriate solutions. Moreover, a conscious effort was made to achieve parity of ethnic representation within the government, as evidenced by the cabinet Buyoya formed in October 1988, which contained a Hutu majority. Finally, and most important, a national commission was established to make specific recommendations to the government to "protect and strengthen the unity of the people of Burundi."

Buyoya's apparent progressive leadership led to the adoption of a new constitution in March 1992, which prohibited political organizations that adhered to "tribalism, divisionalism, or violence" and stipulated that all political parties must include both Hutu and Tutsi representatives. There followed the country's first free, democratic election in June 1993, in which Melchior Ndadaye, a Hutu who ran against Buyoya, was elected president. Ndadaye announced amnesty for many political prisoners and created a carefully balanced government of Hutu and Tutsi, including Sylvie Kinigi, a Tutsi woman, as prime minister.

## CIVIL WAR

Ndadaye was assassinated during an attempted military coup on Oct. 21, 1993, and the wave of violence that followed sparked the country's descent into civil war. As many as 150,000 Tutsi were killed in retribution, and perhaps 50,000 additional people were killed in smaller outbreaks. Amid the violence, leaders of the attempted coup and members of Ndadaye's government vied for power. The main political parties finally chose Cyprien Ntaryamira, a Hutu, as president. Ntaryamira took office in February 1994, but two months later he and Rwandan president Juvénal Habyarimana were killed when the plane they were on crashed near the airport in Kigali, Rwanda. Fighting intensified,

hundreds more were killed, and calls from the United Nations to halt the violence initiated nighttime curfews. In September 1994 a commission agreed to a power-sharing coalition government headed by Sylvestre Ntibantunganya, a Hutu. Fighting continued throughout the country during the nearly two years of coalition government.

The Tutsi-led army staged yet another coup against the government in July 1996 and reinstalled Buyoya as president. He faced considerable internal and international protest, including economic sanctions against the country, and many countries throughout the world had not recognized Buyoya's government by the end of the decade. Economic sanctions were eased in 1997, and an embargo was lifted in 1999.

## THE PATH TOWARD PEACE

Peace talks that began in 1995 among the rival factions were initiated and moderated by Julius Nyerere, former president of Tanzania. The talks were successfully concluded in 2001 under the leadership of former president of South Africa Nelson Mandela, who had assumed the role of mediator after Nyerere's death in 1999. Under the terms of the Arusha Agreement, a multinational, interim security contingent would enforce the peace in Burundi. A new government was installed on Nov. 1, 2001. The country was to be led by a Tutsi president (Buyoya) for 18 months and a Hutu president

*Pierre Buyoya* (right, with Nelson Mandela) *eased restrictions on the church and released prisoners he deemed unfairly detained, raising Hutu hopes but scarcely changing Tutsi practices.*
Marco Longari/AFP/Getty Images

(Domitien Ndayizeye) for the next 18 months. Sporadic fighting continued between Hutu rebel groups and the government, however.

In April 2003 Ndayizeye succeeded Buyoya as president under the terms of the 2001 agreement, and later that year Ndayizeye and rebel leaders signed peace accords that largely ended the civil war. A new power-sharing constitution was promulgated in 2005, and Pierre Nkurunziza, a Hutu, was elected president. Under the terms of the constitution, as the first post-transition president, he was elected by a two-thirds majority of the legislature, rather than by universal suffrage. The following year, the last remaining Hutu rebel group signed a peace agreement with the Burundi government, and there was hope that Burundians would be able to focus on promoting unity and rebuilding the country.

In November 2006 Nkurunziza stewarded Burundi's ascent into the East African Community economic bloc, and in April 2007 he played an important role in reconstituting the Economic Community of the Great Lakes Countries, a trade organization including Burundi, the Democratic Republic of the Congo, and Rwanda. Aided by World Bank funds, he also took the lead on infrastructure projects aimed at increasing the accessibility of water and electricity. These steps toward progress were undercut, however, by accusations that Nkurunziza's administration persecuted journalists critical of its policies as part of its general refusal to acknowledge dissent. Concern by some that the country was moving toward single-party rule mounted in June 2010, when Nkurunziza was reelected with more than 90 percent of the vote following the withdrawal of all six of his challengers. Violence marred the campaign and election proceedings, contributing to a markedly low voter turnout.

# CHAPTER 3

# CENTRAL AFRICAN REPUBLIC

The Central African Republic is a landlocked country in Central Africa. The former French colony became independent in 1960. The capital is Bangui.

## EARLY HISTORY

Diamond prospectors in the Central African Republic have found polished flint and quartz tools that are at least 8,000 years old. About 2,500 years ago local farmers set up megaliths weighing several tons each near Bouar. The cooperation necessary to make and position these monuments suggests that they were built by fairly large social units. By the 15th century CE various groups speaking languages related to those of the present day were living in the area. These peoples lived in relatively isolated small settlements, where they hunted and cleared land for cultivation using the slash-and-burn method. The region also produced such states as Dar al-Kuti, Zande, and Bandi, all founded in the 19th century.

The region of the Central African Republic was not directly connected to external commercial routes until the 17th century. At that time, slavery became an important factor in Central African history as Arabic-speaking slave traders extended the trans-Saharan and Nile River trade routes into the region. Before the mid 19th century these slave traders' captives were sent to northern Africa, where they were eventually sold to countries such as Egypt or Turkey or down the Ubangi and Congo rivers to the Atlantic coast to slave ships that transported them to the Americas.

Later in the mid-19th century, the Bobangi people from the Ubangi River area, who had become major slave traders, raided the nearby Baya and Mandjia peoples for captives. In exchange for captives, the slave traders received arms, which allowed them to continue to raid for more slaves. Though these raids largely ended by the end of the century, they continued in the north until 1912 when Dar al-Kuti fell. The slave trade disrupted the societies in its wake and depopulated the region. It also created lasting tensions between ethnic groups. The ruling elite is still resented today by many in Central Africa because they tend to come from riverine groups akin to the Bobangi.

## THE COLONIAL ERA

During the last two decades of the 19th century, Belgium, Great Britain, Germany, and France competed for control of equatorial Africa. Belgium, Germany, and France each wanted the region that would eventually become the Central African Republic. The French were ultimately successful and named it the French Congo (later French Equatorial Africa), with its capital at Brazzaville. The French colonies included Ubangi-Shari

(Oubangui-Chari; which later became the Central African Republic), Chad, Gabon, and the Middle Congo (which became the Republic of the Congo).

The French government leased large tracts of land to private European companies in order to avoid paying for the development of its Central African possessions; it also placed few controls on their activities. In exchange for an annual rent, these firms exploited the land and dominated the people. Company overseers forced both men and women to gather wild rubber, hunt for ivory and animal skins, and work on plantations. Unable to cultivate their own fields because of the labour demands from European companies, they experienced food shortages and famine. Because they were forced to work in new environments where they were exposed to sleeping sickness, new strains of malaria, and other diseases, the death rate substantially increased.

By the beginning of the 20th century, frontiers had been established for the Ubangi-Shari colony by the European powers. Many Africans resisted French control, and several military expeditions in the first decade of the century were needed to crush their opposition. The Kongo-Wara rebellion (1928–31) was a widespread, though unsuccessful, anticolonial uprising in the western and southwestern parts of the colony. After it was suppressed, its leaders were imprisoned and executed and populations of Central Africans were forcibly relocated to colonially designated villages where they could be supervised.

The French colonial administration did create a network of roads and a mobile health system in Ubangi-Shari to fight disease, and Roman Catholic churches set up schools and medical clinics. However, the French also used the Central Africans for forced labour to increase the cultivation of cotton and coffee, as well as of food crops to supply French troops and labour crews. The French conscripted Central Africans and sent them to southern Congo to construct the Congo-Ocean Railway, which linked Congo to Pointe-Noire.

During World War II, French Gen. Charles de Gaulle called on the residents of the colonial territories to help fight the Germans, and 3,000 responded from Central Africa. After the war these troops returned to their homeland with a new sense of pride and a national, rather than ethnic, identity. After the war de

*In towns such as Bouar, French colonial administration used forced labour to increase production of cotton and other goods.* George Rodger/Time & Life Pictures/Getty Images

Gaulle organized the French Union and created new local assemblies—consisting of French colonists and a handful of Africans—with regional political representatives. In November 1946 Barthélemy Boganda became the first Central African elected to the French National Assembly.

Boganda was a Roman Catholic priest, but he left the priesthood and formed the Social Evolution Movement of Black Africa (Mouvement pour l'Évolution Sociale de l'Afrique Noire; MESAN). MESAN gained control of the Territorial Assembly in 1957, and Boganda became president of the Grand Council of French Equatorial Africa.

## INDEPENDENCE

Boganda had hoped that the French territories of Chad, Gabon, Congo, and Ubangi-Shari could form a single nation. When the others rejected the unification plan, Boganda reluctantly agreed to accept the new constitution offered to Ubangi-Shari by France.

After Boganda's death in March 1959, David Dacko, a government member who claimed a family relationship to Boganda, became president. Ubangi-Shari, renamed the Central African Republic, was granted independence on Aug. 13, 1960.

## THE STRUGGLE FOR LEADERSHIP

Dacko permitted the French to provide the new country with assistance in the areas of trade, defense, and foreign relations. He also added government positions to reward his supporters and increased a number of their salaries, which drained the national budget.

Dacko made MESAN the only legal national political party in 1962. He thus ran unopposed in the elections of early 1964 and was formally elected president. The economy declined rapidly, and the national debt soared. In December 1965—amid impending bankruptcy and a threatened nationwide strike—the commander of the army, Jean-Bédel Bokassa, replaced Dacko in a staged coup.

Bokassa abolished the constitution, dissolved the legislature, and turned over administrative duties to his appointed cabinet. He allowed no opposition. His one forward-thinking act was to appoint Elizabeth Domitien, a prosperous businesswoman, as the country's (and sub-Saharan Africa's) first female prime minister in 1975. France continued to support him and the country's faltering economy because it wanted to retain control of the diamond (and potential uranium) output of the country. Bokassa declared himself president for life in 1972. Four years later he proclaimed himself emperor of the Central African Empire and was crowned the following year as Emperor Bokassa I with lavish ceremonies financed largely by France. While the government's debt mounted, most of the profits for the nation's diamond trade, which was personally administered by Bokassa, remained

# JEAN-BÉDEL BOKASSA

(b. Feb. 22, 1921, Bobangui, Moyen-Congo, French Equatorial Africa [now in Central African Republic]—d. Nov. 3, 1996, Bangui, Central African Republic)

*Jean-Bédel Bokassa was the African military leader who was president of the Central African Republic (1966–76) and self-styled emperor of the Central African Empire (1976–79).*

*The son of a village headman, Bokassa attended local mission schools before joining the French army in 1939. He distinguished himself in the French conflict in Indochina, and by 1961 he had achieved the rank of captain. At the request of Pres. David Dacko, Bokassa left the French armed forces to head the army of the newly independent Central African Republic. On Dec. 31, 1965, Bokassa used his position as supreme military commander to overthrow Dacko and declared himself president of the republic on Jan. 1, 1966. Bokassa initially spearheaded a number of reforms in an effort to develop the Central African Republic. He sought to promote economic development with Operation Bokassa, a national economic plan that created huge nationalized farms and industries, but the plan was stymied by poor management. He later became known for his autocratic and unpredictable policies, and his government was characterized by periodic reshuffles in which the power of the presidency was gradually increased.*

*In December 1976 Bokassa assumed the title Emperor Bokassa I and changed the name of his country to the Central African Empire. He was crowned a year later—in emulation of his hero, Napoleon I—in a lavish ceremony that cost more than $20 million. By this time Bokassa's rule had effectively bankrupted his impoverished country, and his reign as emperor proved to be short-lived. Following the substantiation of international charges that Bokassa had personally participated in a massacre of 100 schoolchildren by his imperial guard, French paratroops carried out a military coup against him that reestablished the republic and reinstated Dacko as president (September 1979). Bokassa went into exile, first traveling to Côte d'Ivoire but later settling in France.*

*Bokassa was sentenced in absentia to death in 1980, but he inexplicably chose to return to the Central African Republic in 1986. He was arrested and put on trial, and in 1987 he was found guilty of the murders of the schoolchildren and other crimes (although he was acquitted of charges of cannibalism). His death sentence was subsequently commuted, and he was freed in 1993.*

with Bokassa. Finally, in September 1979, the French government removed Bokassa—he was eventually allowed to live in France—and restored Dacko as president.

## AUTHORITARIAN RULE UNDER KOLINGBA

Dacko's return was not well received. To maintain his power, Dacko was forced to rely on French paratroops and on administrative officials who had also served in Bokassa's government. As opposition grew, followed by labour strikes and bomb attacks, Dacko increasingly depended on the army to retain power. Finally, in September 1981, Gen. André Kolingba removed Dacko from office in a bloodless coup and established a military government.

The government remained almost completely in military hands until 1985, when Kolingba dissolved the military committee that had ruled the country since the coup and named a new 25-member cabinet that included a few civilians. Under pressure from the World Bank and other international organizations, the National Assembly approved a new constitution early in 1986, adopted following a referendum later that year. Legislative elections were held in July 1987, but the government continued to operate under the direct control of Kolingba, who effectively held all executive and legislative power in the nation.

By the early 1990s Central Africa had become increasingly intolerant of Kolingba's authoritarian control and his lavish lifestyle. Growing democratic movements elsewhere in Africa had gained strength and inspired Central Africans to take action. Riots broke out in 1991, after civil servants had not been paid in more than eight months. It took two more years for Kolingba to give in to demands for open elections, when he allowed other parties to form and slate their own candidates for the presidency. Although he ran for president, Kolingba was rejected by the voters during the first round of balloting. Instead, Ange-Félix Patassé, a former prime minister, became the first democratically elected president since independence as the leader of the Central African People's Liberation Movement (Mouvement pour la Libération du Peuple Centrafricain; MLPC).

## Patassé and the Quest for Democracy

Patassé's tenure as president was far from peaceful. Inheriting a nearly bankrupt treasury and disgruntled civil servants who were still owed back wages, his government endured much civil unrest. Unpaid military factions attempted to stage coups three times in 1996, and Bangui was repeatedly looted, resulting in a significant loss of infrastructure and businesses. Bandit attacks by similar factions in the provinces contributed to unrest there as well as to the interruption of trade and agricultural production. The Patassé government and the military also failed to respect the rights of its citizens. For instance, following the 1996–97 looting, the police created the Squad for the Repression of Banditry and sanctioned the execution of criminals the day after their apprehension. The squad tortured and executed more than 20 suspected bandits without trial. The government also failed to call local elections in the late 1990s, claiming that it was unable to finance them.

The Patassé government, opposition parties, and religious groups signed the Bangui Accords in January 1997. The accords were a series of measures designed to reconcile competing political factions, reform and strengthen the economy, and restructure the military. Although the agreement did not restore peace to the country, French involvement in the Central African Republic ended in October 1997 when France withdrew its troops from Bangui and closed its long-standing military base in Bouar. The United Nations took over the peacekeeping mission and six months later sent in troops under the UN Mission to the Central African Republic (MINURCA). MINURCA's mission was to maintain stability and security, mediate between rival factions in the country, and provide advice and support in the 1998 legislative elections.

In late 1998 the MLPC narrowly retained its majority in the National Assembly when one opposition legislator changed his affiliation. Opposition parties strenuously opposed this change and protested, but MINURCA helped to restore order, and the National Assembly again reconvened. Patassé was reelected in September 1999, and MINURCA continued its peacekeeping operations until February 2000.

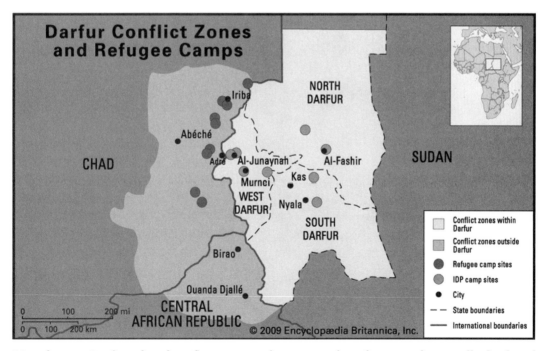

*Map showing Darfur-related conflict zones and campsites for refugees and internally displaced peoples (IDPs) in The Sudan, Central African Republic, and Chad, 2008.*

## THE 21ST CENTURY

The government continued to be plagued by protests over its continuing inability to pay civil servants and the military at the beginning of the new millennium. Attempted military overthrows that troubled the country in the mid-1990s also continued into the 21st century, culminating in the ouster of Patassé in a 2003 coup by former army chief Gen. François Bozizé. Bozizé's transitional government oversaw the drafting of a new constitution that was approved in late 2004 and democratic elections in 2005, in which Bozizé was elected president.

In June 2005, fighting between government and rebel forces in the north caused tens of thousands of people to flee across the border into Chad. This continued in the ensuing years. The north was also subject to violence that emanated from conflict in the Darfur region of neighbouring Sudan and spilled over the border.

# CHAPTER 4

## DEMOCRATIC REPUBLIC OF THE CONGO

The Democratic Republic of the Congo, located in Central Africa, has a 25-mile (40-km) coastline on the Atlantic Ocean but is otherwise landlocked. The former Belgian colony became independent in 1960. The capital is Kinshasa.

### PRECOLONIAL PERSPECTIVES

Before experiencing radical transformations in the colonial era, Congolese societies had already experienced major disruptions. From the 15th to the 17th century several important state systems evolved in the southern savanna region. The most important were the Kongo kingdom in the west and the Luba-Lunda states in the east. They developed elaborate political institutions, buttressed by symbolic kingship and military force. Power emanated from the capital to outlying areas through appointed chiefs or local clan heads. Competition for the kingship often led to civil strife, however, and, with the rise of the slave trade, new sources of instability influenced regional politics. The history of the Kongo peoples in the 16th century, for example, is largely the story of how the Atlantic slave trade created powerful vested interests among provincial chiefs, which over time undermined the kingdom's capacity to resist encroachments by its neighbours. By the late 16th century, the kingdom had all but succumbed to the attacks of the Imbangala (referred to as Jaga in contemporary sources), bands of fighters fleeing famine and drought in the

east. Two centuries later fragmentation also undermined political institutions among the Lunda and the Luba, followed by attacks from interlopers eager to control trade in slaves and ivory.

In the tropical rainforest, the radically different ecological conditions raised formidable obstacles to state formation. Small-scale societies, organized into village communities, were the rule. Corporate groups combining social and economic functions among small numbers of related and unrelated people formed the dominant mode of organization. Exchange took place through trade and gift-giving. Over time these social interactions fostered cultural homogeneity among otherwise distinctive communities, such as Bantu and Pygmy groups. Bantu communities absorbed and intermarried with their Pygmy clients, who brought their skills and crafts into the culture. This predominance of house and village organization stands in sharp contrast to the more centralized state structures characteristic of the savanna kingdoms, which were far more adept at acting in a concerted manner than the segmented societies in the tropical rainforest. The segmented nature of the tropical rainforest societies hindered their ability to resist a full-scale invasion by colonial forces.

In the savanna region, resistance to colonial forces was undermined by internecine raids and wars that followed the slave trade, by the increased devastation wrought on African kingdoms when those forces adopted the use of increasingly sophisticated firearms, and by the divisions between those who collaborated with outsiders and those who resisted. The relative ease with which these Congolese societies yielded to European conquest bears testimony to the magnitude of earlier upheavals.

## THE CONGO FREE STATE

King Leopold II of the Belgians set in motion the conquest of the huge domain that was to become his personal fiefdom. The king's attention was drawn to the region during British explorer and journalist Henry Morton Stanley's exploration of the Congo River in 1874–77. In November 1878 Leopold formed the Committee for Studies of the Upper Congo (Comité d'Études du Haut Congo, later renamed Association Internationale du Congo) to open up the African interior to European trade along the Congo River. Between 1879 and 1882, under the committee's auspices, Stanley established stations on the upper Congo and opened negotiations with local rulers. By 1884 the Association Internationale du Congo had signed treaties with 450 independent African entities and, on that basis, asserted its right to govern all the territory concerned as an independent state.

Leopold's thinly veiled colonial ambitions paved the way for the Berlin West Africa Conference (1884–85), which set the rules for colonial conquest and sanctioned his control of the Congo River basin area to be known as the Congo Free State (1885–1908). Armed with a private mandate from the international community of the time, and under the guise of his African International Association's humanitarian mission of ending slavery and bringing religion and the benefits of modern life to the Congolese, Leopold created a coercive instrument of colonial hegemony.

The name Congo Free State is closely identified with the extraordinary hardships and atrocities visited upon the Congolese masses in the name of Leopold's "civilizing mission." "Without the railroad," said Stanley, "the Congo is not worth a penny." Without recourse to forced labour, however, the railroad could not be built, and the huge concessions that had been made to private European companies would not become profitable, nor could African resistance in the east be overcome without a massive recruitment of indigenous troops. The cruel logic of the revenue imperative led Leopold to transform his nascent administrative system into a machine designed to extract not only the maximum amount of natural resources from the land but also the maximum output of labour from the people. In order to secure the labour necessary to accomplish Leopold's goals, his agents employed such methods as kidnapping the families of Congolese men, who were forced to meet often unrealistic work quotas to secure their families' release. Those who tried to rebel were dealt with by Leopold's private army, the Force Publique—a band of African soldiers led by European officers—who burned the villages and slaughtered the families of rebels. The Force Publique troops were also known for cutting off the hands of Congolese adults as well as children, which further terrorized the Congolese into submission.

In the wake of intense international criticism prompted by exposés by the American writer Mark Twain, the English journalist E.D. Morel, and various missionaries, in 1908 the Belgian Parliament voted to annex the Congo Free State—essentially purchasing the area from King Leopold and thus placing what was once the king's personal holding under Belgian rule. Nevertheless, the destructive effect of the Congo Free State lasted well beyond its brief history. The widespread social disruption complicated the establishment of a viable system of administration and left a legacy of anti-Western sentiment on which subsequent generations of nationalists were able to capitalize.

## BELGIAN PATERNALISM AND THE POLITICS OF DECOLONIZATION

The paternalistic tendencies of Belgian colonial rule bore traces of two characteristic features of Leopoldian rule: an irreducible tendency to treat Africans as children and a firm commitment to political control and compulsion. The elimination of the more brutal aspects of the Congo Free State notwithstanding, Belgian rule remained conspicuously unreceptive to political reform. By placing the inculcation of Western moral

*Historical map of the Belgian Congo (1908–60).*

principles above political education and apprenticeship for social responsibility, Belgian policies virtually ruled out initiatives designed to foster political experience and responsibility.

Not until 1957, with the introduction of a major local government reform (the so-called *statut des villes* ["statute of the cities"]), were Africans afforded a taste of democracy. By then a class of

Westernized Africans (*évolués*), eager to exercise their political rights beyond the urban arenas, had arisen. Moreover, heavy demands made upon the rural masses during the two world wars, coupled with the profound psychological effect of postwar constitutional reforms introduced in neighbouring French-speaking territories, created a climate of social unrest suited for the development of nationalist sentiment and activity.

The publication in 1956 of a political manifesto calling for immediate independence precipitated the political awakening of the Congolese population. Penned by a group of Bakongo *évolués* affiliated with the Alliance des Bakongo (ABAKO), an association based in Léopoldville (now Kinshasa), the manifesto was the response of ABAKO to the ideas set forth by a young Belgian professor of colonial legislation, A.A.J. van Bilsen, in his "Thirty-Year Plan for the Political Emancipation of Belgian Africa." Far more impatient than its catalyst, the ABAKO manifesto stated: "Rather than postponing emancipation for another thirty years, we should be granted self-government today."

Under the leadership of Joseph Kasavubu, ABAKO transformed itself into a vehicle of anticolonial protest. Nationalist sentiment spread through the lower Congo region, and, in time, the nationalist wave washed over the rest of the colony. Self-styled nationalist movements appeared almost overnight in every province. Among the welter of political parties brought into existence by the *statut des villes*, the Congolese National Movement (Mouvement National Congolais; MNC) stood out as the most powerful force for Congolese nationalism. The MNC never disavowed its commitment to national unity (unlike ABAKO, whose appeal was limited to Bakongo elements), and with the arrival of Patrice Lumumba—a powerful orator, advocate of pan-Africanism, and cofounder of the MNC—in Léopoldville in 1958 the party entered a militant phase.

The turning point in the process of decolonization came on Jan. 4, 1959, when anti-European rioting erupted in Léopoldville, resulting in the death of scores of Africans at the hands of the security forces. On January 13 the Belgian government formally recognized independence as the ultimate goal of its policies—a goal to be reached "without fatal procrastination, yet without fatal haste." By then, however, nationalist agitation had reached a level of intensity that made it virtually impossible for the colonial administration to control the course of events. The Belgian government responded to this growing turbulence by inviting a broad spectrum of nationalist organizations to a Round Table Conference in Brussels in January 1960. The aim was to work out the conditions of a viable transfer of power, but the result was an experiment in instant decolonization. Six months later, on June 30, the Congo formally acceded to independence and quickly descended into chaos.

## JOSEPH KASAVUBU

(b. 1910?, Tshela, Belgian Congo [now Democratic Republic of the Congo]—d. March 24, 1969, Boma)

*Joseph Kasavubu was a statesman and the first president of the independent Congo republic from 1960 to 1965, who shortly after independence in 1960 ousted the Congo's first prime minister, Patrice Lumumba, after the breakdown of order in the country.*

*Educated by Roman Catholic missionaries, Kasavubu became a lay teacher. In 1942 he entered the civil service. He attained the rank of chief clerk, the highest position open to Congolese in the Belgian colonial administration.*

*An early leader in the Congo's independence movement, Kasavubu during the late 1940s held important offices in Congolese cultural societies and alumni associations that were actually political organizations operating in defiance of Belgian authorities. As a member of the powerful Bakongo (or Kongo), one of the largest ethnic groups in the country, Kasavubu in the 1950s sought an independent Congo with a federal structure that would ensure a certain measure of Bakongo autonomy.*

*Kasavubu became president (1955) of Abako (Alliance des Ba-Kongo), the powerful cultural-political association of the Bakongo. In 1957 Abako candidates swept the first municipal elections permitted by Belgian authorities in Léopoldville (now Kinshasa), and Kasavubu was elected mayor of the Dendale district.*

*In the Congo's first national elections in 1960, Lumumba's party outpolled Kasavubu's Abako and its allies, but neither side could form a parliamentary coalition. As a compromise measure, Kasavubu and Lumumba formed an uneasy partnership with the former as president and the latter as premier.*

*Shortly after independence, Congo was racked by an army mutiny, Belgian military intervention to protect the remaining Belgian residents, and the secession of the province of Katanga under Moise Tshombe. United Nations aid proved ineffective in restoring order in the country, and there were reports that Prime Minister Lumumba had accepted offers of Soviet military aid to prop up the faltering central government. With the backing of the army under Col. Joseph Mobutu (later Mobutu Sese Seko), Kasavubu dismissed Lumumba and appointed a new government. Kasavubu then tacitly supported Mobuto's first coup in late 1960 and later engineered the accession of Tshombe to the premiership in 1964. Kasavubu's role in Congolese politics effectively ended, however, with Mobutu's second, and final overthrow of the government in 1965. Kasavubu then retired to his farm at Boma on the lower Congo River.*

## THE CONGO CRISIS

The triggering events behind the "Congo crisis" were the mutiny of the army (the Force Publique) near Léopoldville on July 5 and the subsequent intervention of Belgian paratroopers, ostensibly to protect the lives of Belgian citizens.

Adding to the confusion was a constitutional impasse that pitted the new country's president and prime minister against each other and brought the Congolese government to a halt. In the Congo's first national elections, Lumumba's MNC party had outpolled Kasavubu's ABAKO and its allies, but neither side could form a parliamentary coalition. As a compromise measure, Kasavubu and Lumumba formed an uneasy partnership with the former as president and the latter as premier. On September 5, however, Kasavubu relieved Lumumba of his functions, and Lumumba responded by dismissing Kasavubu. As a result of the discord, there were two groups now claiming to be the legal central government.

Meanwhile, on July 11, the country's richest province, Katanga, had declared itself independent under the leadership of Moise Tshombe. The support given by Belgium to the Katanga secession lent credibility to Lumumba's claims that Brussels was trying to reimpose its authority, and on July 12 he and Kasavubu appealed to United Nations (UN) Secretary-General Dag Hammarskjöld for UN security assistance. While intended to pave the way for the restoration of peace and order, the arrival of the UN peacekeeping force added to the tension between President Kasavubu and Prime Minister Lumumba. Lumumba's insistence that the UN should, if necessary, use force to bring Katanga back under control of the central government met with categorical opposition from Kasavubu. Lumumba then appealed to the Soviet Union for logistical assistance to send troops to Katanga. At that point the Congo crisis became inextricably bound up with East-West animosities in the context of the Cold War.

As the process of fragmentation set in motion by the Katanga secession reached its peak, resulting in the breakup of the country into four separate fragments (Katanga, Kasai, Orientale province, and Léopoldville), army Chief of Staff Joseph Mobutu (later Mobutu Sese Seko) took power in a coup d'état: he announced on Sept. 14, 1960, that the army would henceforth rule with the help of a caretaker government. The threat posed to the new regime by the forces loyal to Lumumba was substantially lessened by the capture of Lumumba in December 1960, after a dramatic escape from Léopoldville the previous month, and by his subsequent execution at the hands of the Tshombe government. Although Kasavubu had Lumumba arrested and delivered to the Katanga secessionists, which was intended to pave the way for a reintegration of the province, it was not until January 1963—and only after a violent

*Memorial in Kisangani to Patrice Lumumba, first prime minister of the Democratic Republic of the Congo.* Tomas D.W. Friedmann/Photo Researchers

showdown between the European-trained Katanga gendarmerie and the UN forces—that the secession was decisively crushed. Another secession challenge emerged on Sept. 7, 1964, when the pro-Lumumba government in Stanleyville (now Kisangani) declared much of eastern Congo to be the People's Republic of the Congo. This secession was brought to heel the next year. Meanwhile, following the convening of the parliament in Léopoldville, a new civilian government headed by Cyrille Adoula came to power on Aug. 2, 1961.

Adoula's inability to deal effectively with the Katanga secession and his decision to dissolve the parliament in September 1963 critically undermined his popularity. The dissolution of the parliament contributed directly to the outbreak of rural insurgencies, which engulfed 5 of 21 provinces between January and August 1964, and raised again the prospect of a total collapse of the central government. Because of its poor leadership and fragmented bases of support, however, the rebellion failed to translate its early military successes into effective political power. Even more important in turning the tide against the insurgents was decisive intervention by European mercenaries, who helped the central government regain control over rebel-held areas. Much of the credit for the survival of the government goes to Tshombe, who by July 10, 1964, had replaced Adoula as prime minister. Ironically, then, a year and a half after his defeat at the hands of the UN forces, Tshombe, the most vocal advocate of secession, had emerged as the providential leader of a besieged central government.

## MOBUTU'S REGIME

Mobutu's second coup, on Nov. 24, 1965, occurred in circumstances strikingly similar to those that had led to the first—a struggle for power between the incumbent president, Kasavubu, and his prime minister, this time Tshombe. Mobutu's coup saw to the removal of Kasavubu and Tshombe, and Mobutu proceeded to assume the presidency. Unlike Lumumba, however, Tshombe managed to leave the country unharmed—and determined to regain power. Rumours that the ousted prime minister was plotting a comeback from exile in Spain hardened into certainty when in July 1966 some 2,000 of Tshombe's former Katanga gendarmes, led by mercenaries, mutinied in Kisangani. Exactly one year after the crushing of that first mutiny, a second broke out, again in Kisangani, apparently triggered by the news that

Tshombe's airplane had been hijacked over the Mediterranean and forced to land in Algiers, where he was then held prisoner and later died of a heart attack. Led by a Belgian settler named Jean Schramme and including approximately 100 former Katanga gendarmes and about 1,000 Katangese, the mutineers held their ground against the 32,000-man Congolese National Army (Armée Nationale Congolaise; ANC) until November 1967, when the mercenaries crossed the border into Rwanda and surrendered to the local authorities. Schramme later turned up in Brazil, where he remained in spite of attempts by the Belgian government to have him extradited.

The country settled into a semblance of political stability for the next several years, allowing Mobutu to focus on his unsuccessful strategies for economic progress. In 1971 Mobutu renamed the country Zaire as part of his "authenticity" campaign—his effort to emphasize the country's cultural identity. Officially described as "the nation politically organized," Mobutu's Popular Movement of the Revolution (Mouvement Populaire de la Révolution; MPR), the sole political party from 1970 to 1990, may be better seen as a weakly articulated patronage system. Mobutu's effort to extol the virtues of Zairian "authenticity" did little to lend respectability either to the concept or to the brand of leadership for which it stood. As befit his chiefly image, Mobutu's rule was based on bonds of personal loyalty between himself and his entourage.

*After two coups Joseph Mobutu (later Mobutu Sese Seko) guided the Democratic Republic of the Congo to political stability but made scant economic progress.* Keystone/Hulton Archive/ Getty Images

The fragility of Mobutu's power base was demonstrated in 1977 and '78, when the country's main opposition movement, the Congolese National Liberation Front (Front de la Libération Nationale Congolaise; FLNC), operating from Angola, launched two major invasions into Shaba (which Katanga was called from 1972 to 1997). On both occasions external intervention by friendly governments—primarily Morocco in 1977 and France in 1978—saved the day, but at the price of many African and European casualties. Shortly after the capture of the urban centre of Kolwezi by the FLNC in May 1978, an estimated 100 Europeans lost their lives at the hands of the rebels and the ANC. Apart from the role played by the FLNC in spearheading the invasions, the sharp deterioration of the Zairian economy after 1975, coupled with the rapid growth of anti-Mobutu sentiment among the poor and the unemployed, was a crucial factor in the near success of the invasions of Shaba. The timing of the first Shaba invasion, a full 11 years after the creation of the MPR in 1966, underscored the shortcomings of the single-party state as a vehicle for national integration and of "Mobutism" as an ideology for the legitimization of Mobutu's regime.

Circumstances changed dramatically with the end of the Cold War in the early 1990s. Former supporters on the international scene, such as the United States, France, and Belgium, pressed for democratic reforms; some even openly supported Mobutu's rivals. In April 1990 Mobutu did decide to lift the ban on opposition parties, but he followed that liberalizing act with the brutal repression of student protests at the University of Lubumbashi in May—resulting in the death of 50 to 150 students, according to Amnesty International. In 1991 France reduced its monetary aid to the country, U.S. diplomats criticized Mobutu before the U.S. Congress, and the World Bank cut ties with Mobutu following his appropriation of $400 million from Gécamines, the state mining corporation.

Mobutu grudgingly agreed to relinquish some power in 1991: he convened a national conference that resulted in the formation of a coalition group, the High Council of the Republic (Haut Conseil de la République; HCR), a provisional body charged with overseeing the country's transfer to a multiparty democracy. The HCR selected Étienne Tshisekedi as prime minister. Tshisekedi, an ethnic Luba from the diamond-rich Kasaï-Oriental province, was known as a dissident as early as 1980, when he and a small group of parliamentarians charged the army with having massacred some 300 diamond miners. Tshisekedi's renewed prominence highlighted the key role that natural resources continued to play in national politics.

Meanwhile, Mobutu, resistant to the transfer of authority to Tshisekedi, maneuvered to pit groups within the HCR against each another. He also ensured the support of military units by giving them the right to plunder whole regions of the country and certain sectors of the economy. Eventually, these maneuvers undermined Tshisekedi and resuscitated the regime. Mobutu reached an agreement with the opposition, and Kengo wa Dondo became prime minister in 1994. Mobutu agreed to government reforms set forth in the Transitional Constitutional Act (1994), but real reforms and promised elections never took place.

The Rwandan crisis of 1993–94— rooted in long-running tensions between that country's two major ethnic groups, the Hutu and the Tutsi—and the ensuing genocide (during which more than 800,000 civilians, primarily Tutsi, were killed) afforded Mobutu an opportunity to mend his relationships with the Western powers. Following the late-1993 invasion of Rwanda by the forces of the Rwandan Patriotic Front (Front Patriotique Rwandais; FPR), a Tutsi-led Rwandan exile organization, Mobutu offered logistical and military support to the French and Belgian troops who intervened to support the Hutu-led Rwandan government. This move renewed relations with France and ultimately led Belgium and the United States to reopen diplomatic channels with Mobutu. Business ventures that promised foreign firms privileged access to the country's resources and state enterprises further bolstered external support.

Mobutu also encouraged attacks against Zairians of Rwandan Tutsi origin living in the eastern part of the country, just one of the maneuvers that ultimately sowed the seeds of his downfall. The attacks, coupled with Mobutu's support of a faction of Hutu (exiled in Zaire) who opposed the Rwandan government, ultimately led local Tutsi and the government of Rwanda to join forces with Mobutu's opponent Laurent Kabila and his Alliance of Democratic Forces for the Liberation of Congo-Zaire (Alliance des Forces Démocratiques pour la Libération du Congo-Zaïre; AFDL). Kabila's opposition forces also gained the backing of the governments of Angola and Uganda, because Mobutu had supported rebel movements within those countries. (Mobutu's associates had engaged in diamond trafficking with National Union for the Total Independence of Angola [UNITA] rebels; Mobutu also had allowed supplies for Ugandan rebels to be transported via a Zairian airport.)

In October 1996, while Mobutu was abroad for cancer treatment, Kabila and his supporters launched an offensive from bases in the east and subsequently captured Bukavu and Goma, a city on the shore of Lake Kivu. Mobutu returned to the country in December but failed to stabilize the situation. The rebels continued to advance, and on March 15, 1997, Kisangani fell, followed by Mbuji-Mayi and Lubumbashi in early April. South African-backed negotiations between Mobutu and Kabila in early May quickly failed, and the victorious forces of the AFDL entered the capital on May 17, 1997. By this time, Mobutu had fled. He died in exile a few months later.

# THE DEMOCRATIC REPUBLIC OF THE CONGO

Following Mobutu's departure, Kabila assumed the presidency and restored the country's previous name, the Democratic Republic of the Congo. Initially, Kabila was able to attract foreign aid and provided some order and relief to the country's decimated economy. He also initiated the drafting of a new constitution. The outward appearance of moving toward democracy conflicted with the reality of the situation: Kabila held the bulk of power and did not tolerate criticism or opposition. Political parties and public demonstrations were banned almost immediately following Kabila's takeover of the government, and his administration was accused of human rights abuse.

In August 1998 the new leader was plagued by a rebellion in the country's eastern provinces—supported by some of Kabila's former allies. The rebellion marked the start of what became a devastating five-year civil war that drew in several countries. By the end of 1998, the rebels, backed by the Ugandan and Rwandan governments, controlled roughly one-third of the country. Kabila's government received support from the Angolan, Namibian, and Zimbabwean governments in its fight against the rebels. A cease-fire and the deployment of UN peacekeeping forces were among the provisions of the 1999 Lusaka Peace Accord, an agreement intended to end the hostilities. Although it was eventually signed by most parties involved in the conflict, the accord was not fully implemented, and fighting continued. Meanwhile, long-standing ethnic tensions between the Hema and the Lendu peoples erupted into violence in the Ituri district in the eastern part of the country. Rebel involvement and other political and economic factors further complicated matters, spawning an additional conflict in a region already mired in the civil war.

Kabila was assassinated in January 2001. He was succeeded by his son, Joseph, who immediately declared his commitment to finding a peaceful end to the war. Soon after Joseph Kabila assumed power, the Rwandan and Ugandan governments and the rebels agreed to a UN-proposed pull-out plan, but it was never fully actualized. Finally, in December 2002, an agreement reached in Pretoria, S.Af., provided for the establishment of a power-sharing transitional government and an end to the war. This agreement was ratified in April 2003. A transitional constitution also was adopted that month, and an interim government was inaugurated in July, with Kabila as president. UN peacekeeping troops continued to maintain a presence in the country.

Although the civil war was technically over, the country was devastated. More than three million people had been killed, and survivors were left to struggle with homelessness, starvation, and disease.

The new government was fragile; the economy was in shambles; and societal infrastructure had been destroyed. With international assistance, Kabila was able to make considerable progress toward reforming the economy and began the work of rebuilding the country. With his government unable to exercise any real control over much of the country, he had to cope with fighting that remained in the east, as well as two failed coup attempts in 2004. Nevertheless, a new, formal constitution was promulgated in 2006, and Kabila was victorious in presidential elections held later that year.

In January 2008 a peace agreement aimed at ending the fighting in the eastern part of the country was signed by the government and more than 20 rebel groups. The fragile truce was broken later that year when rebels led by Laurent Nkunda renewed their attacks, displacing tens of thousands of residents and international aid workers. In January 2009 Congolese and Rwandan troops together launched an offensive against rebel groups in the east. They forced Nkunda to flee across the border into Rwanda, where he was arrested and indicted for war crimes by the Congolese government. In May 2009 further efforts to resolve the continuing conflict in the east included an amnesty extended to a number of militant groups there.

# CHAPTER 5

## REPUBLIC OF THE CONGO

The Republic of the Congo is situated astride the Equator in west-central Africa. The former French colony became independent in 1960. The capital is Brazzaville.

### EARLY HISTORY

Human habitation of the Congo basin came relatively late in the Sangoan era (100,000 to 40,000 BCE), perhaps because of the dense forest. The people who used the large-core bifacial Sangoan tools probably subsisted by gathering food and digging up roots. They were not hunters.

Refined versions of this tradition continued through the Lupemban (40,000 to 25,000 BCE) and Tshitolian eras. The early inhabitants of these eras were farmer-trappers, fishing peoples, and Pygmy hunters. People lived in households that included kin and unrelated individuals, with a "big man" at the centre of the household to represent the group. Mobility—of individuals, groups, goods, and ideas—figured prominently and created a common social environment. Such intercommunication is evident from the closely related Bantu languages of the region. Speakers of Adamawa-Ubangi languages lived in the north but maintained ties with their forest neighbours. Research now suggests that agriculture emerged among the western Bantu of the savannas adjacent to the lower Congo River in the 1st millennium BCE—much earlier than previously thought.

Larger-scale societies based on clans whose members lived in different villages, village clusters with chiefs, and small

*The nearly impenetrable forest in the Republic of the Congo likely prevented human population until quite late in the Sangoan era.* Michael Nichols/National Geographic/Getty Images

forest principalities emerged between 1000 and 1500 CE. Chiefdoms on the southern fringes became more complex, and three kingdoms eventually developed: Loango, at the mouth of the Kouilou River on the Atlantic coast; Kongo, in the far southwest; and Tio (Anziku), which grew out of small chiefdoms on the plains north of Malebo Pool. Rulers derived power from control over spirit cults, but trade eventually became a second pillar of power.

In 1483 the Portuguese landed in Kongo. Initially, relations between the Kongolese and Portuguese rulers were good. Characterized by the exchange of representatives and the sojourn of Kongolese students in Portugal, this period was a harbinger of late 20th-century technical assistance. Unfortunately, the need of Portuguese planters on São Tomé for slaves had undermined this amicable arrangement by the 1530s.

Between 1600 and 1800, the slave trade expanded enormously. Local leaders challenged state control. Among the Tio, the western chiefs became more autonomous. Contact with Europeans also introduced New World food crops, such as corn (maize) and cassava (manioc), which allowed greater population densities. This, along with the emergence of a "market" for foodstuffs, led to greater use of slaves, intensified women's work, and changed the division of labour between the sexes.

## THE COLONIAL ERA

By the early 19th century, the Congo River had become a major avenue of commerce between the coast and the interior. Henry Morton Stanley, a British journalist, explored the river in 1877, but France acquired jurisdiction in 1880 when Pierre de Brazza signed a treaty with the Tio ruler. The formal proclamation of the colony of French Congo came in 1891. Early French efforts to exploit their possession led to ruthless treatment of the local people and the subjection of the territory to extreme exploitation by concessionary companies. Brazza returned in 1905 to lead an inquiry into these excesses. In 1910 the French joined Congo with neighbouring colonies, creating a federation of French Equatorial Africa, with its capital at Brazzaville.

The French were preoccupied with acquiring labour. Forced labour, head taxes, compulsory production of cash crops, and draconian labour contracts forced Africans to build infrastructure and to participate in the colonial economy. No project was more costly in African lives than the Congo-Ocean Railway, built between 1921 and 1934 from Pointe-Noire to Brazzaville; between 15,000 and 20,000 Africans died.

In 1940 Congo rallied to the Free French forces. Charles de Gaulle, Gov.-Gen. Félix Éboué, and African leaders held a conference in Brazzaville in 1944 to announce more liberal policies. In 1946 Congo became an overseas territory of France, with representatives in the French Parliament and an elected Territorial Assembly. Ten years later, the loi cadre ("enabling act") endowed the colony with an elected government. Congo became a

# DENIS SASSOU-NGUESSO

(b. 1943, Edou, Rep. of the Congo)

Denis Sassou-Nguesso is a Congolese politician and former military leader who has twice served as president of the Republic of the Congo (1979–92 and 1997– ).

After he left school in 1961, Sassou-Nguesso joined the army, which sent him to Algeria and France for military training. In 1963 Sassou-Nguesso was appointed commander of military forces in Brazzaville and by the early 1970s had risen to the rank of colonel. During this time Sassou-Nguesso took an active role in politics. He joined the Congolese Labour Party (Parti Congolais du Travail; PCT), which embraced a Marxist-Leninist ideology and was designated the country's sole ruling party in 1970. Sassou-Nguesso became a protégé of Pres. Marien Ngouabi (1968–77), who appointed him minister of defense in 1975. After Ngouabi was assassinated in 1977, Sassou-Nguesso's rival within the PCT, Joachim Yhombi-Opango, came to power and appointed Sassou-Nguesso first vice president of the PCT's military committee. Yhombi-Opango was forced to resign in February 1979, and the following month the PCT appointed Sassou-Nguesso president of the republic and head of the party.

Although Sassou-Nguesso's political roots were Marxist-Leninist in nature, as president he adopted a pro-Western approach when it was pragmatic to do so. The country initially enjoyed a period of relative stability under Sassou-Nguesso, and the PCT reelected him to the presidency in 1984 and again in 1989. Falling oil prices in the 1980s contributed to a faltering economy and growing discontent in the country. In response, the PCT officially abandoned its Marxist-Leninist policies in 1990, a move that did not bode well for Sassou-Nguesso. In the country's first multiparty elections, held in August 1992, Sassou-Nguesso was eliminated in the first round of voting.

After a brief alliance with the new ruling party that dissolved in late September, Sassou-Nguesso and the PCT allied itself with the Union for Democratic Renewal (Union pour le Renouveau Démocratique), forming an opposition body and initiating acts of civil disobedience against the new president's administration. In 1993 militias supportive of Sassou-Nguesso clashed with government forces, and escalating violence continued into the next year. Violence erupted again in the months prior to the 1997 presidential and legislative elections, initiating a two-year civil war. In the fall of 1997, the incumbent president was forced into exile and Sassou-Nguesso was once again declared president. He implemented a series of economic and political reforms to rebuild the country from bankruptcy and strengthen the democratic process, although the legitimacy of the democratic reform was often called into question by the opposition.

Sassou-Nguesso was reelected in 2002 in an election clouded by controversy. Some opposition candidates boycotted the race, claiming that democratic reform was still lacking and that the election would not be free and fair. As a result, Sassou-Nguesso faced no real competition, and the legitimacy of his overwhelming victory was disputed by the opposition. The 2009 presidential election was also boycotted by the main opposition candidates, and Sassou-Nguesso was reelected by a wide margin of victory.

republic within the French Community in 1958 and acquired complete political independence on Aug. 15, 1960.

## CONGO SINCE INDEPENDENCE

Two major parties existed at independence: the African Socialist Movement (Mouvement Socialiste Africain; MSA) and the Democratic Union for the Defense of African Interests (Union Démocratique pour la Défense des Intérêts Africains; UDDIA). The two parties pitted the north against the south, an opposition that stemmed from the privileged place occupied by the southern Kongo and Vili in the colonial era. The two parties also had different political philosophies. The MSA favoured a powerful state and a partially publicly owned economy, whereas the UDDIA advocated private ownership and close ties with France. UDDIA leader Fulbert Youlou formed the first parliamentary government in 1958, and in 1959 he became premier and president.

Corruption, incompetence, mass disapproval, general strikes, and lack of French support led to Youlou's ouster in 1963. His successor, Alphonse Massamba-Débat, shifted policies to the left, notably by founding the National Revolutionary Movement (Mouvement National de la Révolution; MNR) as the sole party. The country sought assistance from the Soviet Union and China and voted with the more radical African states in world forums. Regionally, Congo extended concrete support and offered a geographic base for the Popular Movement for the Liberation of Angola (MPLA), the Marxist movement that won independence for that country. Congo also offered asylum to the Patrice Lumumba followers who fled the neighbouring Democratic Republic of the Congo (from 1971 to 1997 called Zaire).

Regionalism and policy failures led the military to replace Massamba-Débat with Maj. Marien Ngouabi in 1968. Ngouabi maintained a socialist line, renaming the country the People's Republic of the Congo on Dec. 31, 1969. The Congolese Labour Party (Parti Congolais du Travail; PCT) replaced MNR as sole ruling party at the same time. Ngouabi was a northerner, and his regime shifted control of the country away from the south. Such moves created opposition among workers and students in the highly politicized environment of Brazzaville and other southern urban centres. Ngouabi was assassinated in March 1977. His successor, the more conservative Col. Joachim Yhombi-Opango, soon clashed with the PCT, and Col. Denis Sassou-Nguesso replaced Yhombi-Opango in 1979.

Although Sassou-Nguesso represented the more militant wing of the PCT—and immediately introduced a new constitution intended as a first step toward building a Marxist-Leninist society—he paradoxically improved relations with France and other Western countries. The regime's political language became more moderate, but inefficient state enterprises created by earlier socialist policies remained in operation in the early 1980s. In the 1970s they had been subsidized by petroleum production, but the subsequent drop in oil and other raw material prices led to economic crisis. The external debt surpassed $1.5 billion in 1985, and debt service consumed 45 percent of state revenue. Negotiations with the International Monetary Fund the following year led to an agreement to help the national economy in exchange for cuts in public spending and in the state bureaucracy.

In 1991 a new constitution was drafted, and it was adopted by referendum in March 1992. Pascal Lissouba defeated Bernard Kolélas and Sassou-Nguesso and acceded to the presidency following elections that August. A period of shaky parliamentary government ensued. Competing politicians built followings by politicizing ethnic differences and sponsoring militias such as the Cocoye, Cobra, and Ninja groups (aligned with Lissouba, Sassou-Nguesso, and Kolélas, respectively), which led to civil conflict in 1994 and 1997. With the support of France and Angola—whose government was troubled by Lissouba's support for the National Union for the Total Independence of Angola (União Nacional para a Independência Total de Angola; UNITA) and other rebels fighting for the independence of the exclave of Cabinda—Sassou-Nguesso led a successful insurrection against the government in 1997 and reclaimed the presidency late in the year. However, violence spiraled beyond the control of the leaders who instigated it. A devastating civil war raged for the next two years, in which

forces loyal to Kolélas and to the ousted Lissouba—both of whom had since left the country—battled government troops for control. A truce was signed between the warring parties in late 1999 in an attempt to reopen a national dialogue. Additional talks held in early 2000 were positive, and by the end of the year the government was able to focus on drafting a new constitution and planning the country's future.

The new constitution was promulgated in January 2002, and Sassou-Nguesso was reelected president in March. Around the same time, rebels resumed fighting in southern Congo, displacing tens of thousands of Congolese by late May. Legislative elections held that month were marred by violence and allegations of fraud. The violence and fighting continued throughout the summer, primarily in the southern part of the country, and finally ceased when a peace agreement was reached in early 2003. Congo's newfound peace provided stability and cultivated the opportunity for progress, and the country enjoyed an improved economic and political climate. Despite these promising steps, sporadic instability continued—especially in the south, in the Pool region in particular—and civilians again faced displacement.

The 2009 presidential election, held on July 12, was boycotted by the main opposition candidates, and Sassou-Nguesso was reelected by a wide margin of victory. Although the opposition and some organizations claimed that there were incidents of fraud and intimidation, international observers from the African Union declared the election free and fair.

# CHAPTER 6

## GABON

G abon is located on the Atlantic coast of west-central Africa, astride the Equator. The former French colony became independent in 1960. The capital is Libreville.

### EARLY COLONIZATION

At the arrival of the first Portuguese navigators to Gabon in 1472, portions of southern Gabon were loosely linked to the state of Loango, which in turn formed a province of the vast Kongo kingdom to the south. From the offshore islands of São Tomé and Príncipe, where the Portuguese established sugar plantations, they developed trade with the mainland. From the late 1500s, Dutch, French, Spanish, and English competitors also exchanged cloth, iron goods, firearms, and alcoholic beverages for hardwoods, ivory, and a few slaves.

The slave trade achieved extensive development only between the 1760s and 1840s, as a result of heightened demand from Brazil and Cuba. Interior peoples sent undesirables from their own societies and captives from warfare down the waterways to the coast, where they were collected in barracoons (temporary enclosures) to await the arrival of European ships. The Orungu clans at Cape Lopez organized a kingdom whose power rested on control of the slave trade through the mouths of the Ogooué River. The Mpongwe clans of the estuary, who were already important traders, also

## THE FANG

*The Fang (also spelled Făn) are Bantu-speaking peoples occupying the southernmost districts of Cameroon south of the Sanaga River, mainland Equatorial Guinea, and the forests of the northern half of Gabon south to the Ogooué River estuary. The Fang speak languages of the Bantu subgroup of the Niger-Congo language family. They can be divided into three linguistic groups: (1) the Beti to the north, the main ethnic groups being the Yaunde, or Éwondo, and Bene; (2) the Bulu, including the Bulu proper, Fong, Zaman, and Yelinda; and (3) the Fang in the south, including the Fang proper, Ntumu, and Mvae.*

*According to tradition, the Fang migrated into the forest from the savanna plateau on the right bank of the Sanaga River at the beginning of the 19th century. They were fine warriors and hunters and cultivated a reputation for cannibalism to repel outsiders and attacks from others. Under colonial rule they engaged in ivory trading, and after World War I they turned to large-scale cocoa farming.*

*The Fang kinship system is strongly patrilineal, with large, patriarchal families and out-marrying clans traced through the male line. Among the southern Fang there is little political organization, whereas in the north some Beti groups have clan chiefs. By 1939 the entire population was reportedly Christian. Since 1945, however, there has been a rapid growth of syncretistic sects combining animistic and Christian beliefs with a cargo-cult element. All their native crafts, including wood carving and their once-reputed work in iron and steatite, have disappeared under Western influence. As a result of educational progress and relative economic prosperity, the Fang have become politically influential, especially in Gabon.*

profited from the slave trade, as did the Vili of Loango, whose activities extended throughout southern Gabon. Only the Fang, who were migrating southward from Cameroon into the forests north of the Ogooué, ordinarily refused to hold slaves or engage in warfare to obtain them. The coastward migrations of the numerous and often warlike Fang nevertheless contributed to the further decimation and dispersion of many interior peoples, particularly during the 19th century.

## FRENCH CONTROL

By 1800 the British were becoming the leading traders in manufactures throughout the Gulf of Guinea. After 1815 the French sought to compete more actively in the commercial sphere and to join Britain in combating the slave trade. To these ends, Capt. Édouard Bouët-Willaumez negotiated treaties with the heads of two Mpongwe clans, King Denis (Antchouwe Kowe Rapontchombo) on the southern bank of the estuary in 1839 and King Louis (Anguile Dowe) on the northern bank in 1841. They agreed to end the slave trade and to accept French sovereignty over their lands. The arrival of American Protestant missionaries on the northern bank in May 1842 to open a school in the lands of King Glass (R'Ogouarowe)—the centre of British, American, and German commercial activity—spurred the French to establish Fort d'Aumale within the territory of King Louis in 1843. In 1844 France brought in Roman Catholic missionaries to promote French cultural influence among the Mpongwe and neighbouring peoples. French agents obtained a treaty from King Glass, recognizing French sovereignty. In 1849 Bouët-Willaumez organized a small settlement of mainly Vili freed slaves called Libreville ("Free Town"), which, combined with the fort, formed the nucleus of the capital.

During the 1850s and '60s the French gradually extended their control along the adjacent coast and sent explorers into the interior. The expeditions of Pierre Savorgnan de Brazza between 1875 and 1885 established French authority on

*Libreville, c. 1900. The city later became the capital of Gabon.* Harlingue/Roger Viollet/ Getty Images

the upper Ogooué, where Franceville was founded in 1880, and on the Loango coast. An enlarged Gabon was attached to the French Congo in 1886 under Brazza as governor.

In 1910 Gabon became one of the four colonies within the federation of French Equatorial Africa. The French delimited the frontier with the Germans in Cameroon in 1885 and with the Spanish in Río Muni, or Spanish Guinea (later Equatorial Guinea), in 1900. French occupation of the Gabon interior brought little opposition, but interference with trade and such exactions as head taxes, labour taxes for public projects, and forced labour provoked considerable resistance, as did the French policy from 1898 to 1914 of developing the economy through monopolistic concessionary companies, which devastated settlement, agricultural production, and trade.

In the period between the two world wars, a pro-French but anticolonialist elite was created, mainly from the graduates of the boys' schools of the Brothers of Saint-Gabriel at Libreville and Lambaréné. From their ranks came most of the politicians who held office during the Fourth French Republic (1946–58), when Gabon became an overseas territory with its own assembly and representation in the French Parliament. During this era France considerably expanded public investment in the economy, health care, and education. In 1958 Gabon became an autonomous republic within the French Community and, after concluding cooperation agreements with France, achieved independence on Aug. 17, 1960.

## GABON SINCE INDEPENDENCE

Gabon favoured close relations with France and the continued use of French language and culture. It opposed political ties with the other states of sub-Saharan Africa, however, because of dissatisfaction with the previous federation and a desire to develop its natural resources for its own benefit.

Attempts by the republic's first president, Léon M'ba, to institute a single-party regime provoked a rebellion by young military officers in February 1964. But M'ba, who had strong backing from French economic interests, was restored to power by French forces sent on orders from Pres. Charles de Gaulle. The intervention made possible the rise of Albert-Bernard (later Omar) Bongo to the presidency after M'ba's death in 1967 and the establishment of a single-party regime in the following year, the only party being Bongo's Gabonese Democratic Party (Parti Démocratique Gabonais; PDG). Under the single-party regime, Bongo was elected to the presidency in 1973 and was reelected in 1979. In 1982 a new opposition group, the Movement for National Renewal (Mouvement de Redressement National), called for multiparty democracy, exercise of civil liberties, and an end to governmental corruption, but it was quickly suppressed. Bongo was again reelected in 1986.

In the mid-1980s, declining petroleum prices caused an economic downturn. Austerity measures imposed by the government led to antigovernment demonstrations in Libreville and Port-Gentil in early 1990. This unrest led to the creation in March of a national conference, which included opposition groups, to discuss political reform. As a result, constitutional amendments adopted in May restored the multiparty system. That same month the death of an opposition leader under mysterious circumstances sparked violent disorders that led to French military intervention at Port-Gentil to protect French nationals and their property. Order was restored, and implementation of the plans for political reform continued. Legislative elections were held in the fall, and, although opposition parties won seats in the new legislative assembly, electoral irregularities allowed the PDG to retain a small majority. The following year a new constitution was promulgated in March.

After the restoration of a multiparty democracy, Bongo was reelected in 1993 and 1998, although both elections were clouded with allegations of fraud. A constitutional amendment passed in 2003 removed presidential term limits and allowed Bongo to stand in the 2005 election, which he also won. In general, the PDG was equally successful during the 1990s and 2000s in legislative and most local elections. However, the

PDG's overall grip on power was briefly threatened by popular dissatisfaction following the December 1993 presidential election and a subsequent 50 percent devaluation of the currency in January 1994, which sparked protests in several cities, during which three dozen people were killed and scores injured. After the demonstrations were suppressed, the government granted modest salary increases and placed controls on soaring prices of largely imported basic commodities.

Many of Gabon's financial problems resulted from protracted and large-scale corruption among government officials and business leaders. Although this group comprised just 2 percent of the population, they came to control some 80 percent of all personal income. In addition to receiving large salaries, they diverted funds from public works and services, as well as the income from at least one-fourth of the oil sales, and transferred vast sums of money to foreign accounts. To counteract this financial drain, the government borrowed money, and by the late 1990s debt service constituted some two-fifths of the national budget. The government turned regularly to France for funds and for help in canceling and rescheduling debts. By the late 1990s, Gabon was under pressure from the International Monetary Fund to privatize state corporations and to eliminate the diversion of state funds, with which the country was able to show some progress during the 2000s. Gabon was able to reschedule a significant amount of debt in 2004.

In 2009 rumours persisted that Bongo was not in good health, particularly in May, when he suspended his presidential duties for the first time since he took office in 1967 and checked into a clinic in Spain—ostensibly to rest and mourn the death of his wife, who had passed away in March. Initial reports of his death on June 7, 2009, were denied by the Gabon government, and an official announcement the next day indicated he died on June 8. Senate president Rose Francine Rogombé was sworn in as interim president two days later, and an election was scheduled for August 30. More than 20 candidates initially announced their intent to stand in the election, including Bongo's son, defense minister Ali Ben Bongo, who was selected to be the PDG's candidate. After a slight delay in the release of the election results and amid allegations of fraud and voting irregularities, Bongo was declared the winner with slightly more than two-fifths of the vote.

# CHAPTER 7

## RWANDA

Rwanda is a landlocked country lying south of the Equator in east-central Africa. The former historical kingdom fell under colonial rule—first by the Germans, then by the Belgians—before it regained its independence in 1962. The capital is Kigali.

### PRE-COLONIAL RWANDA

The area that is now Rwanda is believed to have been initially settled by the Twa, who were closely followed by the Hutu, probably sometime between the 5th and 11th centuries, and then by the Tutsi beginning in the 14th century. Tutsi traditions trace the birth of the Rwanda kingdom to the miraculous feats of its founding hero, Gihanga, whose coming to Rwanda is said to coincide with the advent of civilization. A more historical appraisal, however, would emphasize a long process of Tutsi migrations from the north, culminating in the 16th century with the emergence of a small nuclear kingdom in the central region, ruled by the Tutsi minority, that persisted until the arrival of Europeans in the 19th century. Because of this, Rwanda differs from most countries in sub-Saharan Africa in that its general boundaries were not drawn by European powers but reflect the fully established nation-state that existed until the introduction of German rule.

*Hutu family compound, Burundi.* Sarah Errington/The Hutchison Library

## RWANDA UNDER GERMAN AND BELGIAN CONTROL

From 1894 to 1918, Rwanda, along with Burundi, was part of German East Africa. After Belgium became the administering authority under the mandates system of the League of Nations, Rwanda and Burundi formed a single administrative entity. Although they continued to be jointly administered as the Territory of Ruanda-Urundi until the end of the Belgian trusteeship in 1962, by then the two states had evolved radically different political systems. Rwanda had declared itself a republic in January 1961 and forced its monarch (*mwami*), Kigeri, into exile. Conversely, Burundi retained the formal trappings of a constitutional monarchy until 1966.

The Rwanda revolution was rooted partly in a traditional system of stratification based on an all-embracing "premise of inequality" and partly in a colonial heritage that greatly increased the oppressiveness of the few over the

## THE HUTU AND THE TUTSI

*The Hutu—also called Bahutu or Wahutu—are Bantu-speaking people of Rwanda and Burundi. The Tutsi—also called Batusi, Tussi, Watusi, or Watutsi—are an ethnic group of probable Nilotic origin, whose members also live within Rwanda and Burundi. In both countries, the Hutu comprise the vast majority but were traditionally subject to the Tutsi, who formed the traditional aristocratic minority.*

*When the Hutu first entered the area, they found it inhabited by the Twa, Pygmy hunters whom they forced to retreat. Hutu life centred on small-scale agriculture, and social organization was based on the clan, with petty kings (bahinza) ruling over limited domains. The Tutsi in turn entered the area in the 14th or 15th century, entering from the northeast seeking new rangelands. Though they were skilled warriors, they obtained dominance over the resident Hutu through a slow and largely peaceful infiltration. The Tutsi established a feudal relationship with the Hutu, gaining dominance due to their possession of cattle and their more advanced knowledge of warfare. At the head of the Tutsis' complex hierarchical political structure was the mwami ("king"), who was considered to be of divine origin. Tutsi expansion continued until the European colonial period of the late 19th century. Until then relations between the Hutu and their Tutsi overlords had been fairly amicable, but the favour shown to the Tutsi by the Belgian colonial administration (1916–61) intensified the animosities between the two peoples.*

*For centuries, the Hutu and Tutsi cultures have been largely integrated. The Tutsi adopted the mutually intelligible Bantu languages of Rwanda and Rundi, which were originally spoken by the Hutu. The Hutu's kinship and clan system is probably derived from Tutsi culture, as is the central importance of cattle. The Hutu and the Tutsi adhere essentially to the same religious beliefs, which include forms of animism and (today) Christianity.*

many. Tutsi hegemony was unquestionably more burdensome under Belgian rule than at any time prior to European colonization. By the end of World War II, a growing number of colonial civil servants and missionaries had come to recognize the legitimacy of Hutu claims against the ruling Tutsi minority. The proclamation of the republic a year and a half before the country acceded to independence testifies to the substantial support extended by the trusteeship authorities to the revolution.

## INDEPENDENCE AND THE 1960S

What began as a peasant revolt in November 1959 eventually transformed itself into an organized political movement aimed at the overthrow of the monarchy and the vesting of full political power in Hutu hands. Under the leadership of Grégoire Kayibanda, Rwanda's first president, the Party for Hutu Emancipation (Parti du Mouvement de l'Emancipation du Peuple Hutu) emerged as the spearhead of the revolution. Communal elections were held in 1960, resulting in a massive transfer of power to Hutu elements at the local level. And in the wake of the coup (January 1961) in Gitarama in central Rwanda, which was carried off with the tacit approval of the Belgian authorities, an all-Hutu provisional government came into being. Therefore, by the time that independence was proclaimed in July 1962, the revolution had already run its course. Thousands of Tutsi began fleeing Rwanda, and by early 1964—following a failed Tutsi raid from Burundi—at least 150,000 were in neighbouring countries.

## THE HABYARIMANA ERA

With the elimination of Tutsi elements from the political arena, north-south regional competition among Hutu politicians arose, reflecting the comparatively privileged position of those from the central and southern regions within the party, the government, and the administration. Regional tensions came to a head in July 1973, when a group of army officers from the north overthrew the Kayibanda regime in a bloodless coup and installed a northerner, Maj. Gen. Juvénal Habyarimana. Habyarimana gave a distinctly regional coloration to the institutions of the state during his 21 years in power.

North-south polarities eventually gave way to subregional factions within the northern establishment. By 1980 the principal factions were the Bashiru and Bagoyi elements, respectively identified with the Bushiru and Bugoyi subregions. Habyarimana sided with the Bashiru faction and was the target of an abortive, Bagoyi-inspired coup in April 1980. Thereafter Habyarimana remained in power by holding referenda in 1983 and 1988, thus circumventing the stipulation in the 1978 constitution that the president serve only a single five-year term.

Tension between the Hutu and Tutsi flared in 1990, when the Tutsi-led Rwandan Patriotic Front (Front Patriotique Rwandais; FPR) rebels invaded from Uganda. A cease-fire was negotiated in early 1991, and negotiations between the FPR and the government began in 1992. In the meantime, revisions were made to the 1978 constitution, and the new document, allowing multiparty participation in the government, was promulgated in June 1991. An agreement between the government and the FPR was signed in August 1993 at Arusha, Tanz., that called for the creation of a broad-based transition government that would include the FPR. Hutu extremists strongly opposed this plan.

## GENOCIDE AND AFTERMATH

On April 6, 1994, a plane carrying Habyarimana and Burundi Pres. Cyprien Ntaryamira was shot down over Kigali, and the ensuing crash killed everyone on board. Although the identity of the person or group who fired upon the plane

# WANTED FOR GENOCIDE

ARRESTED ARRESTED ARRESTED

FELICIEN KABUGA | AUGUSTIN BIZIMANA | JEAN-BAPTISTE GATETE | AUGUSTIN BIZIMUNGU | THARCISSE RENZAHO

ARRESTED

IDELPHONSE HATEGEKIMANA | AUGUSTIN NGIRABATWARE | IDELPHONSE NIZEYIMANA | PROTAIS MPIRANYA | CALLIXTE NZABONIMANA

YUSUF JOHN MUNYAKAZI, RYANDIKAYO, CHARLES SIKUBWABO, ALOYS NDIMBATI

## INDICTED

Rewards of up to U.S. $5,000,000 are offered for information that leads to the arrest of persons indicted by the International Criminal Tribunal for Rwanda for serious violations of international humanitarian law and their transfer to Tribunal custody. If you have information about any of the above persons, please contact Rewards for Justice through the telephone number or email below.

CALL NOW - Kinshasa (243)98367160 or (243)8808308 | In the eastern Congo: (00250) 08574066
Nairobi (254)722-298483 or (254)733-250208
WRITE NOW - Kinshasa: JusticeRewards@yahoo.com | Nairobi: Rewards@state.gov
ALL CONTACTS WILL BE KEPT CONFIDENTIAL | www.rewardsforjustice.net

## UP TO U.S. $5,000,000 REWARD

*Poster of fugitives wanted for the genocide in Rwanda in the 1990s.* U.S. Department of State

has never been conclusively determined, Hutu extremists were originally thought to have been responsible. Later allegations suggested that FPR leaders were responsible. The next day Prime Minister Agathe Uwilingiyimana, a moderate Hutu, was assassinated. Her murder was part of a campaign to eliminate moderate Hutu or Tutsi politicians, with the goal of creating a political vacuum and thus allowing for the formation of the interim government of Hutu extremists that was inaugurated on April 9. Over the next several months, the wave of anarchy and mass killings continued, in which the army and Hutu militia groups known as the Interahamwe ("Those Who Attack Together") and Impuzamugambi ("Those Who Have the Same Goal") played a central role. The Tutsi-led FPR responded by resuming their fight and were successful in securing most of the country by early July. Later that month a transitional government was established, with Pasteur Bizimungu, a Hutu, as president and Paul Kagame, a Tutsi, as vice president.

During the genocide more than 800,000 civilians, primarily Tutsi, were killed. As many as 2,000,000 Rwandans, both Hutu and Tutsi, fled, most of them into eastern Zaire (after 1997 called the Democratic Republic of the Congo), most returning to Rwanda in late 1996 and early 1997. The International Criminal Tribunal for Rwanda (ICTR), established by the United Nations Security Council to try the tens of thousands (mostly Hutu) who had committed acts of genocide in 1994, began trying its first cases in 1995. The tremendous number of people to be tried resulted in an inability to proceed in a timely manner, and in 2000 tens of thousands of prisoners continued to await trial. In 2001 the government proposed trying the majority of cases through the traditional *gacaca* legal system. The *gacaca* courts were inaugurated in 2002 and began operating in phases over the next several years. The government also periodically granted mass amnesty to prisoners accused of lesser crimes.

## REGIONAL CONFLICT

Meanwhile, in late 1996 Rwanda's military forces entered neighbouring Zaire to expel Hutu extremists, who had fled there after the genocide and were using that country as a base for launching attacks on Rwanda. Frustrated by the lack of support from Zairean president Mobutu Sese Seko regarding these efforts, Rwanda's troops also intervened in the rebellion taking place in that country: along with Ugandan troops, they lent crucial support to rebel Laurent Kabila, to whom Mobutu eventually relinquished power in 1997. Little more than a year after Kabila became president of what was by then known as the Democratic Republic of the Congo, Rwanda again cited frustration with that country's government over the issue of Hutu extremists and lent support to rebel factions attempting to overthrow Kabila. Rwanda faced much international criticism over its involvement in the war, including a suspension of foreign aid. After many attempts at resolution, a peace agreement was reached in 2002 that provided for the withdrawal of Rwandan troops from the Democratic Republic of the Congo in exchange for the disarmament and repatriation of Hutu extremist rebels in that country.

## MOVING FORWARD

Although Hutu insurgencies continued to occupy Rwanda's government, a new constitution aimed at preventing further ethnic strife in the country was promulgated in 2003. Later that year the first multiparty democratic elections in Rwanda since independence were held. Kagame, who had ascended to the presidency after Bizimungu resigned in 2000, was victorious in securing another term. In 2006 the Rwandan government implemented a significant administrative reorganization, replacing the previous 12 prefectures with 5 larger multiethnic provinces intended to promote power sharing and reduce ethnic conflict. The country's economy, adversely affected by the conflict of the early 1990s, continued to recover gradually. Recovery efforts were aided in 2006, when significant debt relief was granted by the World Bank and the International Monetary Fund, and in 2007, when Rwanda joined the East African Community, a regional trade and development bloc.

In the early 21st century the events of 1994 still weighed heavily in Rwanda. In 2004 Kagame came under fire after a newspaper leaked the findings of a report commissioned by French judge Jean-Louis Bruguière, including allegations that Kagame and other FPR leaders ordered the rocket attack that caused the 1994 plane crash that killed Habyarimana and triggered the genocide (echoing the claims of some Rwandan dissidents). Kagame vehemently denied the allegations. Rwanda severed relations with France in 2006 when Bruguière—claiming jurisdiction because the flight crew members that perished in the crash were French—signed international arrest warrants for several of Kagame's close associates for their alleged roles in the plane crash and requested that Kagame stand trial at the ICTR. (Relations between the two countries were later restored in November 2009.) As before, Kagame denied having anything to do with the crash and countered by alleging that the French government armed and advised the rebels responsible for the genocide. Later that year, Rwanda established a commission to investigate France's role in the genocide. In October 2007, the Rwandan government launched a formal investigation into the 1994 plane crash. The results, released in January 2010, indicated that Hutu extremist soldiers were responsible for shooting down the plane carrying Habyarimana, with the intent of derailing his peace negotiations with Tutsi rebels, and then used the incident as an excuse to initiate the genocide.

Kagame was reelected in August 2010, but amid controversy. Prior to the election, some opposition media outlets were repressed, and many opposition groups were unable to field candidates.

# CHAPTER 8

## SAO TOME AND PRINCIPE

Sao Tome and Principe is located on the Equator in the Gulf of Guinea. It consists of two main islands (São Tomé and Príncipe) and several rocky islets. The former Portuguese colony became independent in 1975. The capital is the city of São Tomé.

### PORTUGUESE COLONIAL RULE

The islands of São Tomé and Príncipe were uninhabited when they were discovered, about 1470, by Portuguese navigators. In the late 15th century the Portuguese sent out settlers (including many convicts and Jewish children who had been separated from their parents and expelled from Portugal) and brought African slaves to the islands to grow sugar.

During the 16th century São Tomé was for a brief time the world's largest producer of sugar, but the rise of Brazilian competition and the poor quality of São Tomé's badly dried product virtually destroyed this industry. The economic decline was accentuated by social instability as slaves escaped to the mountains and raided the plantations. Amador, the self-proclaimed king of the slaves who nearly overran the whole island of São Tomé in 1595, is now regarded by many as a national hero. Foreign pirates were another hazard, and the Dutch briefly captured São Tomé in 1641, only to be expelled seven years later.

After the collapse of the sugar economy, the colony served as an entrepôt for the Portuguese slave trade to Brazil. The cargoes of small slave ships were transferred to larger vessels for the Atlantic voyage, and provisions such as water were obtained. The islanders produced food crops for these ships and for themselves. Because of the frequent political unrest in São Tomé, the capital was moved in 1753 to Santo António on Príncipe, whose harbour was the site of much activity. In 1778 the Portuguese ceded the islands of Fernando Pó (Bioko) and Annobón (Pagalu), on either side of São Tomé and Príncipe, to the Spaniards, who wished to develop their own African slave trade.

The independence of Brazil in 1822, the suppression of the slave trade in the Portuguese territories, and the introduction of coffee and cacao (the source of cocoa beans) cultivation in the 19th century shifted the economic centre of gravity back to São Tomé, and in 1852 São Tomé city once again became the

*Cacao seeds. The introduction of cacao cultivation in the 19th century helped increase economic prosperity in São Tomé.* Martin Van Der Belen/AFP/Getty Images

capital. Cacao replaced coffee as the main cash crop in the 1890s, and during the first two decades of the 20th century the colony was in some years the world's largest producer of the commodity. This led to the maximum expansion of the plantations on the islands. When slavery was legally abolished in 1875, the Portuguese recruited contract workers from such places as Angola, Cape Verde, and Mozambique. However, until 1910 the living and working conditions of these indentured labourers often were little different from slavery.

Cocoa production fell after World War I, and the islands became isolated and notorious for the brutality and corruption that reigned on the plantations belonging to absentee planters and corporations. Attempts to force the local Forros to work on the plantations led to the Batepá Massacre in 1953, an event later often cited by São Toméans in their demands for independence as an example of the violence under Portuguese rule. The Committee for the Liberation of São Tomé and Príncipe was set up in exile in 1960 and changed its name to the Movement for the Liberation of São Tomé and Príncipe (MLSTP) in 1972. However, it consisted of only a small group of exiles, who were unable to mount a guerrilla challenge to the Portuguese on the islands.

The government that took power in Portugal after a coup in 1974 agreed to hand over power to the MLSTP in 1975, and virtually all Portuguese colonists fled to Portugal, fearing an independent black and communist government. Independence was granted on July 12, 1975.

## AFTER INDEPENDENCE

The country's first president, Manuel Pinto da Costa of the MLSTP, was elected in 1975. The government initially followed eastern European models of political and economic organization. Economic decline and popular dissatisfaction, however, led to a process of liberalization that started in 1985 and culminated in the establishment of a multiparty democracy in 1990.

Pinto da Costa was succeeded in 1991 by Miguel Trovoada, a former prime minister who ran for the presidency unopposed in the first free elections in the country's history. In August 1995 Trovoada was deposed in a bloodless coup orchestrated by the military. However, coup leaders reconsidered their demands when faced with the immediate threat of the loss of foreign aid, and Trovoada was reinstated as president a week later.

Trovoada was reelected in 1996 but was barred from seeking a third term in the 2001 election. He was succeeded by businessman Fradique de Menezes of the Independent Democratic Action (ADI), the party with which Trovoada had been affiliated since 1994. Within months of de Menezes's election, a power struggle erupted between the new president and the MLSTP-dominated National Assembly, establishing a pattern of political conflict that continued for some time.

In 2003 de Menezes was deposed in a military coup, but international negotiations were successful in guaranteeing his reinstatement on the condition that the coup leaders would not be punished for their actions. De Menezes was reelected in 2006, representing the Democratic Movement of Forces for Change, the party that had splinted off from the ADI in late 2001.

Although several fair and peaceful legislative and presidential elections were held in the 1990s and 2000s, they did not immediately transform the country's oversized and inefficient public administration from a centre of cronyism and corruption into an efficient bureaucracy that could provide the structural conditions of a functioning market economy. Consequently, the country's tremendous social and economic problems were far from resolved at the start of the 21st century, although the earnings from petroleum concessions beginning in the mid-2000s and the potential for future oil revenues brought a sense of optimism, as did significant debt relief granted in 2007.

# CHAPTER 9

# EASTERN AFRICA

The area commonly referred to as eastern Africa actually comprises two traditionally recognized regions. One is the region of East Africa, made up of the countries of Kenya, Tanzania, and Uganda; the other is the Horn of Africa, made up of the countries of Somalia, Djibouti, Eritrea, and Ethiopia.

## EAST AFRICA

This history of East Africa is long and varied and largely reflects the interactions among indigenous African groups, Arabs, and Europeans. The ethnic fabric of the region is quite fragmented, with many small groups of peoples intermingled or occupying discrete territories, which has at times led to conflict.

### THE COAST UNTIL 1856

The earliest written accounts of the East African coast occur in the *Periplus Maris Erythraei*—apparently written by a Greek merchant living in Egypt in the second half of the 1st century CE—and in Ptolemy's *Guide to Geography*, the East African section of which, in its extant form, probably represents a compilation of geographic knowledge available at Byzantium about 400. The *Periplus* describes in some detail the shore of what was to become northern Somalia. Ships sailed from there to western India to bring back cotton cloth, grain, oil, sugar, and ghee, while others moved down the Red Sea to the East African coast bringing cloaks, tunics, copper, and tin. Aromatic gums, tortoiseshell, ivory, and slaves were traded in return.

## AZANIA

Because of offshore islands, better landing places, and wetter climate, Arab traders from about 700 seem to have preferred the East African coast to the south of modern Somalia. They sailed there with the northeast monsoon, returning home in the summer with the southwest. They dubbed the part of the coast to which they sailed Azania, or the Land of Zanj—by which they meant the land of the blacks and by which they knew it until the 10th century. South of Sarapion, Nikon, the Pyralaae Islands, and the island of Diorux (about whose precise location only speculation seems possible), the chief town was Rhapta, which may lie buried in the Rufiji delta of present-day Tanzania. Here the situation differed somewhat from that in the north, and, though tortoiseshell and rhinoceros horn were exported from there—as were quantities of ivory and coconut oil—no mention is made of slaves. Rhapta's main imports were metal weapons and iron tools—suggesting that iron smelting was not yet known. Mafia Island, which lies out to sea here, could perhaps be Menouthias, the only island named in both the *Periplus* and the *Guide*, although this could also be either Pemba or Zanzibar (perhaps there has been a conflation of all three in the one name).

There is little information concerning the period until the 8th century. Greek and Roman coins have been found, and there are some accounts of overseas migrations to the coast. No settlements from this period have been found.

A new period opened, it seems, in the 9th century. The first identifiable building sites are dated from this time, and, according to Arab geographers, the East African coast was then generally thought of as being divided into four: (1) Berber (Amazigh) lands, which ran down the Somalian coast to the Shabeelle River, (2) Zanj proper, (3) the land of Sofala in present-day Mozambique, whence gold was beginning to be shipped by about the 10th century, and (4) a vaguely described land of Waq waq, beyond. The only island that is mentioned is Qanbalu, which appears to have been what is now Tanzania's Pemba Island. Though there is some suggestion that in the 10th century the Muslims had not yet begun to move farther south than Somalia, on Qanbalu they soon became rulers of a pagan population, whose language they adopted. Moreover, at Zanzibar an extant Kūfic inscription (the only one) recording the construction of a mosque by Sheikh al-Sayyid Abū 'Imrān Mūsā ibn al-Ḥasan ibn Muḥammad in 1107 confirms that by this time substantial Muslim settlements had been established.

The main coastal settlements were situated on islands, largely, no doubt,

*By the 11th century, East Africans used cowrie shells as their main currency.* Jupiterimages/ Photos.com/Thinkstock

because of the greater security these provided against attacks from the mainland. Their populations seem mostly to have been made up from migrants from the Persian Gulf—some from the great port of Sīrāf, others from near Bahrain—though conceivably some too came from Daybul, at the mouth of the Indus River, in northwestern India. They exported ivory (some of it went as far as China) and also tortoiseshell, ambergris, and leopard skins. Such trade goods as they obtained from the interior were apparently bought by barter at the coast.

Ruins at Kilwa, on the southern Tanzanian coast, probably date from the 9th or perhaps from the 8th century. They have revealed an extensive pre-Muslim settlement standing on the edge of what was the finest harbour on the coast. Though there is little evidence to suggest that its inhabitants had any buildings to begin with, wattle-and-daub dwellings appeared in due course, and by the 10th century short lengths of coral masonry wall were being built. The inhabitants, whose main local currency was cowrie shells, traded with the peoples of the Persian Gulf and, by the early 11th century, had first come under Muslim influence. By 1300, like the inhabitants of neighbouring Mafia, they were living in Muslim towns, the rulers of which were Shī'ites. Although no houses were being built of coral, stone mosques were being constructed.

External trade was increasing: glass beads were being imported from India, and porcelains, transshipped either in India or in the Persian Gulf, were arriving from China. There appears also to have been a rather extensive trade with the island of Madagascar.

The most important site of this period yet to have been found is at Manda, near Lamu, on the Kenyan coast. Apparently established in the 9th century, it is distinguished for its seawalls of coral blocks, each of which weighs up to a ton. Though most of its houses were of wattle and daub, there were also some of stone. Trade, which seems to have been by barter, was considerable, with the main export probably of ivory. Manda had close trading connections with the

Persian Gulf—with Sīrāf in particular. It imported large quantities of Islamic pottery and, in the 9th and 10th centuries, Chinese porcelain. There is evidence of a considerable iron-smelting industry at Manda and of a lesser one at Kilwa.

## THE SHIRAZI MIGRATION

For much of the 13th century the most important coastal town was Mogadishu, a mercantile city on the Somalian coast to which new migrants came from the Persian Gulf and southern Arabia. Of these, the most important were called Shirazi, who, in the second half of the 12th century, had migrated southward to the Lamu islands, to Pemba, to Mafia, to the Comoro Islands, and to Kilwa, where by the end of the 12th century they had established a dynasty. Whether they were actually Persian in origin is somewhat doubtful. Though much troubled by wars, by the latter part of the 13th century they had made Kilwa second in importance only to Mogadishu. When the Kilwa throne was seized by Abū al-Mawāhib, major new developments ensued. Kilwa captured Mogadishu's erstwhile monopoly of the gold trade with Sofala and exchanged cloth—much of it made at Kilwa—and glass beads for gold. With the resulting great wealth, new pottery styles were developed, a marked increase in the import of Chinese porcelain occurred, and stone houses, which had hitherto been rare, became common. The great palace of Husuni Kubwa, with well over 100 rooms, was built at this time and had the distinction of being the largest single building in all sub-Saharan Africa. Husuni Ndogo, with its massive enclosure walls, was probably built at this time, too, as were the extensions to the great mosque at Kilwa. The architectural inspiration of these buildings was Arab, their craftsmanship was of a high standard, and the grammar of their inscriptions was impeccable. Kilwa declined in the late 14th century and revived in the first half of the 15th, but then—partly because of internal dynastic conflict but also partly because of diminishing profits from the gold trade—it declined again thereafter.

Elsewhere, especially on the Kenyan coastline, the first half of the 15th century seems to have been a period of much prosperity. Whether at Gede (south of Malindi) or at Songo Mnara (south of Kilwa), architectural styles were relatively uniform. Single-story stone houses, mostly of coral, were common. Each coastal settlement had a stone mosque, which typically centred on a roofed rectangular hall divided by masonry pillars. Chinese imports arrived in ever larger quantities, and there are signs that eating bowls were beginning to come into more common use. Mombasa became a substantial town, as did Pate, in the Lamu islands. The ruling classes of these towns were Muslims of mixed Arab and African descent who were mostly involved in trade. Beneath them were African labourers who were often slaves and a transient Arab population. The impetus in this society was Islamic rather than African. It was bound by sea to the distant Islamic world, whence immigrants still arrived to settle on the East African coast, to intermarry with local people, and to adopt the Swahili language. The effect of these settlements was limited, while their influence upon the East African interior was nonexistent.

During the 15th century, Shirazi families continued to rule in Malindi, Mombasa, and Kilwa and at many lesser places along the coast. They also dominated Zanzibar and Pemba. The Nabahani, who were of Omani origin, ruled at Pate and were well-represented in Pemba as well. Coastal society derived a certain unity by its participation in a single trading network, by a common adherence to Islam, and by the ties of blood and marriage among its leading families. Politically, however, its city-states were largely independent, acknowledging no foreign control, and their limited resources confined their political activities to East Africa and to a variety of local rivalries—Zanzibar and Pemba, for example, appear frequently to have been divided between several local rulers. Mombasa occupied the premier position on this part of the coast, although its control over the area immediately to the north was disputed by its main rival, Malindi. Close connections seem to have existed between Mombasa and a number of places to the south. Its Shirazi rulers were able to mobilize military support from some of the inland peoples, and as a result of the place it had won in the trade of the northwestern Indian Ocean they had turned Mombasa into a prosperous

town. Its population of about 10,000 compared with only 4,000 at Kilwa.

## THE PORTUGUESE INVASION

This was the situation on the East African coast when Portuguese ships under Vasco da Gama arrived in 1498. The manifestly superior military and naval technology of the Portuguese and the greater unity of their command enabled them, in the years that lay ahead, to mount assaults upon the ill-defended city-states. As early as 1502 the sheikh at Kilwa was obliged to agree to a tribute to the Portuguese, as the ruler of Zanzibar was later. Shortly afterward the Portuguese sacked both Kilwa and Mombasa and forced Lamu and Pate to submit. Within eight years of their arrival they had managed to dominate the coast and the trade routes that led from there to India.

The Portuguese became skilled at playing one small state against another, but their global enterprise was such that they did not immediately impose direct rule. This changed toward the end of the 16th century, however, when Turkish expeditions descending the northern coast with promises of assistance against the Portuguese encouraged the coast north of Pemba to revolt. This prompted the dispatch of Portuguese fleets from Goa, one of which, in 1589, sacked Mombasa and placed that city much more firmly under Portuguese control. This was helped by the death of Mombasa's last Shirazi ruler, Shah ibn Mishhan, who, in leaving no clear successor, gave the Portuguese the

*To further bolster their control of Mombasa, in 1593 the Portuguese built the mighty Fort Jesus and staffed it with 100 men a year later.* Brian Miller/Time & Life Pictures/Getty Images

opportunity to install Sheikh Aḥmad of Malindi in his place. In 1593, with an architect from Italy in charge and with masons from India to assist them, the Portuguese set about building their great Fort Jesus at Mombasa. In the following year it was occupied by a garrison of 100 men.

With Mombasa's downfall, the major hindrance to Portuguese power on the East African coast was overthrown. They installed garrisons elsewhere than at Mombasa and brought about the downfall of a number of Shirazi dynasties.

And although they did not exercise day-to-day control over local rulers, they did make these rulers dependent on them for their position. (Local rulers were in particular required to pay regular tribute to the Portuguese king on pain of dethronement and even of death.)

Portugal's chief interests were not imperial but economic. With Mombasa in their grip, they controlled the commercial system of the western Indian Ocean. Customs houses were opened at Mombasa and Pate, and ironware, weapons, beads, jewelry, cotton, and silks were imported. The main exports were ivory, gold, ambergris, and coral. There was a flourishing local trade in timber, pitch, rice, and cereals but few signs of any considerable traffic in slaves. Individual Portuguese traders often developed excellent relations with Swahilis in the coastal cities.

Though the Portuguese managed to ride out local rebellions into the 17th century, their authority over a much wider area was undermined by the rise of new powers on the Persian Gulf. Portugal lost Hormuz to the Persians in 1622 and Muscat to the imam of Oman in 1650. Two years later the Omanis launched their first major intervention into East Africa's affairs when in response to a Mombasan appeal the imam sent ships to Pate and Zanzibar and killed their Portuguese inhabitants. As a consequence, Pate became the centre of East Africa's resistance to Portuguese rule. The Portuguese responded in an equally bloody manner, but eventually, in 1696, in alliance with Pate, the imam of Oman sailed to East Africa with a fleet of more than 3,000 men to lay siege to Mombasa. Although Fort Jesus was reinforced, the great Portuguese stronghold finally fell to Sayf ibn Sulṭān in December 1698. A few years later Zanzibar, the last of Portugal's allies in eastern Africa, also fell to the imam.

## THE OMANI ASCENDANCY

There ensued, after the Omani victory, a century during which, despite a succession of Omani incursions, the East African coast remained very largely free from the dominance of any outside power. Oman itself suffered an invasion by the Persians and was long distracted by civil conflict. Its originally successful Ya'rubid dynasty lost prestige as a consequence, fell from power, and was then superseded by the Āl Bū Saʿīdīs, who quickly found themselves preoccupied by conflicts at home. Moves against them also originated along the East African coast.

In 1727 Pate joined with the Portuguese to expel the Omanis, especially from Mombasa, where in 1728–29 Portuguese authority was momentarily restored. But the Mombasans wanted as little to be controlled by Portugal as by Muscat and soon evicted the Portuguese once again. Thereafter, Kilwa, Zanzibar, Lamu, and Pate largely kept themselves free from both Omani and Portuguese control. Distracted though it was by protracted internecine quarrels, Pate was preeminent in the Lamu archipelago and, like all the other coastal towns, was ambitious to preserve its independence.

Even so, Mombasa, in quite new circumstances, in the 18th century reached the apogee of its power as an independent city-state. The architects of this achievement were the Mazrui, an Omani clan who had provided some of the imam's governors to Mombasa but who, because they were opposed to the Āl Bū Saʿīdīs, did not long persist in their allegiance to Muscat. They owed their authority in Mombasa itself to an ability to hold the balance between the rival factions in the Swahili population and also to their ability peacefully to overcome all but one of their dynastic successions. In 1746 a Mazrui notable, 'Alī ibn Uthman al-Mazrui, overthrew an Omani force that had murdered his brother. Soon after he seized Pemba and, but for a family quarrel, might have won Zanzibar. His successor, Mas'ūd ibn Nāṣir, initiated a pattern of cooperation with Pate, maintained close links with inland Nyika peoples, and established Mazrui dominance from the Pangani River to Malindi.

Both Mombasa and Pate were disastrously defeated by Lamu in the battle of Shela, about 1810. Pate's preeminence in the Lamu islands was destroyed, Mombasa's authority on the coast was diminished, and the way was open to Muscat's great intrusion into East African affairs. Lamu appealed to Oman for a garrison to assist it, to which Sayyid Sa'īd of Muscat very soon responded.

The Āl Bū Sa'īdīs, who had captured Kilwa in 1785, maintained their principal footing upon the coast in Zanzibar, which had long held to its association with them. Thanks to the city's growing success, from the end of the 18th century onward, in turning itself into the main entrepôt for the trade in the area south of Mombasa, Zanzibar soon rivaled Mombasa as the focal point for the whole coastline. As such, it was both developed and used by Sayyid Sa'īd ibn Sulṭān of Oman as the base for his growing ambitions. Having won the succession to Muscat after an internecine struggle following his father's death in 1804, Sa'īd spent much

of the next two decades establishing his authority there. (In this he was assisted by the British, who were much concerned to safeguard their route to India, which ran close to Muscat on its way past the Persian Gulf.) Then, in 1822, he wrested Pemba from Mazrui control and by 1824 had installed a Muscat garrison in Pate as well, thus bringing to an end the previous influence that the Mazrui had exercised.

Sensing the increasing threat from Muscat, the Mazrui appealed to the British for assistance. Though their application was formally denied, a British naval officer, Capt. W.F. Owen, on his own initiative raised a British flag of protection over Mombasa in 1824. Because the British had no desire formally to extend their authority to East Africa at this time, let alone to break with their ally Sa'īd, it was hauled down in 1826. This gave Sa'īd his opportunity, and in 1828, 1829, and 1833 he mounted assaults upon Mombasa. But it was only when he successfully intervened in a dynastic dispute among the Mazrui, which followed on the death of a *liwali* in 1835, that he was able in 1837 to fasten his control over Mombasa and to topple the Mazrui from their position. His dominion along the whole coastline thus became assured, and after over a century's interval the East African littoral once more found itself dominated by a single outside power. Though this outcome owed much to the inability of the coastal towns to unite against an invader, it owed much as well to the striking personality of Sa'īd himself, his investment in a navy, his force of Baloch soldiers (with which he supplemented his Omani levies), and the support he received from the British.

It also stemmed from his intimate association with the major economic developments then taking place along the East African coast. These began with a marked growth in the previously marginal slave trade, particularly at first in the Kilwa region, more especially from 1780 to 1810 as a result of French demand for slaves in Mauritius and Bourbon. This was succeeded by the discovery that cloves could be successfully grown on Zanzibar and by the development of flourishing plantations. British pressure on Sa'īd to end the export of slaves to "Christian" markets came to fruition in 1822, when he reluctantly signed what became known as the Moresby Treaty. In the event, however, it scarcely made a difference, either on the coast or in the interior, because slaves were required in growing numbers for the plantations on both Zanzibar and Pemba and for export to the Persian Gulf and beyond.

Increasing commercial activity brought Sayyid Sa'īd sufficient wealth to buy ships and pay troops. It also attracted to the East African coast migrant Indians, who became heavily involved in the country's economic expansion. Together with the Arabs, who were beginning to make profits from their clove plantations, Indians helped to finance the new upcountry trading caravans.

The increased economic activity that centred upon the islands of Zanzibar and Pemba served to enhance the importance of the smaller towns that stood on the mainland opposite. It also attracted an influx of European traders, of which the most important were the Americans. They were the first Westerners to conclude a trade agreement with Sa'īd (1833) and the first also to establish a consul at Zanzibar (1837). (Their prime achievement was to capture the cloth trade to East Africa—so that cheap cotton cloth thenceforth came to be known there as Americani.) The British followed with a trade agreement in 1839 and a consul in 1841. The French made similar provisions in 1844, and some Germans from the Hanseatic towns moved in at about the same time. British trade, however, never flourished and in fact died away; but by 1856 the United States and France were both making purchases in East Africa of more than $500,000 a year, while exports to India, particularly British India, were higher still. Some of the main items of trade, such as ivory, were traditional, but copal, sesame, cloves, cowries, hides, and coconut oil were also important. Because of this increased activity, Sa'īd's economy in due course depended less on the export of slaves, and he therefore showed himself more ready than he might otherwise have been to accept the so-called Hamerton Treaty of 1845, by which the export of slaves to his Arabian dominions was forbidden.

Because by this time the revenues from Sa'īd's East African territories had overtaken those he received from Oman, it is understandable that in 1840 he should have transferred his own capital from Muscat to Zanzibar. At his death in 1856, Zanzibar was firmly established as the East African coast's main centre, from which major new incursions into the interior had begun to radiate extensively.

## THE INTERIOR BEFORE
## THE COLONIAL ERA

The coast was never more than East Africa's fringe. Beyond the harsh *nyika*, or "wilderness," which lay immediately inland and was nowhere pierced by a long, navigable river, thornbush country extended to the south, sometimes interspersed with pleasanter plains toward the centre, while to the north cooler forested highlands ran into harsher country. Westward lay the Great Rift Valley and, beyond, the regions of the great lakes whence the Nile ran northward through its usually impassable marshes.

Because there are no written records antedating the last century or so for this region, its history has to be deduced from often uncertain linguistic, cultural, and anthropological evidence; from oral traditions—where they are available, which at best is only for recent centuries; and from archaeological findings. With investigations and analyses still at an exceedingly early stage and the first hypotheses proving vulnerable to criticism, the following statements must be only tentative. Furthermore, all accounts of the migration of ethnic groups must allow for innumerable short-run moves and may refer only to small—if important—minorities. They must also

take account of probable interactions with other peoples en route and often, indeed, of extensive absorption. Above all, care must be exercised over anachronistic concepts of *tribe*. Moreover, bolder categories such as *Bantu* are strictly only linguistic and must be treated with caution.

Two features of the pre-19th-century period may be stressed: first, although it seems to have been in this part of Africa that humans first developed, in the three or four most recent millennia the key innovations in human evolution seem to have occurred elsewhere; second, the extensive agricultural revolution in East Africa, which took place during this time, had the vital consequence that sizable populations grew up in areas of adequate rainfall, which could not be easily brushed aside by subsequent alien invaders.

During the earlier stages of the Stone Age down to about 50,000 BCE, hand-ax industries were established in the Rift Valley areas of Kenya and of Tanzania (especially at Olduvai Gorge) and along the Kagera River in Uganda. During the Mesolithic period (thence to c. 10,000 BCE), new stone-tool-making techniques evolved, and the use of fire was mastered. Spreading to other parts of East Africa, in the Neolithic period humans clustered into specialized hunting-and-gathering communities from which may have developed some still-existing ways of life. The largest number of relevant sites is close to the homeland of the Hadzapi—the last contemporary hunters and gatherers—and to that of the

Sandawe, who are physically and linguistically akin to the San of Southern Africa. Remnants of other hunting and gathering communities—such as the Twa and Mbuti of western Uganda—or at least the memory of them, are found in many places. Latterly, they often lived in precisely those highland regions where agriculture and animal domestication in East Africa first occurred.

Food production and the keeping of cattle seem to have begun in the highland and Rift Valley regions of Kenya and of northern Tanzania in the 1st millennium BCE and to have derived from peoples who were probably southern Cushites from Ethiopia. Some traces of these interlopers remain among, for example, the Iraqw of Tanzania, and it may be that the age-old systems of irrigation found throughout this region owe their origins to this period as well. Agriculture preceded the smelting of iron in these areas, and hunting and gathering continued to be important for the domestic economy. It looks as if in due course southern Cushites spread deep into what is now southern Tanzania, but, so far as has been ascertained, food production did not develop in the period BCE elsewhere in Tanzania, nor in what is now Uganda.

## THE SPREAD OF IRONWORKING AND THE BANTU MIGRATIONS

It is still far from clear when and whence iron smelting spread to the East African interior. Certainly there was no swift or complete transfer from stone to iron.

At Engaruka, for example, in that same region of the Rift Valley in northern Tanzania, a major Iron Age site, which was both an important and concentrated agricultural settlement using irrigation, seems to have been occupied for over a thousand years. Significantly, its styles of pottery do not seem to have been related to those that became widespread in the 1st millennium CE. It is a reasonable assumption that its inhabitants were Cushitic speakers, but it seems that its major period belongs to the middle of the 2nd millennium CE.

The major occurrences of the 1st millennium CE involved the spread of agriculture—more particularly, the cultivation of the banana—to the remaining areas of East Africa. Simultaneously or perhaps previously went the spread of ironworking, and fairly certainly too the diffusion of Bantu languages—except in the core of the Cushitic wedge and to the north of an east-west line through Lake Kyoga. If, as seems probable, proto-Bantu languages had their origins in the eastern interior of western Africa, it does not seem inconceivable that over a lengthy period of time some of its speakers, probably carrying with them a knowledge of grain agriculture and conceivably a knowledge of ironworking, should have diffused along the tributaries of the Congo River to the savanna country south of the Congo forest into what is now the region of Katanga (Shaba) in the Democratic Republic of the Congo. Nor does it seem inconceivable that the banana, originally an Indonesian plant particularly suitable in tropical conditions, should have spread to that same region up the Zambezi valley (certainly the Malayo-Polynesian influences in Madagascar in the 1st millennium CE are well attested in other respects). At all events, the linguistic and archaeological arguments for a fairly rapid eastward and northward expansion during the 1st millennium CE from the Katanga area now have wide acceptance. Bantu languages came to dominate most of this region (many Cushitic speakers in what is now Tanzania seem to have switched over to them or to have been eliminated). More varieties of banana developed in East Africa than anywhere else in the world. Ironworking was soon prevalent, and, where rainfall, soil nutrients, and the absence of the tsetse fly allowed, population growth increased decisively.

## THE EARLY INTERLACUSTRINE KINGDOMS

Sometime before the middle of the 2nd millennium CE, some of the most interesting developments were occurring in the interlacustrine area (i.e., the region bounded by Lakes Victoria, Kyoga, Albert, Edward, and Tanganyika). Vague accounts of rulerships in various parts of this area date from the first half of the 2nd millennium CE, and it is at least possible that they existed—though they may well have been judicial arbitrators or ritual leaders rather than more strictly political figures. Whether they had their origins in roving Cushitic or Nilotic cattle keepers

from the north or northeast—as has been variously suggested—is impossible to say, though some such explanation would not be difficult to believe. What seems certain is that about the middle of the present millennium a sudden cultural political climax was marked by a short-lived, though widely acknowledged, dynasty of Chwezi rulers.

The Chwezi people are frequently associated with the great earthwork sites at Bigo, Mubende, Munsa, Kibengo, and Bugoma, in western Uganda. That at Mubende seems to have been a religious centre. The largest is at Bigo, where a ditch system, more than 6.5 miles (10.5 km) long, some of it cut out of rock, encloses a large grazing area on a riverbank. It looks as if it comprised both a royal capital and a well-defended cattle enclosure. Its construction must certainly have required a considerable mobilization of labour—which, apart from indicating that it must have been the work of a substantial political power, would support the view that the distinction between cultivators and a pastoral aristocracy, which later became typical of this area, is of very long standing. Radioactive carbon dating suggests Bigo was occupied from the mid-14th to the early 16th century. This correlates with the evidence of oral tradition that around the turn of the 15th century the Chwezi were supplanted in the north by Luo rulers of the Bito clan (who provided the dynasties that ruled in Bunyoro, Koki, Buganda, and parts of Busoga) and that they were superseded to the south by various Hima rulers of the Hinda clan (in Ankole, Buhaya, Busubi, and around to the southeast of Lake Victoria). Under these, and the corresponding Nyiginya dynasty in Rwanda, powerful traditional rulerships among the interlacustrine Bantu persisted after the middle of the 20th century.

Their relatively common experience was reinforced in the aftermath of the Chwezi dynasty by the prevalence among them of a variety of (often commemorative) Chwezi religious movements. In some areas these took the form of spirit-possession cults, while pantheons of deities were developed in others. In various guises—sometimes in support of the existing political order, sometimes against it—they spread into Bunyoro, Buganda, Busoga, Ankole, Buha, Rwanda, Burundi, and even to Nyamwezi country, in what is now Tanzania. So extensive a diffusion of a basically common religious tradition in any other part of the East African interior before the much later arrival of Islam and Christianity was rare indeed.

## THE CHIEFTAINSHIPS OF THE SOUTHERN SAVANNA

In northwestern Tanzania, dynasties of a pre-Chwezi kind apparently spread from the interlacustrine area during the middle centuries of the present millennium. *Ntemi* (as the office was called) became prevalent among both the Sukuma and the Nyamwezi. The *ntemi* were probably as much ritual leaders as political rulers. Certainly, they do not seem to have

exercised before the 19th century a "state" authority that was characteristic of the later interlacustrine rulers. By roughly the 16th century there may have been an extension of this style of chieftainship southward into southwestern Tanzania. At all events, the chiefly groups among the Nyamwanga, the Nyika, the Safwa, the Ngonde, the Kinga, the Bena, the Pangwa, the Hehe, and the Sangu have common traditions of origin. And it seems clear that they are to be distinguished from their significantly different, matrilineal neighbours in southern Tanzania, Zambia, and the Democratic Republic of the Congo. There also seem to have been secondary movements of *ntemi*-like institutions in the 18th century to Ugogo, Safwa, Kaguru, Kilimanjaro, and Usambara. At the same time, the development of chieftainships in these other areas of Tanzania may originally have occurred independently of influences from elsewhere.

## NORTHEASTERN BANTU

The spread of some Bantu to the northern coast of East Africa during the 1st millennium CE is supported by the memory of a settlement area named Shungwaya situated to the north of the Tana River. Shungwaya appears to have had its heyday as a Bantu settlement area between perhaps the 12th and the 15th centuries, after which it was subjected to a full-scale invasion of Cushitic-speaking Oromo peoples from the Horn of Africa. There is controversy as to whether the ancestors of the present Kamba and Kikuyu of Kenya were from Shungwaya, but it would seem that they probably broke away from there some time before the Oromo onslaught. It has been suggested, indeed, that the Kikuyu spread through their present territories from 1400 to 1800. The old Cushitic wedge checked them from spreading farther westward. This extended, as it would seem to have done for two or more millennia past, over both sides of the Kenyan and northern Tanzanian Rift Valley, but in the middle of the present millennium it was subjected to one of the multiple waves of invading Nilotic peoples—who were partly agriculturists and partly pastoralists—that moved into much of the northern and northwestern parts of East Africa.

## THE NILOTIC MIGRATIONS

The supersession of the Chwezi by Luo dynasties in the northern interlacustrine region at about the end of the 15th century resulted from the migrations of Nilotic peoples southward—in this instance, it has seemed, from a cradleland in what is now the country of Sudan.

For some 18 generations or so Bito rulers of Luo origin held sway over the kingdom of Bunyoro-Kitara, to the east of Lake Albert. Though at first their dominion seems to have been widely extended, they began to be rivaled in the 16th and 17th centuries by the rise of Buganda, under its ruler, or *kabaka*. Working on interior lines and based upon a particularly fertile region, Buganda developed a strength and cohesion that from the 18th century onward was to make it—with Rwanda—one of the two most formidable kingdoms of the region.

The Luo rulers and such followers as had accompanied them were soon fully absorbed into the Bantu population of these kingdoms. Immediately to the north (where the Bantu did not extend) there occurred the greatest independent expansion of the Luo peoples, who formed the Acholi; provided ruling groups for peoples to the west who came to be called Alur; and bred the Jopaluo and Jopadhola to the east and also the sizable Luo populations who, between the mid-16th and the mid-18th centuries, came to settle on the northern side of Winam Bay to the northeast of Lake Victoria and spread thereafter to its southern shore as well.

Over to the east, into the former Cushitic domain that centred upon the Rift Valley, there appears to have been, in about the middle of the present millennium, a great expansion of Kalenjin peoples. These Highland Nilotes (as distinguished from, among others, River-Lake Nilotes such as the Luo), seem to have absorbed most of the previous southern Cushites who remained there and also to have successfully held the core of this ancient wedge, if not its earlier dimensions, against further Bantu incursions. By 1700, however, a second expansion into this old protrusion was beginning. During the 18th century the Maasai (Plains Nilotes, as they are sometimes called) spread over most of the area,

## BUGANDA

*The kingdom of Buganda is located in East Africa along the northern shore of Lake Victoria in present-day south-central Uganda. It was one of the most powerful kingdoms of East Africa during the 19th century.*

*Buganda is one of several small principalities founded by Bantu-speaking peoples in what is now Uganda. It was founded in the late 14th century, when the kabaka, or ruler, of the Ganda people came to exercise strong centralized control over his domains, called Buganda. By the 19th century Buganda had become the largest and most powerful kingdom in the region. The local chiefs of conquered areas ruled as personal appointees of the kabaka, who had a sizable army at his disposal.*

*Foreign influences, including the Islamic and Christian religions, began to reach Buganda in the 19th century, especially during the rule of Mutesa I (1856–84). After his death the kingdom was riven by a number of politico-religious factions. In 1894 Buganda became part of the British sphere of influence, and in 1900 the Buganda Agreement made it formally a British protectorate. The Ganda people subsequently played a major role in assisting the British administration in East Africa.*

*When Uganda achieved independence in 1962, the Buganda kingdom was given considerable autonomy and was accorded special federal status within the new country. Buganda's insistence upon its separate political identity generated worsening tensions with the central government, however. In 1966 open conflict broke out between the Bugandan ruler, Mutesa II, and the prime minister of Uganda, Milton Obote, who in 1967 abolished Buganda and the country's three other traditional kingdoms. The Buganda kingdom was not restored until 1993.*

until they came to be found as far south as Gogo country in central Tanzania. Already divided into pure-pastoralist and mixed-agriculturist subgroups, they were soon to be found to the east near Kilimanjaro. The earlier Kalenjin thus found themselves confined to the hillier country between the Rift Valley and Lake Victoria, where—constituting the Keyu (Elgeyo), the Suk (Pokot), the Nandi, the Kipsikis, and the Tatoga of more recent times—they entered into a variety of interactions with their various Luo and Bantu neighbours. Farther to the north in the areas beyond Mount Elgon a shorter-run series of migrations by other Plains Nilotes was simultaneously taking place. First, in the 17th century, the Lango began moving southwestward (and became much affected by their River-Lake Nilotic neighbours, the Acholi). Then, in the 18th century, the Teso, Karimojong, and others began also to move in various southward directions.

It has been suggested that all these Highland and Plains Nilotic migrations were set off, both before and after the middle of the present millennium, by successive pressures from the Oromo to the north. Like the Oromo, the Nilotic peoples lacked any firmly institutionalized political power, and their leaders were often less important than the elders of their clans. Indeed, Nilotes established "states" only where, as in the interlacustrine area over to the west, they came to rule other peoples who may very well have had traditions of rulership before they arrived. Such distinctions were to be of immense importance for the future.

## PRESSURE ON THE SOUTHERN CHIEFTAINSHIPS

With the breakup of their main body, at the north end of Lake Nyasa, after 1845, some parties of Ngoni moved northward. Some Ngoni groups made their way to Songea, while another struck north to Lake Victoria. They carried, to the area west of Lake Tanganyika, a new style of raiding and appear to have precipitated among such peoples as the Holoholo and the Ndendehule, the Sangu, and the Bena—in part, at least, as a safeguard against Ngoni raids—the creation of new political institutions, including more powerful rulerships. The most notable of such developments were, in the first place, among the Hehe, where, under Munyigumba and then on his death, in 1879, under his son Mkwawa, a powerful state was built up; then among the Nyamwezi, where between 1870 and 1884 the warrior chief Mirambo established a powerful personal rulership; and also among the Kimbu, where, between 1870

and 1884, Nyungu and his *ruga-rugas* (or bands of warriors) created a dominion that survived his death.

Nothing quite so striking occurred to the northeast. Conflict persisted between the smaller Chaga rulers on Kilimanjaro. In the mid-19th century, Kimweri enjoyed a considerable dominion in the region of the Usambara Mountains, but on his death in the 1860s his rulership disintegrated. Further such disintegrations occurred in the 19th century among the rulerships of Buha and Buzinza, at the south end of Lake Victoria, and among the Buhaya kingdoms on its eastern shore. The kingdom of Mpororo, to the west of Buhaya, had already broken up. By the 1890s its neighbour Nkore seems to have been in danger of disintegrating as well. Earlier in the century Toro, to its north, had broken away from Bunyoro, previously the most extensive of the kingdoms in this area, while fragmentation was almost endemic among the Busoga kingdoms to the east.

### RWANDA AND BUGANDA

But there were also growing points in the interlacustrine area, where one of the largest kingdoms, Rwanda, consolidated its rear by annexing Lake Kivu, then, in the aftermath of a succession war, swallowed the small kingdom of Gissaka, to its east. It failed to defeat Burundi, to the south, but under its *mwami*, or ruler, Kigeri IV (who reorganized its military forces) it extended its control by raiding to the north.

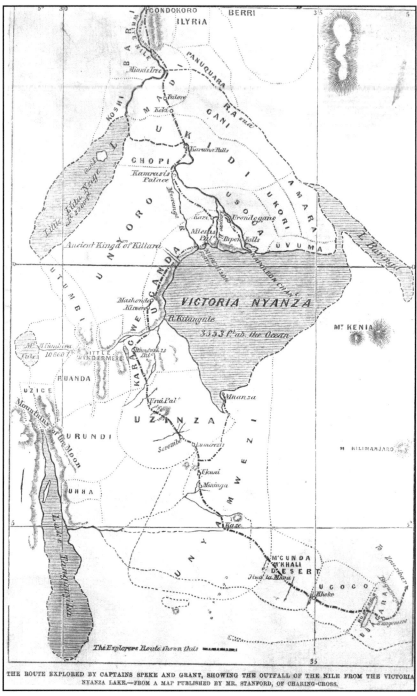

THE ROUTE EXPLORED BY CAPTAINS SPEKE AND GRANT, SHOWING THE OUTFALL OF THE NILE FROM THE VICTORIA NYANZA LAKE.—FROM A MAP PUBLISHED BY MR. STANFORD, OF CHARING-CROSS.

*Making satellites rather than subjects of the people, the kingdom of Buganda successfully worked their way southward along Lake Victoria's substantial western shore.* Hulton Archive/Getty Images

Its power was equaled in this region only by the kingdom of Buganda. Having annexed the large area of Buddu, to its southwest, in the late 18th century, Buganda thereafter generally refrained from any further territorial extensions. Its rulers steadily increased their authority at home by enhancing the power of appointed chiefs at the expense of the clan leaders, while abroad they preferred to make satellites rather than subjects of their neighbours. They had a good deal of success eastward in Busoga and southward along the western shore of Lake Victoria and around its southern rim. In the 1870s and '80s Buganda's protégés were on several occasions installed in petty rulerships in Busoga. In 1869 Bunyoro successfully survived Buganda interference in one of its succession conflicts (as Nkore did in 1878) and indeed in the 1870s and '80s was renewing its strength. Bunyoro's improved position turned much on its new military formations, the *abarasura*, while Buganda's successful predation owed a good deal to its new military efforts under the *mujasi*, or military commander, as well as to the building of a formidable fleet of canoes.

## THE LUO AND MAASAI

To the north and northeast the previous migrations of the Luo from west to east were followed in the 19th century by a new wave of migrations from east to west. The Lango, for example, further expanded in two southward and westward waves toward Lake Kyoga and toward the Victoria Nile, where they ran up against the Acholi. To their south the Teso and the Kumam were also moving west and south. A flourishing trading network developed around Lake Kyoga.

Activity was rife also among the pastoral peoples to the east. In about 1850 the Turkana began to migrate from a base west of Lake Rudolf. Southward stood the Maasai, the warrior people of the plains and open plateaus north and south of the string of Rift Valley lakes west of Mount Kenya. From 1830 onward their various subgroups were engaged, under the auspices of their rival *laibon*s, or ritual leaders—among whom Mbatian, who succeeded his father, Subet, in 1866, was the most famous—in a succession of internecine conflicts largely over cattle and grazing grounds. Their wars denuded the Laikipia and Uasin Gishu plateaus of their former Maasai, the so-called Wakwavi, who, being deprived of their cattle, switched to agriculture. They also helped the Nandi, who, with the Uasin Gishu Maasai now troubling them no more, took to raiding on their own account from a base between the Rift Valley and Lake Victoria. Under the leadership of their *laibon*-like *orkoiyot*s, the Nandi and their kinfolk, the Kipsikis, were soon the new powers in the land. Some of their neighbours who lived in open country put up defense works against them—the Baluyia, to the west, for example, built mud walls around their villages—while others, such as the Teita, the Kamba, and the Kikuyu, who lived on higher ground and in forest country, were rather better placed and from their carefully guarded fastnesses could defy the Maasai. On the edges of their country they even entered into some permanent trade and marriage relations with the Maasai. Where the soil was fertile, moreover, such people considerably increased their populations. Though they had no chiefs, "prominent men" were accorded a recognized status among them, and by the close of the century some of these were fighting each other for local supremacy.

## TRADE WITH THE COAST

On the coast, following the death, in 1856, of Sayyid Sa'īd, his erstwhile dominions in East Africa were split off from the imamate of Muscat. By 1873 the authority of the Āl Bū Sa'īdī sultans on Zanzibar itself became complete, although there were still revolts against them on the coast—particularly at Pate and Mombasa (where the Mazrui retained their preeminence despite successive defeats)—and at Kilwa, to the south. This arose chiefly from the sultan's acceptance of the further measures against the East African slave trade pressed upon him by the British consul at his court. By the 1860s some 7,000 or so slaves were being sold annually in the Zanzibar slave market, but in 1873 a treaty with the British closed the market at Zanzibar, and Sultan Barghash, by two proclamations in 1876, reduced the export from the mainland to a trickle. As it happened, however, there was then a final period of unprecedented slaving on the mainland, where the trade in slaves had generally been closely connected with the trade in ivory and the demand for porters was still considerable.

Trade in the East African interior began in African hands. Disa, Yao, Tipa, and Nyamwezi traders were long active over a wide area in the southern regions. By the early 19th century Kamba traders had begun regularly to move northwestward between the Rift Valley and the sea. Indeed, it was Africans who usually arrived first to trade at the coast, rather than the Zanzibaris, who first moved inland. Zanzibari caravans had, however, begun to thrust inland before the end of the 18th century. Their main route thereafter struck immediately to the west and soon made Tabora their chief upcountry base.

From there some traders went due west to Ujiji and across Lake Tanganyika to found, in the latter part of the 19th century, slave-based Arab states upon the Luapula and the upper reaches of the Congo. In these areas some of those who crossed the Nyasa-Tanganyika watershed (which was often approached from farther down the East African coast) were involved as well, while others went northwestward and captured the trade on the south and west sides of Lake Victoria. Here they were mostly kept out of Rwanda, but they were welcomed in both Buganda and Bunyoro and largely forestalled other traders who, after 1841, were thrusting up the Nile from Khartoum. They forestalled, too, the coastal traders moving inland from Mombasa, who seemed unable to establish themselves beyond Kilimanjaro on the south side of Lake Victoria. These Mombasa traders only captured the Kamba trade by first moving out beyond it to the west. By the 1880s, however, they were operating both in the Mount Kenya region and around Winam Bay and were even reaching north toward Lake Rudolf.

## THE COLONIAL ERA

Suggestions that he might at this time establish his dominion over the East African interior prompted Sultan Barghash to send a Baloch force to Tabora, but the idea was never pursued. A comparable notion, however, led Khedive Isma'il Pasha of Egypt to appoint in 1869 the Englishman Samuel White Baker as governor of the Equatorial Province of the Sudan, so that Baker might carry the Egyptian flag to the East African lakes. Though Baker reached as far south as Bunyoro in 1872, he was soon obliged to leave. His successor, Charles George Gordon, proposed to circumvent both Bunyoro and Buganda by going straight up the Nile's banks. But Mutesa I, *kabaka* of Buganda, frustrated Gordon's efforts on the Nile, and by the early 1880s, with bankruptcy in Egypt and the Mahdist revolt in the Sudan, only remnants of the Egyptian enterprise remained.

The Egyptian incursion had been the climax to the search by many European explorers for the headwaters of the Nile—a quest that had obsessed the later years of the Scottish missionary David Livingstone and had prompted the

discovery in 1858 of Lake Tanganyika by the English expedition of Richard Burton and John Hanning Speke. Speke returned first to discover Lake Victoria in 1858 and then with James Grant in 1862 became the first white man to set eyes on the source of the Nile, which Speke named Ripon Falls. By circumnavigating Lake Victoria 12 years later, Henry Morton Stanley stilled the controversy that had ensued in Europe over Speke's claim.

### MISSIONARY ACTIVITY

The revelations of these explorers, the example of David Livingstone, concern in western Europe over the East African slave trade, and the Roman Catholic and evangelical fervour that existed there inspired the invasion of the East African interior by a motley collection of Christian missionary enterprises. Johann Ludwig Krapf and Johannes Rebmann of the Church Missionary Society, who had worked inland from Mombasa and had, in the 1840s and '50s, journeyed to the foothills of Mount Kenya and Kilimanjaro, were followed by a British Methodist mission. Roman Catholic missionaries reached Zanzibar in 1860 and settled at Bagamoyo in 1868. An Anglo-Catholic mission first tried to establish itself in the Shire highlands, then in 1864 transferred to Zanzibar. Anglican missionaries arriving in Buganda in the mid-1870s at the request of Kabaka Mutesa were soon followed by Catholic White Fathers—there and elsewhere on Zanzibar's Tabora route—while the London Missionary

*The work of Scottish explorer and missionary David Livingstone was one inspiration for a diverse and zealous crew of missionaries to penetrate the East African interior.* Popperfoto/ Getty Images

Society sent men both to Unyamwezi and to Lake Tanganyika.

There were, of course, a number of localized religious movements among the peoples of East Africa during the 19th century. These included the Mbari cult among the Nyakyusa, the Nyabingi in Rwanda, and the Yakany movement north of Mount Ruwenzori. None of them, however, spread in quite the way that the Chwezi movement had earlier. Islam, however—spread widely at the instance of the Zanzibari traders and long established on the coast—had secured a scattering of converts in the interior as in the key kingdom of Buganda.

This was the scene onto which Christian missionaries first entered. Although by 1885 there were nearly 300 of them in East Africa, they did not initially win many converts, and those they at first obtained came only from among freed slaves and refugees from local wars. After 1880, however, they made important conversions in Buganda, and by the end of the century Christianity was spreading in the Lake Victoria area over most of the region in which the Chwezi movement had previously percolated—and before very long over a much larger area as well.

## PARTITION BY GERMANY AND BRITAIN

Philanthropic, commercial, and eventually imperialist ventures followed these evangelical endeavours. Nothing of great moment, however, occurred until 1885, when a German, Carl Peters, riding a tide of diplomatic hostility between Germany and Britain in Europe, secured the grant of an imperial charter for his German East Africa Company. With this the European "scramble for Africa" began. In east-central Africa the key occurrence was the Anglo-German Agreement of 1886, by which the two parties agreed that their spheres of influence in East Africa should be divided by a line running from south of Mombasa, then north of Kilimanjaro to a point on the eastern shore of Lake Victoria. This began the extraordinary process by which the territories and subsequently the nations of East Africa were blocked out first upon the maps far away in Europe and only later upon the ground in East Africa itself. The agreement put the area to the north (most of modern Kenya) under British influence and the area to the south (Tanganyika; modern mainland Tanzania) under German influence. The Anglo-German Agreement of 1890 placed additional territory (most of modern Uganda) under British influence.

Kenya was proclaimed a British protectorate in 1895 and a crown colony in 1920. Most of what is now Uganda was formally proclaimed a British protectorate in 1894, with additional areas being added to the protectorate in the following years. Tanganyika was declared a German protectorate in 1891. During World War I, Britain captured the German holdings, which became a British mandate in 1920. Britain retained control of Tanganyika after World War II when it became a United Nations trust territory. Tanganyika gained independence in 1961 and in 1964 merged with Zanzibar,

## GERMAN EAST AFRICA

*German East Africa was a former dependency of imperial Germany, corresponding to present-day Rwanda and Burundi, the continental portion of Tanzania, and a small section of Mozambique. Penetration of the area was begun in 1884 by German commercial agents, and German claims were recognized by the other European powers in the period 1885–94. In 1891 the German imperial government took over administration of the area from the German East Africa Company. Although its subjugation was not completed until 1907, the colony experienced considerable economic development before World War I. During the war it was occupied by the British, who received a mandate to administer the greater part of it (Tanganyika Territory) by the Treaty of Versailles (signed June 1919; enacted January 1920). A smaller portion (Ruanda-Urundi) was entrusted to Belgium.*

later taking the name Tanzania. Uganda gained its independence in 1962, and Kenya became fully independent in 1963.

## HORN OF AFRICA

The history of the Horn of Africa has largely been dominated by Ethiopia and has been characterized by struggles between Muslim and other herdsmen and Christian farmers for resources and living space. The Christians mostly spoke Semitic languages and the Muslims Cushitic tongues. Although these languages were derived from the same Afro-Asiatic origin, the more apparent differences between the peoples often were excuses for war.

### AKSUM

When the Ethiopian empire of Aksum emerged into the light of history at the end of the 1st century CE, it was as a trading state known throughout the Red Sea region. Its people spoke Ge'ez, a Semitic language, and they mostly worshipped Middle Eastern gods, although here and there a traditional African deity survived. Its port of Adulis received a continuous stream of merchants who offered textiles, glassware, tools, precious jewelry, copper, iron, and steel in return for ivory, tortoiseshell, rhinoceros horn, gold, silver, slaves, frankincense, and myrrh. Aksum, the capital, was five days' march from the coast onto the Tigray Plateau, from which position it dominated trade routes into the south and west, where the commodities originated.

By the 4th century Aksum had become a regional power and an ally of Constantinople, whose language and culture attracted the ruling elites. Sometime around 321 Emperor Ezana and the Aksumite court converted to

## BRITISH EAST AFRICA

*British East Africa is the name used to refer to a collection of territories that were once under British control in eastern Africa—namely Kenya, Uganda, and Zanzibar and Tanganyika (now Tanzania). British penetration of the area began at Zanzibar in the last quarter of the 19th century. In 1888 the Imperial British East Africa Company established claims to territory in what is now Kenya. In 1890 and 1894 British protectorates were established over the sultanate of Zanzibar and the kingdom of Buganda (Uganda), respectively, and in 1895 the company's territory in Kenya was transferred to the crown as the East Africa Protectorate (after 1920, the Kenya Colony and the Kenya Protectorate). Under the Treaty of Versailles (signed June 1919; enacted January 1920), Britain was awarded the former German territory of Tanganyika as a League of Nations mandate. All of these territories achieved political independence in the 1960s, and Zanzibar united with Tanganyika to form what is now Tanzania in 1964.*

the monophysitic Christianity—a belief that Christ had one nature that was both divine and human—of Alexandria's See of St. Mark. During the next 200 years Christianity penetrated the masses, as foreign and native-born monks proselytized the interior, building churches and establishing monasteries wherever they found pagan temples and shrines.

Through the first half of the 6th century, Aksum was the most important state in the Red Sea–Indian Ocean region and even extended its power over the kingdom of the Ḥimyarites on the Arabian Peninsula. In the Horn, Aksum dominated Welo, Tigray, Eritrea, and the important trade routes to and from the Sudan. The capital's stone buildings, monuments, churches, and 20,000 inhabitants were supported by tribute and taxes extracted from vassals and traders.

In 543 Abraha, the general in charge of Ḥimyar, rebelled and weakened

Aksum's hold over South Arabia. This event marked the end of the empire's regional hegemony, allowed Persia to assume supremacy, and forced Constantinople into an overland trade route with India and Africa. Aksum's international trade diminished, a shift reflected in the debasement of the state's coins. The rise of Islam in Arabia a century later almost completely devastated Aksum, as Muslim sailors swept Ethiopian shipping from the sea-lanes.

Aksum lost its economic vitality, and Adulis and other commercial centres withered. State revenues were greatly reduced, and the government could no longer maintain a standing army, a complex administration, and urban amenities. The culture associated with the outside world quickly became a memory, and Ethiopia learned to exist in local terms. The Christian state moved southward into the rich grain-growing areas of the interior, where the rulers could sustain themselves. There they and the local Cushitic-speaking population, the Agew, worked out a new political arrangement for Ethiopia.

## THE SOMALI

Meanwhile, another Cushitic people, the Somali, had separated themselves from the Oromo in what is now north-central Kenya. For their livelihood, they depended upon the one-humped Arabian camel, sheep, and goats. During the first centuries CE they migrated in a southeastern direction, finally following the Tana River to the Indian Ocean. They then turned north and peopled the entire Somali peninsula, coming into contact on the coast with Arab and Persian trading communities, from whom they took Islam and a mythological Arabian origin. By the 12th century the entire northern Somali coast was Islamized, providing a basis for proselytism in the interior. But, as the Somali migration and Islam moved westward, they encountered a resurgent Christian Ethiopia.

## THE SOLOMONIDS

An amalgamated Christian state, led by Semitized Agew, had reappeared in the 12th century. This Zagwe dynasty gave way in the late 13th century to a dynasty that claimed descent from King Solomon and the Queen of Sheba, a genealogy providing the legitimacy and continuity

so honoured in Ethiopia's subsequent national history. During the 14th and 15th centuries, the Solomonid monarchs expanded their state southward and eastward. By then Muslims dominated Ethiopia's trade, which exited via Mitsiwa in Eritrea or through Seylac on the northern Somali coast.

The Solomonids permitted Muslim business activities in return for submission and taxes. In 1332 Ifat, a large Muslim polity with its port at Seylac, fed up with being a Christian vassal, declared a holy war against Ethiopia and invaded its territory, destroying churches and forcing conversions to Islam. The Ethiopian emperor, Amda Tseyon, fought back hard, routed the enemy, and carried the frontier of Christian power to the edge of the Shewan Plateau, overlooking the largely Muslim-inhabited Awash valley. One hundred years later, under Emperor Zara Yakob, the Solomonid empire extended its authority southward to modern Bale and Sidamo.

By then Ethiopia faced a challenge from Adal, Ifat's militant successor. Located in the semidesert Harer region, Adal employed highly mobile Somali and Afar cavalry, whose raiding Ethiopia could not control. Meanwhile, the Solomonid state had begun to decay, owing to succession problems and the sheer complexity of governing a large empire. The Muslims consequently stopped paying tribute and a percentage of their trading profits to the hated Christians. Thereafter, they grew stronger and more daring, responding in part to overpopulation among the Somali.

The distress was exploited by the charismatic Aḥmad ibn Ibrāhīm al-Ghāzī, known to the Ethiopians as Aḥmad Grāñ ("Aḥmad the Left-handed"). A pious, indeed rigorous, Muslim, Aḥmad railed against the secular nature of Adal, mobilized men to purify the state, and trained his enlistees to use the modern tactics and firearms recently introduced by the Ottomans into the Red Sea region. After he took over Adal about 1526, his refusal to pay tribute triggered a Solomonid invasion in 1527, which his army easily repulsed.

Aḥmad thereupon declared a holy war, led his men into Ethiopia, and won battle after battle, fragmenting the Solomonid state into its component parts. During 1531–32 the Muslims pushed northward, traversing the rich Amhara Plateau north of the Awash and destroying churches and monasteries. Aḥmad Grāñ built a civil administration composed of his own men, remnants of the pre-Solomonid ruling classes, and collaborators. By 1535 he headed a vast Islamic empire stretching from Seylac to Mitsiwa on the coast and including much of the Ethiopian interior, but not the staunchly Christian mountain fastnesses.

There, in 1541, Emperor Galawdewos learned that 400 Portuguese musketeers had disembarked at Mitsiwa in response to pleas for assistance. Though they lost half their strength moving inland, their weapons and tactics inspired Galawdewos to exploit Ethiopia's difficult terrain by undertaking hit-and-run warfare. Aḥmad never knew where his adversaries would strike and therefore placed his forces in defensive positions, where they lost their mobility, while he and his personal guard acted as a rapidly deployed reserve. Encamped at Weyna Dega near Lake Tana, Aḥmad's unit was attacked on Feb. 21, 1543, by Galawdewos and a flying column. During the hard-fought battle Aḥmad was killed, and that single death ended the war.

Christian Ethiopia was reprieved, but at a great cost. The country had lost hundreds of thousands of lives, confidence in itself and its religion, and its store of capital. Unable to follow Europe into commercial and then industrial capitalism, Ethiopia rebuilt feudalism, because the state simply had to restore affordable administration. By the early 1550s Galawdewos had fashioned a reasonable facsimile of the high Solomonid empire. Muslims, especially in the border provinces of Ifat, Dawaro (in the modern Arsi region), and Bale, remained disaffected. Christian converts along the periphery of the heartland, south of the Blue Nile and the Awash River, chafed under renewed exploitation, and the Judaized Falasha, to the north of Lake Tana, returned to their life of dispossession and economic marginalization. Finally, south of Lake Tana, in modern Gojam, Welega, Ilubabor, Kefa, Gamo Gofa, and Sidamo, a whole range of people remained tributary to the Christian kingdom. From among this last category emerged a new and more fundamental threat to old-fashioned Ethiopia.

## RISE OF THE OROMO

The challenge came from the Oromo, a Cushitic-speaking pastoralist people whose original homeland was located on the Sidamo-Borena plain. From there, the related Afar and Somali peoples had hived off northeastward to the Red Sea coast, the Indian Ocean, and the Gulf of Aden, perhaps in some way causing the pressures that finally erupted in Aḥmad Grāñ's invasion of the Solomonid state. Some Oromo may have climbed onto the high Christian plateaus as early as the late 13th century, only to be repulsed. Garrisons established along the empire's periphery by Amda Tseyon and Zara Yakob were designed to keep the Oromo out, but, when these defenses were destroyed during the war with Aḥmad Grāñ, the Oromo naturally resumed infiltrating.

The Oromo had an age-set form of government that changed every eight years, when a new warrior class sought its fortune by raiding and rustling in order to provide resources that the natural environment lacked. Every eight years, from the 1540s on, they advanced farther into the well-watered, fertile highlands—a sharp contrast with their arid bush country. Helped by their adversary's war-weariness, demoralization, and depopulation, the Oromo invariably won territory after territory. By the beginning of the 17th century they had pushed northwestward into the modern regions of Arsi, Shewa, Welega, and Gojam and northeastward into Harerge and Welo,

stopping only where they were blocked by forest, high population density, or effective mobilization of Christian forces.

## ABYSSINIA

The Christians retreated into what may be called Abyssinia, an easily defensible, socially cohesive unit that included mostly Christian, Semitic-speaking peoples in a territory comprising most of Eritrea, Tigray, and Gonder and parts of Gojam, Shewa, and Welo. For the next two centuries Abyssinia defined the limits of Ethiopia's extent, but not its reach, for the Christian highlands received the hinterland's trade in transit to the Red Sea and the Nile valley. A complex caravan network linked Mitsiwa (now Massawa, Eritrea) on the Red Sea coast with the highlands of the interior.

Gonder, the new capital, became a regional centre, doing business with the Sudanese cities of Sannār and Fazughli for slaves and gold, bought and paid for with coffee obtained from the Oromo-dominated lands. Demand for Ethiopian products increased considerably during the last quarter of the 17th century, as Yemen, a major trading partner on the Arabian Peninsula, sought increasing amounts of coffee for trans-shipment to Europe.

## REVIVAL OF THE ETHIOPIAN EMPIRE

By the late 19th century the northernmost Oromo had been assimilated

## THE OROMO

*One of the two largest ethnolinguistic groups of Ethiopia, the Oromo constitute about one-third of the population and speak a language of the Cushitic branch of the Afro-Asiatic family. Originally confined to the southeast of the country, they migrated in waves of invasions in the 16th century CE. They occupied all of southern Ethiopia, with some settling along the Tana River in Kenya; most of the central and western Ethiopian provinces, including the southern parts of the Amhara region; and, farther north, the Welo and Tigre regions near Eritrea. Wherever the Oromo settled in these physically disparate areas, they assimilated local customs and intermarried to such an extent that the Oromo people's original cultural cohesiveness was largely lost. Also, the resultant political division of the Oromo facilitated their own eventual subjugation by the people whom they had driven northward, the Amhara, the other major ethnolinguistic group in Ethiopia.*

*The Oromo pursued pastoralism before the great migration, and this way of life still prevails for the great numbers of people in the southern provinces. In the east and north, however, long mingling and intermarrying with the Sidamo and Amhara resulted in the adoption of a sedentary agriculture.*

*The southern groups, such as the Arusi and Boran (Borana) Oromo, have remained pagan, believing in a sky god. They have retained virtually intact the gada, or highly formalized age-set system (a system in which all members of society are included in separate age groups for life). These traditions have been diluted in the north, where the Oromo are either Muslim or Ethiopian Orthodox Christian and where many Oromo have, through acculturation, become social equals to the dominant Amhara. The influence of the Oromo increased after the Ethiopian revolution of 1974.*

into Christian culture, and Abyssinia's national unity had been restored after a century of feudal anarchy that ended with the accession of Yohannes IV in 1872. Yohannes forced the submission of Ethiopia's princes, repulsed Egyptian expansionism in 1875–76, pushed back Mahdist invasions in 1885–86, and limited the Italians to the Eritrean coast. Meanwhile, the ambitious King Menilek II of Shewa began a reconquest of Ethiopia's southern and eastern peripheries to acquire commodities to sell for the weapons and ammunition he would need in his fight for the Solomonid crown. Italian adventurers, scientists, and missionaries helped organize a route, outside imperial control, that took Shewan caravans to the coast, where Menilek's ivory, gold, hides, and furs could be sold for a sizable (and untaxed) profit.

The economy of the Red Sea region had been stimulated by the opening of the Suez Canal, by the establishment of a British base in Aden, and by the opening of a French coaling station at Obock on the Afar coast. Britain sought to close off the Nile valley to the French by facilitating Rome's aspirations in the Horn. Thus, after 1885, Italy occupied coastal positions in Ethiopia and in southern Somalia. This limited the French to their mini-colony, leaving the British in control of ports in northern Somalia from which foodstuffs were exported to Aden. After Yohannes' death in March 1889, the Italians hoped to translate a cordial relationship with the new emperor, Menilek, into an Ethiopian empire.

On May 2, 1889, Menilek signed at Wichale (known as Ucciali to the Italians) a treaty of peace and amity with Italy. The Italians' famous mistranslation of Article XVII of the Treaty of Wichale provided them with an excuse to declare Ethiopia a protectorate. To Italy's dismay, the new emperor promptly wrote to the great powers, rejecting Rome's claim. Since neither France nor Russia accepted the new protectorate status, Ethiopia continued to acquire modern weapons from these countries through Obock. When, by 1894–95, Italy not only refused to rescind its declaration but also reinforced its army in Eritrea and invaded eastern Tigray, Menilek mobilized.

In late February 1896 an Ethiopian army of approximately 100,000 men was encamped at Adwa in Tigray, facing a much smaller enemy force some miles away. The Italians nevertheless attacked and were defeated on March 1, 1896, in what became known to Europeans as the Battle of Adwa. Menilek immediately withdrew his hungry army southward with 1,800 prisoner-hostages, leaving Eritrea to Rome in the hope that peace with honour would be restored quickly. On Oct. 26, 1896, Italy signed the Treaty of Addis Ababa, conceding the unconditional abrogation of the Treaty of Wichale and recognizing Ethiopia's sovereign independence.

During the next decade, Menilek directed Ethiopia's return into the southern and western regions that had been abandoned in the 17th century. Most of the newly incorporated peoples there lived in segmented societies, practiced animal husbandry or cultivation with digging stick or hoe, followed traditional religions or Islam, and spoke non-Semitic languages. In practically every way but skin colour, the northerners were aliens. Their superior weapons and more complex social organization gave them a material advantage, but they also were inspired by the idea that they were regaining lands that had once been part of the Christian state. Menilek and his soldiers believed that they were on a holy crusade to restore Ethiopia to its historic grandeur, but they did not realize that they were participating in Europe's "scramble for Africa" and that they were creating problems among nationalities that would afflict the Horn of Africa throughout the 20th century.

# CHAPTER 10

## DJIBOUTI

D jibouti is a small eastern African country located along the northeast coast of the Horn of Africa, on the Gulf of Aden at the entrance to the Red Sea. Once under French colonial administration, it became independent in 1977. The capital is the city of Djibouti.

### EARLY HISTORY

Settled by the Arab ancestors of the Afars, the area that is now known as Djibouti was later populated by Somali Issas. In 825 CE Islam was brought to the area by missionaries, and Arabs controlled the trade in this region until the 16th century. It was made a French protectorate in the 19th century and became known as French Somaliland. It was made a French overseas territory in 1946 and assumed the name French Territory of the Afars and Issas in 1967.

### INDEPENDENCE AND THE GOULED PRESIDENCY

On June 27, 1977, the French Territory of the Afars and the Issas became independent. The new country took the name Djibouti, and Hassan Gouled Aptidon was the first president.

### BALANCING ETHNIC TENSIONS

On the eve of independence, Djibouti's viability as a sovereign state was questionable. However, fears that the Afar and

the Issa Somali would become pawns in a struggle between the republic's rival neighbours, Ethiopia and Somalia, did not materialize. No Djiboutian political leader, either Afar or Somali, ever condoned unification with either of the larger states. Indeed, Djibouti established a peaceful international profile through a policy of strict neutrality in regional affairs. In keeping with friendship treaties with both Somalia and Ethiopia, the government refused to support armed groups opposing the neighbouring regimes, and it hosted negotiations between Somalia's and Ethiopia's leaders that resulted in a series of accords in 1988.

Djibouti's balanced posture in external relations was reflected in its internal politics. Gouled, an Issa Somali, was elected to two consecutive terms as president in 1981 and 1987. Barkat Gourad Hamadou, an Afar serving as prime minister since 1978, was reappointed in 1987. Power appeared to be shared, with ministry appointments following a formula designed to maintain ethnic balance.

In the first years of self-government, though, ethnic tensions were evident. By 1978 the state had experienced two cabinet crises and changes of prime minister. Those ousted were Afars accused of fomenting ethnic strife. After opposition parties were banned in 1981, ethnic conflict in the political arena was for the most part minimal. However, Issa predominance in the civil service, the armed forces, and the Popular Assembly for Progress (Rassemblement Populaire pour le Progrès; RPP)—now the only legally

recognized political party—was only slightly masked, and occasional tremors of social unrest disturbed Djibouti's superficial calm.

## URBAN DEVELOPMENT AND CHALLENGES

Challenges to Djibouti's stability could not be reduced to traditional Afar and Issa enmity. Signs of the serious problems facing the young nation were also to be found in the urban demography of its capital. On the outskirts of the city, an expansive squatter community known as Balbala, which originally developed just beyond the barbed-wire boundary erected by the French colonial administration to prevent migration to the capital, tripled in size within a decade after independence. In 1987 it was officially incorporated into the city, with the promise of development of basic water and sanitary services. Its growth continued because of a high birth rate, rural migration, and displacement of persons from the urban core.

Conditions in some of the densely populated quarters of Djibouti city were only marginally better than in Balbala. Structures were limited to wood and corrugated iron by colonial, and later national, restrictions on the construction and location of permanent dwellings. Distinct ethnic enclaves were identifiable: the retail centre surrounding the main mosque (Hamoudi Mosque) and the former caravan terminus (Harbi Square) housed the Arab community; the neighbourhoods radiating beyond this area were settled by the Isaaq, Gadaboursi, and Issa Somali; and the quarter known as Arhiba was built by the French to house the Afar dockworkers recruited from the north of the colony in the 1960s.

As the urban infrastructure was developed, and because government-subsidized housing was realized through international aid programs, conditions in the old districts of the city improved. Yet the needs remained immense, and progress was accompanied by perceptions of ethnic favouritism. Discontent was also fostered by a high cost of living, unemployment, and a widening gap in living conditions between the majority of the population and the new urban elite.

## MULTIPARTY POLITICS AND CIVIL WAR

Djibouti's status as a single-party state ended when a new constitution promulgated in 1992 introduced multiparty politics, although the number of political parties allowed to participate in the political process was initially limited to four. In the subsequent multiparty presidential election held the following year, Gouled emerged victorious over opposition candidates by a wide margin of victory.

Meanwhile, the country's ethnic tensions had continued to simmer, and in late 1991 the Afar Front for the Restoration of Unity and Democracy (Front pour la Restauration de l'Unité et de la Démocratie; FRUD) took up arms against the Issa-dominated government; the conflict quickly developed into civil war. By mid-1992 FRUD forces occupied some two-thirds of the country, although the territory that they held consisted of sparsely populated rural areas. In 1994 internal dissent within FRUD's leadership caused the group to splinter. Later that year a power-sharing agreement signed by the government and primary FRUD group largely ended the conflict, although the final peace agreement would not be signed until 2001. As part of the 1994 agreement, some FRUD leaders became ministers in the government, and FRUD was allowed to register as a legal political party in 1996.

## DJIBOUTI UNDER GUELLEH

In 1999 Gouled announced that he would not stand in the presidential election scheduled for April, and the RPP nominated Ismail Omar Guelleh, a former cabinet secretary and Gouled's nephew, easily beat his opponent, Moussa Ahmed Idriss, who represented a small coalition of opposition parties. In 2001 the long-serving prime minister Hamadou resigned for health reasons, and Guelleh named Dileita Muhammad Dileita, an accomplished public servant, to the post. Dileita, like his predecessor, was an Afar, and Guelleh's appointment of him to the post maintained the balance of power between the Afars and Somali Issas that Gouled had established after independence.

In 2002 the previous restriction on the number of political parties was lifted, which allowed for the creation of many

*Ismail Omar Guelleh became president of Djibouti in 1999.* Patrick Kovarik/AFP/Getty Images

new legally recognized political parties and offered the potential for change in Djibouti's political landscape. One such change was the creation of the Union for the Presidential Majority (Union pour la Majorité Présidentielle; UMP) coalition, which included both RPP and FRUD and was formed in preparation for the 2003 legislative elections. Despite the problems affecting Djiboutians at the time, including a serious drought and food shortage, it was the presence of U.S. troops in the country that appeared to be the dominant campaign issue. U.S. troops had been in Djibouti since 2002 to use the country's strategic location during the U.S.-led global campaign against terrorism. The opposition argued against the government's decision to allow the troops in the country, saying it could provoke acts of terrorism against Djiboutians. Despite the argument, the UMP prevailed in the election, taking all parliamentary seats. Although Guelleh continued to cultivate diplomatic ties with the United States, he was openly critical of its role in the Iraq War that began in 2003, citing the lack of UN approval for the operation, and he did not allow the U.S. to launch any attacks from Djibouti. Whether the presence of U.S. troops would be an issue in future elections was not immediately known: the next scheduled election—the 2005 presidential poll—was boycotted by the opposition, who cited the need for greater transparency and electoral change. As a result, Guelleh was the only candidate, and he won 100 percent of the vote.

Djibouti's somewhat acrimonious relationship with neighbouring Eritrea (a former Ethiopian province that had gained independence in 1993) worsened in April 2008 when Eritrea amassed troops along the Ras Doumeira border area of Djibouti; this action resulted in border skirmishes that in June led to the deaths of more than 30 people and injuries to many more. Eritrea's actions were widely criticized, notably by the African Union, the United Nations Security Council, and the Arab League.

# CHAPTER 11

# ERITREA

Eritrea is an eastern African country located on the northeast coast of the Horn of Africa, on the Red Sea. It became an independent country in 1993. The capital is Asmara.

## PRECOLONIAL ERITREA

Beginning about 1000 BCE, Semitic peoples from the south Arabian kingdom of Saba' (Sheba) migrated across the Red Sea and absorbed the Cushitic inhabitants of the Eritrean coast and adjacent highlands. These Semitic invaders, possessing a well-developed culture, established the kingdom of Aksum, which, by the end of the 4th century CE, ruled the northern stretches of the Ethiopian Plateau and the eastern lowlands. An important trade route led from the port of Adulis, near modern Zula, to the city of Aksum, the capital, located in what is now the Ethiopian province of Tigray.

### RULE FROM THE HIGHLANDS

After extending its power at times as far afield as modern Egypt and Yemen, Aksum began to decline into obscurity in the 6th century CE. Beginning in the 12th century, however, the Ethiopian Zagwe and Solomonid dynasties held sway to a fluctuating extent over the entire plateau and the Red Sea coast. Eritrea's central highlands, known as the *mereb melash* ("land beyond the Mereb River"), were the northern frontier region of the Ethiopian kingdoms and were ruled by a governor titled *bahr negash* ("lord of the sea"). The control exercised by the crown over this region was never firm, and it became even more tenuous as the centre of Ethiopian power moved steadily southward to Gonder and Shewa. Highland Eritrea became a vassal fiefdom of the lords of Tigray, who were seldom on good terms with the dominant Amhara branch of the Ethiopian family.

## CONTESTING FOR THE COASTLANDS AND BEYOND

Off the plateau, the pastoralist peoples in the west and north knew no foreign master until the early 19th century, when the Egyptians invaded the Sudan and raided deep into the Eritrean lowlands. The Red Sea coast, having its strategic and commercial importance, was contested by many powers. In the 16th century the Ottoman Turks occupied the Dahlak Archipelago and then Massawa, where they maintained with occasional interruption a garrison for more than three centuries. Also in the 16th century, Eritrea as well as Ethiopia was affected by the invasions of Aḥmad Grāñ, the Muslim leader of the sultanate of Adal. After the expulsion of Aḥmad's forces, the Ottoman Turks temporarily occupied even more of Eritrea's coastal area. In 1865 the Egyptians obtained Massawa from the Turks. From there they pushed inland to the plateau, until in 1875 an Egyptian force that reached the Mereb River was annihilated by Ethiopian forces.

Meanwhile, the opening of the Suez Canal in 1869 had made the Red Sea a scene of rivalry among the world's most powerful states. Between 1869 and 1880 the Italian Rubattino Navigation Company purchased from the local Afar sultan stretches of the Red Sea coast adjoining the village of Asseb. In 1882 these acquisitions were transferred to the Italian state, and in 1885 Italian troops landed at Massawa, Asseb, and other locations. There was no resistance by the Egyptians at Massawa, and protests made by the Turks and Ethiopians were ignored. Italian forces then systematically spread out from Massawa toward the highlands.

The Italians' expansion onto the plateau was initially opposed by Emperor Yohannes IV, the only Tigray to wear the Ethiopian crown in modern times, but Yohannes's successor, Menilek II, in return for weapons that he needed to fight possible rivals, acquiesced to Italian occupation of the region north of the Mereb. In the Treaty of Wichale, signed on May 2, 1889, Menilek recognized "Italian possessions in the Red Sea," and on Jan. 1, 1890, the Italian colony of Eritrea was officially proclaimed. From Eritrea the Italians launched several incursions into Ethiopia, only to be decisively defeated by Menilek's army at the Battle of Adwa on March 1, 1896. Menilek did not pursue the defeated enemy across the Mereb. Soon afterward he signed the Treaty of Addis Ababa, obtaining Italian recognition of Ethiopia's sovereignty in

*Following the 1869 opening of the Suez Canal, an Italian company purchased sections of the Red Sea coast, which were later transferred to the Italian government. Thus Italian expansion commenced.* Apic/Hulton Archive/Getty Images

return for his recognition of Italian rule over Eritrea.

## COLONIAL ERITREA

In precolonial times there were no towns on the Eritrean plateau, urban centres being limited to the Red Sea coast. Under Italian rule, however, Eritrea's urban sector flourished.

### RULE BY ITALY

Tens of thousands of Italians arrived, bringing with them modern skills and a new lifestyle. Asmara grew into a charming city in the Mediterranean style, the port of Massawa was modernized and the port of Asseb improved, and a number of smaller towns appeared on the plateau. Road and rail construction linked the various regions of the colony, and a modest manufacturing sector also appeared, in which Eritreans acquired industrial skills.

At the same time, a sizable portion of Eritrea's best agricultural land was reserved for Italian farmers (although only a few actually settled on the land), and a small plantation sector was established to grow produce for the urban

## AḤMAD GRĀÑ

(b. c. 1506—d. 1543)

*Aḥmad Grāñ was the byname of Aḥmad Ibn Ibrāhīm al-Ghāzī, the leader of a Muslim move-ment that all but subjugated Ethiopia. At the height of his conquest, Aḥmad Grāñ (also called Aḥmad the Left-handed) held more than three-quarters of the kingdom, and, according to the chronicles, the majority of men in these conquered areas had converted to Islam.*

*Once Aḥmad Grāñ had gained control of the Muslim Somali state of Adal (Adel), where he installed his brother as a puppet king, he launched a jihad (Islamic holy war) against Christian Ethiopia. He created an army out of the masses of heterogeneous and nomadic Somalis who had joined him, motivated by religion and the prospects of wealth. He also made skillful use of firearms, introduced by the Turks, and employed a small body of Turkish troops.*

*Although Aḥmad Grāñ defeated an Ethiopian army in Adal in 1526–27, it was not until 1531 that he felt ready for a large-scale invasion. By 1535 he had conquered the southern and central areas of the state and had even invaded the northern highlands, leaving a trail of devastation behind him. The Ethiopian king and a few followers retreated and begged for Portuguese aid. But when a small Portuguese force tried to relieve them in 1541, they were first delayed and later soundly defeated by Aḥmad Grāñ, who had meanwhile been able to obtain Turkish reinforcements. The few remaining Portuguese, however, with the new Ethiopian ruler, Galawdewos (Claudius), were soon able to rearm themselves and rally a large number of Ethiopians. Aḥmad Grāñ, who had sent most of his Turkish troops back, was killed in the cru-cial battle that followed, and Galawdewos was able to regain his kingdom in 1543, though the conversion to Islam and reconversion of most of his subjects may have left a spiritual crisis less easily resolved.*

market. Eritrea's population grew rap-idly during this period. Combined with the appropriation of land for Italian use, population growth created a shortage of land for Eritrean farmers. This in turn stimulated a drift to the cities, which fur-ther expanded the urban population and produced an Eritrean working class.

Still, Eritrea had no valuable resources for exploitation and was not a wealth-producing colony for Italy. In fact, the colony was subsidized by the Italians, an extraneous factor that gave the local economy an artificial glow. Investment in education for Eritreans was negligible. There were very few schools for them, and these were limited to the primary level. Also, Eritreans were not employed in the colonial service except as labour-ers and soldiers. As preparations for the Italian invasion of Ethiopia got under way in the mid-1930s, several thousand Eritreans were recruited to serve in the invading army.

## FROM ITALIAN TO ETHIOPIAN RULE

Italy's invasion and occupation of Ethiopia beginning in 1935—including Ethiopia's annexation and incorporation into Italian East Africa in 1936—marked the last chapter in Italian colonial history. The chapter came to an end with the eviction of Italy from the Horn of Africa by the British in 1941, during World War II. The following decade, during which Eritrea remained under British administration, was a period of intense political and diplomatic activity that shaped the future of Eritrea.

Landlocked Ethiopia, coveting Eritrea's two seaports, launched an early campaign to annex the former colony, claiming that it had always been part of Ethiopia's domain. Lobbying of the Allied powers was carried out, and within Eritrea, with the help of Ethiopian Orthodox clergy, support for annexation was mobilized on the basis of religious loyalty. To promote the union of Eritrea with Ethiopia, a Unionist Party was formed in 1946. It was financed and guided from the Ethiopian capital, Addis Ababa.

Eritrea's Muslims had every good reason to oppose union with Ethiopia, where Christianity was the official religion and Muslims suffered discrimination in many areas of life. To counter Christian mobilization for union, a Muslim League was founded in 1947 to campaign for Eritrean independence. Thus, although there were some Christians who favoured independence and a few Muslims who were favourable to union with Ethiopia, the political division was drawn largely along sectarian lines.

## FEDERATION WITH ETHIOPIA

In 1950 the United Nations (UN), under the prompting of the United States, resolved to join Eritrea to Ethiopia within two years. The proposed federation would provide Eritrea with autonomy under its own constitution and elected government. Elections to a new Eritrean Assembly in 1952 gave the Unionist Party the largest number of seats but not a majority. The party thus formed a government in coalition with a Muslim faction. The Eritrean constitution, prepared by the UN in consultation with Emperor Haile Selassie I of Ethiopia, was adopted by the Eritrean Assembly on July 10, 1952, and ratified by Haile Selassie on August 11. The act of federation was ratified by the emperor on September 11, and British authorities officially relinquished control on September 15.

The federal scheme was short-lived, mainly because the imperial government in Addis Ababa was unwilling to abide by its provisions. First, the Eritrean constitution sought to establish an equilibrium between ethnic and religious groups. It made Tigrinya and Arabic the official languages of Eritrea, and it allowed local communities to choose the language of education for their children. In the spirit of the constitution, it became a practice to ensure parity between Christians and Muslims in appointment to state office.

This delicate balance was destroyed by Ethiopian interference, and Muslims were the initial losers, as Arabic was eliminated from state education and Muslims were squeezed out of public employment.

Furthermore, the Ethiopians were anxious to eliminate any traces of separatism in Eritrea, and to that end they harassed the leaders of the independence movement until many of them fled abroad. With the collaboration of their Unionist allies and in express violation of the constitution, they also suppressed all attempts to form autonomous Eritrean organizations. Political parties were banned in 1955, trade unions were banned in 1958, and in 1959 the name Eritrean Government was changed to "Eritrean Administration" and Ethiopian law was imposed. Eventually, even Ethiopia's Eritrean allies were alienated—by crude intervention in the running of the Eritrean Administration, financial disputes between Asmara and Addis Ababa, and mounting pressure on the Eritreans to renounce autonomy. The federation was already dead when, on Nov. 14, 1962, the Ethiopian parliament and Eritrean Assembly voted unanimously for the abolition of Eritrea's federal status, making Eritrea a simple province of the Ethiopian empire. Soon afterward Tigrinya was banned in education; it was replaced by Amharic, which at the time was the official language of Ethiopia.

## THE WAR OF INDEPENDENCE

Muslims had been the first to suffer from Ethiopia's intervention in Eritrea, and it was they who formed the first opposition movement. In 1960, leaders of the defunct independence movement who were then living in exile announced the formation of the Eritrean Liberation Front (ELF). The founders, all Muslims, were led by Idris Mohammed Adam, a leading political figure in Eritrea in the 1940s. By the mid-1960s the ELF was able to field a small guerrilla force in the western plain of Eritrea, and thus it began a war that was to last nearly three decades. In the early years the ELF drew support from Muslim communities in the western and eastern lowlands as well as the northern hills. It also sought support from Sudan, Syria, Iran, and other Islamic states; used Arabic as its official language; and adopted Arab nomenclature in its organization. Ethiopian authorities portrayed the movement as an Arab tool and sought to rally Eritrean Christians to oppose it. Deteriorating economic and political conditions in Eritrea, however, combined to produce the opposite result.

During the 1930s and '40s the Eritrean economy had been stimulated by Italian colonial activity and by the special conditions created by World War II. After the war the local economy deflated, and it remained stagnant during the entire period of federation with Ethiopia. Many thousands of Eritreans were forced to emigrate to Ethiopia and the Middle East in search of employment. The suppression of the nascent trade union movement further embittered this class, and many Eritrean workers—Muslims and Christians alike—rallied to the nationalist movement. In addition, the banning of Tigrinya in state education helped to turn an entire generation of Eritrean Christian students toward nationalism. Christians began to join the ELF in significant numbers at the end of the 1960s. Among them were students who had become politically radicalized in the Ethiopian student movement, which itself became a centre of opposition to the regime of Haile Selassie in the 1960s and '70s.

The ELF was now able to extend its operations to the central highlands of Eritrea—the home of the Tigray. However, the arrival of the radical students coincided with the emergence of a serious rift between the leadership of the ELF, which was permanently resident in Cairo, and the rank and file, which remained in the field. The newcomers joined the opposition to the leadership, and in 1972 several groups that had defected from the ELF joined forces to form the Eritrean Liberation Front–People's Liberation Forces (ELF–PLF). For several years the two rival organizations fought each other as well as the Ethiopians. After a series of splits and mergers, the ELF–PLF came under the control of former students, among whom Christians predominated, and was renamed the Eritrean People's Liberation Front (EPLF), a Marxist and secular organization.

The EPLF had made its presence felt by 1974, when the imperial regime in Ethiopia collapsed. While a power struggle for the succession was waged in Addis Ababa, the two Eritrean fronts liberated most of Eritrea. By 1977 the nationalist revolution seemed on the verge of victory. Yet it was not to be. A military dictatorship—also espousing Marxism—emerged in Addis Ababa, and, armed and assisted by the Soviet bloc, the new Ethiopian regime was able to regain most of Eritrea in 1978. Warfare on a scale unprecedented in sub-Saharan Africa raged for the next two decades. The Ethiopians made enormous efforts with massive land attacks and heavy weaponry, but they had no success against the small and lightly armed guerrilla forces.

The violence of war and indiscriminate oppression in their homeland turned most Eritreans against Ethiopia, thereby producing a steady stream of young recruits for the nationalist movement. Throughout the 1980s the fighting was carried out by the EPLF, which by 1981 had succeeded in eliminating the ELF and had emerged as the unchallenged champion of Eritrean nationalism. In the latter part of the decade, the Soviet Union terminated its military aid to Ethiopia. Unable to find another patron and faced with armed rebellion in other parts of the country, the regime in Addis Ababa began to falter. The final act occurred in 1991, when a rebel military offensive, led by the Tigray People's Liberation Front (a group that had long been fighting for the autonomy of Tigray in Ethiopia), swept toward the capital. The Ethiopian army disintegrated, and in May the EPLF assumed complete control of Eritrea.

Three decades of war had produced among Eritreans a sense of unity and

*An Eritrean People's Liberation Front (EPLF) fighter. The EPLF formed an alliance with other guerrilla groups and eventually overthrew Ethiopian rule in the early 1990s.* Alex Bowie/Hulton Archive/Getty Images

solidarity that they had not known before. Indeed, an entire generation had come of age during the struggle for independence, which was now to become a reality. The new regime in Ethiopia supported Eritrea's independence, and a separation was effected amicably. In a referendum held two years after liberation, on April 23–25, 1993, the overwhelming majority of Eritreans voted for independence. On May 21 Isaias Afwerki, the secretary-general of the EPLF, was made president of a transitional government, and on May 24 he proclaimed Eritrea officially independent.

## INDEPENDENT ERITREA

Following independence, Eritrea enjoyed a thriving economy but maintained poor relations with neighbouring countries—with the noteworthy exception of Ethiopia. Tension with Sudan throughout the 1990s centred on mutual allegations that each had attempted to destabilize the other. In late 1995 and 1996 Eritrea engaged in a brief but violent conflict with Yemen over the Ḥanīsh Islands, an archipelago in the Red Sea claimed by both countries but ultimately recognized as Yemeni.

Postindependence relations with Ethiopia, initially warm and supportive, became strained over trade issues and the question of Ethiopia's access to Eritrea's Red Sea ports. In 1998 relations deteriorated rapidly when a border dispute, centred around the hamlet of Badme, exploded into violence. Following two years of bloodshed, a

peace was negotiated in December 2000, and the UN established a peacekeeping mission along the border in question. An international boundary commission agreed on a border demarcation, but Ethiopia rejected the decision and refused to leave territory that the commission had recognized as Eritrean. Meanwhile, tension had been growing between the UN peacekeepers and the Eritrean government, which accused several UN workers of being spies. The UN withdrew its mission in 2008. In the same year, another boundary dispute, this one with Djibouti, escalated when Eritrea amassed troops along the Ras Doumeira border area. Fighting between Eritrean and Djiboutian soldiers led to the deaths of more than 30 people.

The postindependence conflicts shattered Eritrea's earlier economic and political progress. Amid economic distress, loss of life, and a new flood of displaced persons, voices of discontent with the government leadership were raised in the late 20th and early 21st centuries. Calls were made to promulgate the country's constitution, which had been ratified in 1997, and to hold parliamentary and presidential elections, which had been postponed indefinitely. Opposition was hampered, however, by the closure of the national press in 2001 and a ban on the formation of new political parties. President Afwerki and his party, the People's Front for Democracy and Justice—the successor to the EPLF—remained firmly in power.

# CHAPTER 12

## ETHIOPIA

Ethiopia is a landlocked country in eastern Africa on the Horn of Africa. As one of the world's oldest countries, it long maintained its independence until the 20th century, when it was briefly occupied by Italy (1936–41). The capital is Addis Ababa.

### FROM PREHISTORY TO THE AKSUMITE KINGDOM

That life is of great antiquity in Ethiopia is indicated by the Hadar remains, a group of skeletal fragments found in the lower Awash River valley. The bone fragments, thought to be 3.4 to 2.9 million years old, belong to *Australopithecus afarensis*, an apelike creature that may have been an ancestor of modern humans.

Sometime between the 8th and 6th millennia BCE, pastoralism and then agriculture developed in northern Africa and southwestern Asia, and, as the population grew, an ancient tongue spoken in this region fissured into the modern languages of the Afro-Asiatic (formerly Hamito-Semitic) family. This family includes the Cushitic, Semitic, and Omotic languages now spoken in Ethiopia. During the 2nd millennium BCE, cereal grains and the use of the plow were introduced into Ethiopia, possibly from the region of the Sudan, and peoples speaking Ge'ez (a Semitic language) came to dominate the rich northern highlands of Tigray. There, in the 7th century BCE, they established the kingdom of D'mt (Da'amat). This kingdom dominated lands to the west, obtaining ivory,

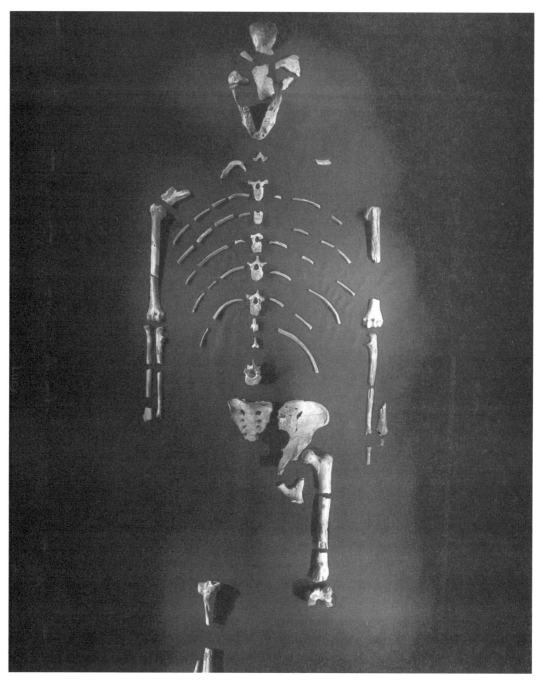

*Australopithecus afarensis bone fragments thought to be 3.4 to 2.9 million years old were found in Ethiopia's lower Awash River valley.* Dave Einsel/Getty Images

tortoiseshell, rhinoceros horn, gold, silver, and slaves and trading them to South Arabian merchants.

After 300 BCE, D'mt deteriorated as trade routes were diverted eastward for easier access to coastal ports, and a number of smaller city-states arose in its place. Subsequent wars of aggrandizement led to unification under the inland state of Aksum, which, from its base on the Tigray Plateau, controlled the ivory trade into the Sudan, other trade routes leading farther inland to the south, and the port of Adulis on the Gulf of Zula. Aksum's culture comprised Ge'ez, written in a modified South Arabian alphabet, sculpture and architecture based on South Arabian prototypes, and an amalgam of local and Middle Eastern dieties. Thus, evidence exists of a close cultural exchange between Aksum and the Arabian peninsula, but the traditional scholarly view, that South Arabian immigrants actually peopled and created pre-Aksumite northern Ethiopia, is increasingly under siege. Nevertheless, the ancient cultural exchange across the Red Sea became enshrined in Ethiopian legend in the persons of Makeda—the Queen of Sheba—and the Israelite king Solomon. Their mythical union was said to have produced Menilek I, the progenitor of Ethiopia's royal dynasty.

By the 5th century CE, Aksum was the dominant trading power in the Red Sea. Commerce rested on sound financial methods, attested to by the minting of coins bearing the effigies of Aksumite emperors. In the anonymous Greek travel book *Periplus Maris Erythraei*, written in the 1st century CE, Adulis is described as an "open harbour" containing a settlement of Greco-Roman merchants. It was through such communities, established for the purposes of trade, that the Christianity of the eastern Mediterranean reached Ethiopia during the reign of Emperor Ezanas (c. 303–c. 350). By the mid-5th century, monks were evangelizing among the Cushitic-speaking Agew people to the east and south. The Ethiopian Church opted to follow the leadership of the Coptic Church (in Alexandria, Egypt) in rejecting the Christology proposed at the Council of Chalcedon in 451 and breaking with the bishops of Rome and Constantinople (relations would not resume until the second half of the 20th century).

At its height, Aksum extended its influence westward to the kingdom of Meroe, southward toward the Omo River, and eastward to the spice coasts on the Gulf of Aden. Even the South Arabian kingdom of the Himyarites, across the Red Sea in what is now Yemen, came under the suzerainty of Aksum. In the early 6th century, Emperor Caleb (Ella-Asbeha; reigned c. 500–534) was strong enough to reach across the Red Sea to protect his coreligionists in Yemen against persecution by a Jewish prince. However, Christian power in South Arabia ended after 572, when the Persians invaded and disrupted trade. They were followed 30 years later by the Arabs, whose rise in the 7th and 8th centuries cut off Aksum's trade with the Mediterranean world.

## THE ZAGWE AND SOLOMONIC DYNASTIES

As Christian shipping disappeared from the Red Sea, Aksum's towns lost their vitality. The Aksumite state turned southward, conquering adjacent grain-rich highlands. Monastic establishments moved even farther to the south. For example, a major church was founded near Lake Hayk in the 9th century. Over time, one of the subject peoples, the Agew, learned Ge'ez, became Christian, and assimilated their Aksumite oppressors to the point that Agew princes were able to transfer the seat of the empire southward to their own region of Lasta. Thus, the Zagwe dynasty appeared in Ethiopia. Later ecclesiastical texts accused this dynasty of not having been of pure "Solomonic" stock (i.e., not descended from the union of Solomon and the Queen of Sheba), but it was in the religious plane that the Zagwe nonetheless distinguished themselves. At the Zagwe capital of Roha (modern-day Lalibela), Emperor Lalibela (reigned c. 1185–1225) directed the hewing of 11 churches out of living rock—a stupendous monument to Christianity, which he and the other Zagwes fostered along with the Ethiopianization of the countryside.

However, Zagwe hegemony was never complete, and opposition continued among the Semitic-speaking elite of Tigray, to the north, and the newly emergent Amhara people, to the south. The opposition increasingly focused on questions of "Solomonic" legitimacy. In 1270 a leading nobleman of the province of Shewa, Yekuno Amlak, rebelled. He was supported by an influential faction of monastic churchmen, who condoned his regicide of Emperor Yitbarek and legitimated his descent from Solomon. The genealogy of the new Solomonic dynasty was published in the early 14th century in the *Kebra negast* ("Glory of the Kings"), a collection of legends that related the birth of Menilek I, associated Ethiopia with the Judeo-Christian tradition, and provided a basis for Ethiopian national unity through the Solomonic dynasty, Semitic culture, and the Amharic language. Well-armed ideologically, the Ethiopian state was prepared for a struggle impending in its eastern and southern provinces, where Christianity was meeting increasing resistance from the forces of Islam.

Islamic preaching had converted many of the people living on the peripheries of Ethiopian rule. In the late 13th century, various Muslim sultanates on Ethiopia's southern border fell under the hegemony of Ifat, located on the eastern Shewan Plateau and in the Awash valley. The Ethiopian emperor Amda Tseyon proved a vigorous campaigner, waging wars in all directions—to the Red Sea in the north, unincorporated areas in the south and eastward against the Muslim state of Ifat. He established strategic garrisons to consolidate the newly

*House of Giorgis, rock-hewn church in Lalibela, Ethiopia.* Richard Abeles

conquered regions, creating a system of *gult*s, or fiefs, in which the holders of a *gult* were paid tribute by the *gult*'s inhabitants. His heavy taxation of exports, especially of gold, ivory, and slaves that were transshipped from Ifat to Arabia, met with resistance. Amda Tseyon and his successors replied with brutal pacification campaigns that carried Solomonic power into the Awash valley and even as far as Seylac (Zeila) on the Gulf of Aden.

Aggrandizement into non-Christian areas was accompanied by internal reform and consolidation of the Christian state. As heads of the church, the Solomonic monarchs actively participated in the development of religious culture and discipline by building and beautifying churches, repressing "pagan" practices, and promoting the composition of theological and doctrinal works. Nevertheless, the relations between church and state were marked by conflict as well as cooperation. The rise of the Shewan Solomonics had been preceded by a revival of monasticism in the Amhara areas, and the monks had an uneasy relationship with the new dynasty. The bolder ones among them condemned the dynasty's practice of polygyny, and not until the late 14th century was the conflict resolved, the royal court winning over the monks with rich grants of land. Other conflicts also arose. The monk Ewostatewos (*c.* 1273–1352) preached isolation from corrupting state influences and a return to biblical teachings—including observance of the Judaic Sabbath on Saturday in addition

to the Sunday observance, an idea apparently already widely diffused in Ethiopia. The great emperor Zara Yaqob (Zara Yakob; reigned 1434–68) conceded the latter point in 1450 at the Council of Debre Mitmaq, but he also initiated severe reforms in the church, eliminating abuses by strong measures and executing the leaders of heretical sects. Zara Yaqob also conducted an unsuccessful military campaign against the Beta Israel, or Falasha, a group of Agew-speaking Jews who practiced a non-Talmudic form of Judaism.

Zara Yaqob valued national unity above all and feared Muslim encirclement. In 1445 he dealt Ifat such a crushing military defeat that hegemony over the Muslim states passed to the sultans of Adal, in the vicinity of Harer. About 1520 the leadership of Adal was assumed by Aḥmad ibn Ibrāhīm al-Ghāzī, a Muslim reformer who became known as Sahib al-Fath ("the Conqueror") to the Muslims and Aḥmad Grāñ ("Ahmad the Left-Handed") to the Christians. Aḥmad drilled his men in modern Ottomon tactics and led them on a jihad, or holy war, against Ethiopia, quickly taking areas on the periphery of Solomonic rule. In 1528 Emperor Lebna Denegel was defeated at the battle of Shimbra Kure, and the Muslims pushed northward into the central highlands, destroying settlements, churches, and monasteries. In 1541 the Portuguese, whose interests in the Red Sea were imperiled by Muslim power, sent 400 musketeers to train the

Ethiopian army in European tactics. Emperor Galawdewos (reigned 1540–59) opted for a hit-and-run strategy and on Feb. 21, 1543, caught Aḥmad in the open near Lake Tana and killed him in action. The Muslim army broke, leaving the field and north-central Ethiopia to the Christians.

## CHALLENGE, REVIVAL, AND DECLINE

Meanwhile, population pressures had mounted among the Oromo, a pastoral people who inhabited the upper basin of the Genalē (Jubba) River in what is now southern Ethiopia and northern Kenya. Oromo society was based upon an "age-set" system known as *gada*, in which all males born into an eight-year generation moved together through all the stages of life. The warrior classes (*luba*) raided and rustled in order to prove themselves, and in the 16th century they began to undertake long-distance expeditions, availing themselves of the collapse of the frontier defenses of both the Christian and Muslim states. By 1600 the Oromo had spread so widely in Ethiopia that Emperor Sarsa Dengel (reigned 1563–97) limited his government to what are now Eritrea, the northern regions of Tigray and Gonder, and parts of Gojam, Shewa, and Welo, areas that included the bulk of the Christian Semitic-speaking agriculturalists. Meanwhile, the church had barely revived following the destruction and mass apostasy of the jihad era, when

it found itself facing a different kind of threat from Roman Catholicism.

Following close upon the Portuguese musketeers were missionaries who, sent by the Jesuit founder St. Ignatius of Loyola, sought to convert Ethiopia to the Western church. The most successful of these was the Jesuit Pedro Páez. His personal authority and eminent qualities were such that Emperor Susenyos (reigned 1607–32) was persuaded to accept the doctrine of the dual nature of Christ and to notify the pope of his submission. This apostasy was joined by many in the royal court but met with violent resistance from the provincial nobles, the church, and the people at large. Susenyos was forced to abdicate in favour of his son Fasilides (reigned 1632–67).

Fasilides established a new capital at Gonder, a trading centre north of Lake Tana that connected the interior to the coast. At its height about 1700, the city supported the arts and educational, religious, and social institutions as well as Beta Israel craftspeople, Muslim traders, and a large population of farmers, day labourers, students, and soldiers. Fasilides was succeeded by his son, Yohannes, and then by a grandson, Iyasu the Great. The court sponsored secular and religious construction, manuscript writing and copying, the verbal arts, and painting. A second wave of cultural productivity followed, in the middle decades of the 18th century under the sponsorship of Empress Mentewwab (reigned 1730–69), a remarkable woman who ruled jointly with her son and grandson. However, ethnic, regional, and religious factionalism undermined the kingdom and led in 1769 to its collapse. The Zamana Masafent ("Age of the Princes"; 1769–1855), an era of feudal anarchy, had commenced.

For most Ethiopians, life during the Age of the Princes was difficult. Power had shifted from the central court to the courts of regional princes, and they vied with one another in battle. There were no significant changes in the social order, but the oppression of the farming population increased as armies traversed the highlands, ruining the countryside and plundering the harvests of farmers. Nevertheless, significant developments were taking place in the south.

Agricultural development in the Gībē River basin led to the formation of Oromo states to the southwest of Shewa; the Gonga people developed their own states in the Kefa highlands on the west bank of the Omo River; and a line that claimed Solomonic descent established a formidable regional kingdom in northern Shewa. Shewa prospered in the growing trade of the Gībē states, and Shewa's self-proclaimed king, Sahle Selassie (reigned 1813–47), and his successors expanded southward. By 1840 they controlled most of Shewa to the Awash River and enjoyed suzerainty as far south as Guragē.

To the north, Kassa Hailu was in the process of ending the Age of the Princes. After serving as a mercenary in Gojam, Kassa returned to his native Qwara on the extreme edge of the western highlands, where he prospered as a highwayman and built a good small army. By 1847 he had monopolized the lowlands' revenues from trade and smuggling, forcing Gonder's leading magnates to integrate him into the establishment. Finally, in April 1853 at Takusa, Kassa defeated Ras (Prince) Ali, the last of a succession of the Oromo lords who had played a central role in the Age of the Princes.

## EMERGENCE OF MODERN ETHIOPIA

After defeating the ruler of northern Ethiopia, Kassa was crowned Emperor Tewodros II on Feb. 9, 1855. Later that year he marched south and forced the submission of Shewa. His consolidation of power over the formerly separate states established the modern Ethiopian country.

### Tewodros II

Although Tewodros's first years were marked by attempts at social reform, his effort to establish garrisons nationwide lost the allegiance of the already heavily taxed peasantry, and he alienated parish clergy by converting "excess" church land to military and secular tenure. Such measures gave heart to the regional aristocrats, who returned to rebellion. The emperor held Ethiopia together only through coercion. In 1861 he conceived a bold foreign policy to bolster his kingdom and promote his reforms. In 1862 Tewodros offered

Britain's Queen Victoria an alliance to destroy Islam. The British ignored the scheme, and, when no response came, Tewodros imprisoned the British envoy and other Europeans. This diplomatic incident led to an Anglo-Indian military expedition in 1868. Sir Robert Napier, the commander, paid money and weapons to Kassa, a *dejazmatch* (earl) of Tigray, in order to secure passage inland, and on April 10, on the plains below Āmba Maryam (or Mek'dela), British troops defeated a small imperial force. In order to avoid capture, Tewodros committed suicide two days later.

## YOHANNES IV

After a period of conflict that saw the brief and self-proclaimed rule of Tekle Giorgis (1868–72), the Tigrayan Kassa took the imperial crown as Yohannes IV on Jan. 21, 1872. After having ejected two Egyptian armies from the highlands of Eritrea in 1875–76, Yohannes moved south, forcing Shewa's king Sahle Miriam to submit and to renounce imperial ambitions. Yohannes thus became the first Ethiopian emperor in 300 years to wield authority from Tigray south to Guragē. He then sought to oust the Egyptians from coastal Eritrea, where they remained after the Mahdists had largely taken over the Sudan, but he was unable to prevent Italy from disembarking troops at Mitsiwa (now Massawa) in February 1885. In order to weaken the emperor, Rome tried to buy Sahle Miriam's cooperation with thousands of rifles; the Shewan

king remained faithful to Yohannes but took the opportunity in January 1887 to incorporate Harer into his kingdom. Meanwhile, Yohannes repulsed Italian forays inland, and in 1889 he marched into the Sudan to avenge Mahdist attacks on Gonder. On March 9, 1889, with victory in his grasp, he was shot and killed at Metema.

## MENILEK II

Sahle Miriam declared himself emperor of Ethiopia on March 25, taking the name Menilek II, and at Wichale (or Ucciali, as the Italians called it) in Wallo on May 2 he signed a treaty of amity and commerce granting Italy rule over Eritrea. The Italian version of Article XVII of the Treaty of Wichale made Rome the medium for Ethiopia's foreign relations, whereas the Amharic text was noncommital. Both texts agreed that in the case of differences the Amharic text was to prevail. Learning that Rome had used the mistranslation to claim a protectorate over all of Ethiopia, Menilek first sought a diplomatic solution. Meanwhile, during 1891–93 he sent expeditions south and east to obtain gold, ivory, musk, coffee, hides, and slaves to trade for modern weapons and munitions. In December 1895, after two years of good harvests had filled Ethiopia's granaries, Menilek moved his army into Tigray.

Rome believed that as few as 35,000 soldiers could control Ethiopia, but it was proved wrong on March 1, 1896, at the Battle of Adwa, where Gen. Oreste

## TREATY OF WICHALE

*The Treaty of Wichale (also spelled Ucciali) was a pact signed at Wichale, Eth., on May 2, 1889, by the Italians and Menilek II of Ethiopia, whereby Italy was granted the northern Ethiopian territories of Bogos, Hamasen, and Akale-Guzai (modern Eritrea and northern Tigray) in exchange for a sum of money and the provision of 30,000 muskets and 28 cannons.*

*Article XVII of the Treaty of Wichale stated that the emperor of Ethiopia "could" have recourse to the good offices of the Italian government in his dealings with other foreign powers, but the Italian text of the treaty had the word "must." Based on their own text, the Italians proclaimed a protectorate over Ethiopia. In September 1890, Menilek II repudiated their claim, and in 1893 he officially denounced the entire treaty. An attempt by the Italians to impose a protectorate over Ethiopia by force was finally confounded by their defeat at the Battle of Adwa on March 1, 1896. By the Treaty of Addis Ababa (Oct. 26, 1896), the country south of the Mareb and Muna rivers was restored to Ethiopia, and Italy acknowledged the absolute independence of Ethiopia.*

Baratieri led 14,500 Italian troops on a poorly organized attack against Menilek's well-armed host of some 100,000 fighters. The Italian lines crumbled, and at noon retreat was sounded. The emperor retired into Ethiopia to await negotiations, and on Oct. 26, 1896, he signed the Treaty of Addis Ababa, which abrogated the Treaty of Wichale.

Menilek subsequently directed the Solomonic state into areas never before under its rule. Between 1896 and 1906 Ethiopia expanded to its present size, taking in the highlands, the key river systems, and a buffer of low-lying zones around the state's central core. Revenues from the periphery were used to modernize the new capital of Addis Ababa, to open schools and hospitals, and to build communication networks. Menilek contracted with a French company to

construct a railway between Addis Ababa and Djibouti, which thus spurred the exploitation of the country's produce by foreign merchants in cooperation with the ruling elites.

## IYASU

As Menilek aged, he appointed a cabinet to act for his grandson and heir designate, Iyasu (Lij Yasu), a son of the Muslim Oromo ruler of Wallo. Upon the emperor's death in 1913, Iyasu took power in his own right. Seeking a society free of religious and ethnic divisions, he removed many of Menilek's governors and integrated Muslims into the administration, outraging Ethiopia's Christian ruling class. During World War I, Iyasu dallied with Islam and with the Central Powers in the hope of regaining Eritrea and freeing

## RAS TAFARI

(b. July 23, 1892, near Harer, Eth.—d. Aug. 27, 1975, Addis Ababa)

*Ras Tafari—better known as Haile Selassie—served as the emperor of Ethiopia (1930–74). Tafari was a son of Ras (Prince) Makonnen, a chief adviser to Emperor Menilek II. After Menilek's daughter, Zauditu, became empress, Ras Tafari (who had married Menilek's great-granddaughter) was named regent and heir apparent to the throne. When Zauditu died in 1930, Tafari took the name of Haile Selassie ("Might of the Trinity") to mark his imperial status. As emperor he sought to modernize his country and steer it into the mainstream of African politics. He brought Ethiopia into the League of Nations and the UN and made Addis Ababa the centre for the Organization of African Unity (now the African Union). Through most of his reign he remained popular among the majority Christian population. He was deposed in 1974 in a military coup by Mengistu Haile Mariam and kept under house arrest. He was apparently killed by his captors. Haile Selassie was regarded as the messiah by the Rastafarian movement.*

himself still further from the dominance of the Shewan aristocrats. After the Allied Powers formally protested, the Shewan aristocrats met, accused Iyasu of apostasy and subversion, and deposed him on Sept. 27, 1916.

## THE RISE AND REIGN OF HAILE SELASSIE I

Iyasu was replaced by Menilek's daughter, Zauditu. Since it was considered unseemly for a woman to serve in her own right, Ras Tafari, the son of Ras Makonnen and a cousin of Menilek, served as Zauditu's regent and heir apparent.

### REGENT AND HEIR APPARENT

The prince developed the rudiments of a modern bureaucracy by recruiting the newly educated for government service. He also engineered Ethiopia's entry into the League of Nations in 1923, reasoning that collective security would protect his backward country from aggression. To brighten Ethiopia's external image, he hired foreign advisers for key departments and set about abolishing slavery—a process possibly helped by the stirrings in Ethiopia of a market economy.

By 1928, when Zauditu named Tafari king, the economy was booming, thanks mainly to the export of coffee. In the countryside, local officials built roads and improved communications, facilitating the penetration of traders and entrepreneurs. Ethiopians remained in charge of the economy, since Tafari forced foreigners to take local partners and maintained tight control over concessions.

*Emperor from 1930 to 1974—and regarded by Rastafarians as the messiah—Haile Selassie (Ras Tafari) endeavored to move Ethiopia into the political mainstream.* AFP/Getty Images

## EMPEROR

On April 1, 1930, Zauditu died, and Tafari declared himself emperor. He was crowned Haile Selassie I ("Power of the Trinity"; his baptismal name) on November 2. In July 1931 the emperor promulgated a constitution that enshrined as law his prerogative to delegate authority to an appointed and indirectly elected bicameral parliament, among other modern institutions. During 1931–34 Haile Selassie instituted projects for roads, schools, hospitals, communications, administration, and public services. The combined effect of these projects was to increase the country's exposure to the world economy. By 1932 revenues were pouring into Addis Ababa from taxes applied to 25,000 tons of coffee exported each year.

## CONFLICT WITH ITALY

Haile Selassie's success persuaded Italy's ruler Benito Mussolini to undertake a preemptive strike before Ethiopia grew too strong to oppose Italian ambitions in the Horn of Africa. After an Ethiopian patrol clashed with an Italian garrison at the Welwel oasis in the Ogaden in November–December 1934, Rome began seriously preparing for war. Haile Selassie continued to trust in the collective security promised by the League of Nations. Only on Oct. 2, 1935, upon learning that Italian forces had crossed the frontier, did he order mobilization. During the

subsequent seven-month Italo-Ethiopian War, the Italian command used air power and poison gas to separate, flank, and destroy Haile Selassie's poorly equipped armies. The emperor went into exile on May 2, 1936.

For five years (1936–41) Ethiopia was joined to Eritrea and Italian Somaliland to form Italian East Africa. During this period Italy carried out a program of public works, concentrating especially on highways and on agricultural and industrial development. Resistance to the occupation continued, however. The Italians dominated the cities, towns, and major caravan routes, while Ethiopian patriots harried the occupiers and sometimes tested the larger garrison towns. When Italy joined the European war in June 1940, the United Kingdom recognized Haile Selassie as a full ally, and the emperor was soon in Khartoum, Sudan, to help train a British-led Ethiopian army. This joint force entered Gojam on Jan. 20, 1941, and encountered an enemy quick to surrender. On May 5 the emperor triumphantly returned to Addis Ababa. Defying the British occupation authorities, he quickly organized his own government.

## RETURN TO POWER

In February 1945 at a meeting with U.S. Pres. Franklin D. Roosevelt, Haile Selassie submitted memoranda stressing the imperative for recovering Eritrea and thereby gaining free access to the sea. In 1948 and again in 1949, two commissions established by the wartime Allied Powers and by the United Nations (UN) reported that Eritrea lacked national consciousness and an economy that could sustain independence. Washington, wishing to secure a communications base in Asmara (Asmera) and naval facilities in Massawa—and also to counter possible subversion in the region—supported Eritrea's federation with Ethiopia. The union took place in September 1952.

During the 1950s Ethiopia's coffee sold well in world markets. Revenues were used to centralize the government, to improve communications, to develop a national system of education based on the western model, and to modernize urban centres. In November 1955 the emperor promulgated a revised constitution, which permitted the parliament to authorize finances and taxes, to question ministers, and to disapprove imperial decrees. The constitution also introduced an elected lower house of parliament, a theoretically independent judiciary, separation of powers, a catalog of human rights, and a mandate for bureaucratic responsibility to the people. At the same time, the emperor retained his power of decree and his authority to appoint the government. Among his ministers, he subtly established competing power factions—a stratagem that had the ultimate effect of retarding governmental functioning and bureaucratic modernization.

## INTERNAL CONFLICTS AND THE FALL OF THE MONARCHY

Some officials concluded that the country would move ahead only when the imperial regime was destroyed. In December 1960, while the emperor was abroad, members of the security and military forces attempted a coup d'état. The coup rapidly unraveled, but not before the country's social and economic problems had been described in radical terms. Even then, the emperor ignored the coup's significance. In February 1961 he began to name a new government that reflected the status quo ante by depending on the landowning military, aristocracy, and oligarchy for authority. Haile Selassie showed himself unable to implement significant land reform, and, as a result, progressives and students opposed the regime. The monarchy gradually lost its credibility, especially as it became embroiled in intractable conflicts in Eritrea and with Somalia.

Somalia's independence in 1960 stimulated Somali nationalists in Ethiopia's Ogaden to rebel in February 1963. When Somalia joined the fighting, the Ethiopian army and air force smashed its enemy. Somalia's consequent military alliance with the Soviet Union upset the regional balance of power, driving up Ethiopia's arms expenditures and necessitating more U.S. assistance. Meanwhile, an insurrection in Eritrea, which had begun in 1960 mainly among Muslim pastoralists in the western lowlands, came to attract highland Christians disaffected by the government's dissolution of the federation in 1962 and the imposition of Amharic in the schools. At the same time, an increasingly radical student movement in Addis Ababa identified Haile Selassie as an agent of U.S. imperialism and his landowning oligarchs as the enemy of the people. Under the motto "Land to the tiller," the students sought to limit property size and rights, and, by fostering debate on the issue of ethnicity, they confronted a problem marginalized by Haile Selassie. Some students espoused the Leninist notion that nationalities had the right to secede and, in so doing, gave strength and ideological justification to the Eritrean rebellion.

By the early 1970s one-third of Ethiopia's 45,000 soldiers were in Eritrea, and others were putting down rebellions in Balē, Sīdamo, and Gojam. In January 1974, there began a series of mutinies led by junior officers and senior noncommissioned officers, who blamed the imperial elites for their impoverishment and for the country's economic and social ills. For the government, the situation was greatly worsened by drought and famine in the north, the denial of which became an international scandal. In June representatives of the mutineers constituted themselves as the Coordinating Committee (Derg) of the Armed Forces, Police, and Territorial Army. Maj. Mengistu Haile Mariam, of Harer's 3rd Division, was elected chairman. The Derg proceeded to dismantle the monarchy's institutions and to arrest

Haile Selassie's cronies, confidantes, and advisers. It then campaigned against the old and senile emperor, who was deposed on Sept. 12, 1974. The Provisional Military Administrative Council (PMAC) was established. The PMAC was administered by the Derg and assumed the functions of government, with Lieut. Gen. Aman Andom as chairman and head of state and Mengistu as the first vice-chairman. Tensions within the Derg soon fueled a power struggle and led to Bloody Saturday (Nov. 23, 1974), when as many as 60 leaders, including Andom, were executed; Andom was replaced by Brig. Gen. Teferi Banti. The new government issued a Declaration of Socialism on Dec. 20, 1974.

## SOCIALIST ETHIOPIA

The Derg borrowed its ideology from competing Marxist parties, all of which arose from the student movement. One of them, the Ethiopian People's Revolutionary Party (EPRP), believed so strongly in civilian rule that it undertook urban guerrilla war against the military rulers, and anarchy ensued in the following years.

In February 1977 Mengistu (now a lieutenant colonel) survived a battle between his supporters and those of rivals on the PMAC. Andom and several other members were killed, and Mengistu seized complete power as chairman and head of state. A series of EPRP attacks against Derg members and their supporters, known as the White Terror, was countered by Mengistu's Red Terror, a bloody campaign that crushed armed opponents among the EPRP and other groups, as well as members of the civilian populace. As a result of the campaign, which continued into 1978, thousands of Ethiopia's best-educated and idealistic young people were killed or exiled. In all, as many as 100,000 people were killed, and thousands more were tortured or imprisoned.

Meanwhile, in May and June 1977, Somalia's army advanced into the Ogaden. The U.S.S.R. labeled Somalia the aggressor and diverted arms shipments to Ethiopia, where Soviet and allied troops trained and armed a People's Militia, provided fighting men, and reequipped the army. Unable to entice the United States into resupplying its troops and faced with renewed Ethiopian military vigor, Somalia withdrew in early 1978. Mengistu quickly shifted troops to Eritrea, where by year's end the Eritrean nationalists had been pushed back into mountainous terrain around Nak'fa.

## LAND REFORM AND FAMINE

Mengistu sought to transform Ethiopia into a command state led by a disciplined and loyal party that would control all organs of authority. To this end a land-reform proclamation of 1975 transferred ownership of all land to the state and provided allotments of no more than 25 acres (10 hectares) to individual peasants who farmed the land themselves. Extensive nationalization of industry, banking, insurance, large-scale trade, and urban land and extra dwellings completed the reforms and wiped out the economic base of the old ruling class. To implement the reforms, adjudicate disputes, and administer local affairs, peasants' associations were organized in the countryside and precinct organizations (kebele) in the towns. In 1984 the Workers' Party of Ethiopia was formed, with Mengistu as secretary-general, and in 1987 a new parliament inaugurated the People's Democratic Republic of Ethiopia, with Mengistu as president.

Despite initial expectations, farmers failed to generate the high yields expected from the land reform, for there was little incentive for them to do so. Moreover, their plots were tiny, rendering the legal limit of 25 acres irrelevant. Holdings varied according to the country's different regions, but overall probably averaged not much more than 3.7 acres (1.5 hectares). In order to feed Ethiopia's cities and the army, the government tried to force the peasants' associations to deliver grain at below-market prices, a measure that alienated the peasants and did nothing to stimulate production. Meanwhile, drought intensified yearly from 1980, building to a climax in 1984, when the small rains were scanty and the main rains failed altogether. Famine ensued, government controls limiting the mobility with which peasants had responded to previous shortfalls. Ideological suspicions precluded the West from responding to alarms that the Ethiopian government put forward in the spring of 1984 following the small rains, and its own preoccupation with celebrating its 10th anniversary and founding the Workers' Party led the government to cover up the developing famine in the fall of that same year. With one-sixth of Ethiopia's people at risk of starvation, Western countries made available enough surplus grain to end the crisis by mid-1985. Donors were not so forthcoming for a mammoth population-resettlement program that proposed to move people from the drought-prone and crowded north to the west and south, where supposedly surplus lands were available. The Mengistu regime handled the shift callously and did not have the necessary resources to provide proper housing, tools, medical treatment, or food for the 600,000 farming families it moved. Resources were also lacking for a related villagization program, which had the putative aim of concentrating scattered populations into villages where they might receive modern services. As late as 1990 most villages lacked the promised amenities, in part because of resource-draining civil strife in the north.

## Challenges to the Regime

By 1985–86 the government was embattled throughout most of Eritrea and Tigray, but Mengistu simply stepped up recruitment and asked the U.S.S.R. for more arms. In December 1987 the Eritrean People's Liberation Front (EPLF) broke through the Ethiopian lines before Nak'fa and waged an increasingly

successful war with weapons captured from demoralized government troops. In early 1988 the EPLF began to coordinate its attacks with the Tigray People's Liberation Front (TPLF), which had long been fighting for the autonomy of Tigray and for the reconstitution of Ethiopia on the basis of ethnically autonomous regions. The Soviets refused to ship more arms, and in February 1989 a series of defeats and a worsening lack of weaponry forced the government to evacuate Tigray. The TPLF then organized the largely Amhara Ethiopian People's Democratic Movement. Together, these two groups formed the Ethiopian People's Revolutionary Democratic Front (EPRDF), and their forces easily advanced into Gonder and Welo provinces. The following year the EPLF occupied Massawa, which broke the Ethiopian stranglehold on supplies entering the country and demonstrated that the government no longer ruled in Tigray and Eritrea. Shortly thereafter, when the TPLF cut the Addis Ababa–Gonder road and put Gojam at risk, Mengistu announced the end of many of the regime's most unpopular socialist measures.

The peasants immediately abandoned their new villages for their old homesteads, dismantled cooperatives, and redistributed land and capital goods. They ejected or ignored party and government functionaries, in several cases killing recalcitrant administrators. The regime was thus weakened in the countryside—not least in southern Ethiopia, where the long-dormant Oromo

Liberation Front (OLF) became active. By May 1991, with EPRDF forces controlling Tigray, Welo, Gonder, Gojam, and about half of Shewa, it was obvious that the army did not have sufficient morale, manpower, weapons, munitions, and leadership to stop the rebels' advance on Addis Ababa. Mengistu fled to Zimbabwe, and on May 28 the EPRDF took power.

## TRANSITION

The new government, led by a Tigrayan, the EPRDF chairman Meles Zenawi, claimed that it would democratize Ethiopia through recognition of the country's ethnic heterogeneity. No longer would Ethiopia be maintained by force. Rather, it would be a voluntary federation of its many peoples. To this end the EPRDF and other political groups, including the OLF, agreed to the creation of a transitional government that would engineer a new constitution and elections, to a national charter that recognized an ethnic division of political power, and to the right of nationalities to secede from Ethiopian—thus paving the way for Eritrea's legal independence, which was official on May 24, 1993.

The new regime began to lay the foundations for Ethiopia's first federal administrative structure, the component units consisting of ostensibly ethnically homogeneous regions. There was little lessening of control from the centre, however, as the ruling parties of the regional governments intimately affiliated politically and ideologically with the EPRDF.

Many of the country's elite feared that the regime was weakening the country's unity. The Amhara, identified by the EPRDF as colonizers and unaccustomed to thinking of themselves as but one of the country's many different ethnic groups, were particularly affronted by the apparent fragmentation of the country. The government fought back by denouncing Amhara leaders as antidemocratic chauvinists and by muzzling the press through the application of a new law, which, ironically, primarily served to end decades of systematic censorship under previous regimes but also established media regulations and penalties. In the provinces the government did not bother to maintain even the guise of freedom: there the suppression of anti-EPRDF forces, especially the OLF, was so blatant as to be noticed by the members of an international team sent to observe hastily called regional elections in June 1992. The OLF left the government over the conduct of these elections and has been in increasingly armed opposition ever since.

Throughout 1992–93 the transitional government worked with donor governments and the World Bank to forge a structural-adjustment program. This program devalued the Ethiopian currency, sharply reduced government intervention in the economy, dictated redundancies in the civil service, and made it easier for foreign companies to invest in Ethiopia and repatriate their profits. However, the government refused to denationalize land, and foreign investment was slow to return. The economy grew modestly but experienced no structural transformations. Yet another famine, stemming from a lack of national integration and the stifling overregulation of business, and again accompanied by drought, was signaled in 1994. Millions of Ethiopians were put at risk, largely in the north and east. The government called upon the international donor community for help, but, by failing to find measures to stimulate agricultural production, Ethiopia remained unable to finance its own development and to create the surplus needed to relieve its own population. Meanwhile, population growth had reduced the size of the average Ethiopian farm to under 2.5 acres (1 hectare).

## FEDERAL DEMOCRATIC REPUBLIC OF ETHIOPIA

In 1994 the EPRDF adopted Ethiopia's third constitution in 40 years. It was promulgated in 1995, creating the Federal Democratic Republic of Ethiopia. This constitution enshrined the principles of regionalism and ethnic autonomy, devolving power to regional states, several of them coalitions of smaller ethnic groups. It also enshrined, for the first time as a constitutional principle, national ownership of land. The country's first multiparty elections were also held in 1995, but they were boycotted by most opposition groups in protest against the harassment, arrests, and other actions instigated by the EPRDF-led government. As a result, the multiethnic EPRDF

easily retained control of the federal government and most of the regional states. Negasso Gidada, a Christian Oromo who had served as minister of information in the transitional government, became president, and Meles became prime minister. The ethnic balance of the country was reflected in the careful selection of members for the Council of Ministers.

The economic-reform efforts that had begun in 1991 were somewhat successful, as the economy showed improvement in the mid-1990s. However, some aspects of reform, such as privatization of state-owned enterprises, progressed slowly, and the government's cautious approach to economic liberalization remained an obstacle for foreign investment, as did the issue of nationalized property, which continued to be a source of consternation.

In 1998 simmering border tensions between Eritrea and Ethiopia erupted into war. At the heart of the dispute was some 250 square miles (640 square km) of land near Badme, but the conflict quickly spread to two other areas, Zela Ambesa and the important Eritrean port city of Assab. A cease-fire signed in June 2000 provided for a UN mission (United Nations Mission in Eritrea and Ethiopia; UNMEE) to monitor the cease-fire and deploy troops in a buffer zone between the two countries while the border was being demarcated. A peace agreement signed in Algeria in December ended the conflict, although relations between Ethiopia and Eritrea remained tense, and UNMEE troops stayed to monitor the truce and supervise the withdrawal of Ethiopian troops from Eritrean territory. The Ethiopian government was not pleased with the border demarcation proposed in 2002, as the town of Badme was awarded to Eritrea, and Meles protested this decision. Discussions continued during the next few years. UNMEE troops remained until July 2008 but ultimately left with the issue of demarcation still unsettled.

Meanwhile, the EPRDF remained in power into the 2000s, although it was weakened by internal dissent in 2001 when the EPRDF's TPLF faction split over the government's anticorruption policies and Meles's embrace of more-liberal economic policies. The TPLF members who opposed Meles were purged from the party and held under house arrest. When President Negasso sided with the TPLF splinter group, he was ousted from the leadership of his own party, the Oromo People's Democratic Organization (OPDO). He did, however, keep his position as federal president until his term was up in September 2001. He was succeeded by Girma Wolde-Giyorgis, who, like Negasso, was an Oromo, although he was not affiliated with the OPDO. Against the backdrop of political infighting, drought and famine continued to periodically plague the country, particularly in 2003, when the crisis was exacerbated by widespread incidence of waterborne illnesses and a malaria epidemic.

A strong performance by opposition parties in the May 2005 elections greatly increased the number of seats they held in the legislature. The EPRDF remained in power but with less of a majority and amid questionable circumstances. Although the elections were initially found to have been generally credible, there were reports of voter intimidation and other problems, and allegations of irregularities from more than half the country's electoral constituencies delayed the announcement of the results for eight weeks. Accusations of fraud, as well as the final outcome of the elections, led to considerable protests and demonstrations in Addis Ababa. Ensuing clashes between protesters and security forces left more than three dozen people dead, hundreds injured, and 3,000 arrested. This was followed in November by additional rioting, which left dozens more dead. Some of the victorious opposition candidates refused to take their legislative seats, in protest against the questionable circumstances surrounding the elections and aftermath, and some were arrested for "violent activities aimed at subverting the constitutional order." Tensions continued into the next year, with thousands of Ethiopians—including activists, journalists, and other legislators—being detained across the country. Many detainees were released periodically throughout 2006, often without having had any charges filed against them. In May 2006 the EPRDF reached an agreement with the two primary opposition political parties, which then took their seats in the parliament.

More than a decade after his ouster, former Derg ruler Mengistu and his legacy still weighed heavily in the Ethiopian consciousness. To the dismay of many, Mengistu continued to live in exile in Zimbabwe, despite the Ethiopian government's repeated attempts beginning in the 1990s to lobby for his extradition. Nevertheless, he was tried, in absentia, on charges of genocide for his role in the Red Terror campaign. In December 2006 he was found guilty, and the next year he was given a life sentence. Following a successful appeal from the prosecution, he was sentenced to death in May 2008.

Also in 2006, Ethiopia sent troops to neighbouring Somalia to defend that country's beleaguered transitional government against rebel forces, and in December Ethiopia began a coordinated air and ground war there. Ethiopian troops had withdrawn from the country by January 2009, although they remained close to the Ethiopian-Somali border in case future intervention was deemed necessary. The intervention in the Somali crisis heightened the existing tensions with Eritrea, which supported Somalia's rebels.

# CHAPTER 13

## KENYA

Kenya is an eastern African country located along the coast of the Indian Ocean. The former British colony became independent in 1963. The capital is Nairobi.

### EARLY AND PRECOLONIAL HISTORY

It is known that human history in Kenya dates back millions of years, because it is there that some of the earliest fossilized remains of hominids have been discovered. Among the best-known finds are those by anthropologist Richard Leakey and others in the Koobi Fora area along the shore of Lake Rudolf that have included portions of *Australopithecus boisei* and *Homo habilis* skeletons. The following discussion, however, covers the history of Kenya only from the 18th century.

### MAASAI AND KIKUYU

The Maasai moved into what is now central Kenya from an area north of Lake Rudolf sometime in the mid-18th century. Their southward advance was checked about 1830 by the Hehe people from what is now Tanzania, but their raiding parties continued to range widely and even reached the coast south of Mombasa in 1859. The Maasai *moran* ("warrior") prepared for war under the spiritual direction of the *laibon* ("medicine man"). Although not particularly numerous, the Maasai were able to dominate a considerable region because the Bantu-speaking inhabitants offered little effective resistance to their raids. The Nandi, who inhabited the escarpment to the west of the Maasai, were equally warlike and were relatively undisturbed by their predatory neighbours. Another group, the Taveta, took refuge in the forest on the eastern slopes of Mount Kilimanjaro, while the Taita, who were farther east, used the natural strongholds provided by their mountainous homeland to resist the Maasai raiders.

The Kikuyu, who were far more numerous than the Maasai, also looked to the mountains and forests for protection against Maasai war parties. The Kikuyu had expanded northward, westward, and southward from their territory in the Fort Hall area of present-day Central province, where they cleared the forests to provide themselves with agricultural land. Toward the end of the 19th century, however, they had reached the limits imposed by the presence of the Maasai to the north and south and by the upper slopes of the Aberdare Range to the west.

Famine and smallpox in the 1890s compelled the Kikuyu to vacate much of the land in what is now Kiambu district (in Central province) as they withdrew northward. The Maasai too were passing through a difficult period. An outbreak of disease, either pleuro-pneumonia or rinderpest, attacked their cattle in 1883. Further infestations in 1889–90 continued to decimate their herds, while the Maasai themselves were overwhelmed by epidemics of smallpox. Simultaneously, the death

of Mbatian, their great *laibon*, split the group into warring factions, and it was some time before his younger son, Lenana, was able to restore order. Power was never revived, however, since their problems coincided with the arrival of European traders and administrators who eventually gained control of the region.

## CONTROL OF THE INTERIOR

Trading relations had existed for centuries between southern Arabia and the coastline of what is now Kenya. Some Arab traders remained in the area and contributed to the language that came to be known as Swahili. During the 19th century, Arab and Swahili caravans in search of ivory penetrated the interior. One route went from Mombasa to Kilimanjaro and Lake Victoria and then toward Mount Elgon, but this route was less popular as the caravan trails farther south, both because of the difficulty of crossing the desert country of the Taru Plain and because of the hostility of the Maasai. The first Europeans to penetrate the interior were two German agents of the Church Missionary Society, Johann Ludwig Krapf and Johannes Rebmann. They established a mission station at Rabai, a short distance inland from Mombasa. In 1848 Rebmann became the first European to see Kilimanjaro, and in 1849 Krapf ventured still farther inland and saw Mount Kenya. These were isolated journeys, however, and more than 30 years elapsed before any other Europeans attempted to explore the country dominated by the Maasai.

## THE BRITISH EAST AFRICA COMPANY AND EAST AFRICA PROTECTORATE

As Germany, Britain, and France were carving up East Africa in the mid-1880s, they recognized the authority of the sultan of Zanzibar over a coastal strip 10 miles (16 km) wide between the Tana (in Kenya) and Ruvuma (in Tanzania) rivers. The hinterland, however, was divided between Britain and Germany: the British took the area north of a line running from the mouth of the Umba River, opposite Pemba Island, and skirting north of Kilimanjaro to a point where latitude 1° S cut the eastern shore of Lake Victoria; the German sphere, Tanganyika (present-day Tanzania), lay to the south of that line. In 1887 the sultan's territory on the mainland was conceded to the British East Africa Association (later Company) for a 50-year period; this was later made a permanent grant. Because the British government was reluctant to become involved in the administration of East Africa, in 1888 it granted the company a royal charter that authorized it to accept existing and future grants and concessions relevant to the administration and development of the British sphere in that part of the world. The financial resources of the company, however, were inadequate for any large-scale development of the region. The company

also administered territory in what is now Uganda. When it became involved with the kingdoms of Buganda and Bunyoro, it incurred a great debt and therefore was forced to limit its activities to regions nearer the coast. This financial problem was finally resolved in 1895 when the British government made Buganda a protectorate and paid the company £250,000 to surrender its charter to the area that is now Kenya. The East Africa Protectorate was then proclaimed, with Sir Arthur Hardinge as the first commissioner. Initially the British government did not attach much importance to the new protectorate because Hardinge continued to reside in Zanzibar, where he already functioned as the consul general.

## RESISTANCE TO EUROPEAN RULE AND EARLY ADMINISTRATION

During the early years, the new administration largely focused on asserting authority over the territory. The Mazrui family (a Swahili family) along the coast actively resisted the usurpation of its authority by the British administrators, as did the Kikuyu and the Kamba. Farther west the Nandi did not accept their new overlords until 1905, after a series of British military columns had ranged through their territory. The Maasai were one of the few groups who offered no resistance to British authority, and they even served in the military during the British campaigns against the Kikuyu. Although this caused lasting enmity between the two groups, the Maasai behaved as they did largely because they had been so devastated by disease at the end of the 19th century.

The extension of British administration into the more remote areas of the protectorate was slowed by the lack of communication infrastructure and the limited financial resources available. When administration was introduced, though, it was direct rule because the British did not find the centralized African political system that had existed in other parts of Africa that they came to control.

## THE UGANDA RAILWAY AND EUROPEAN SETTLEMENT

The East Africa Protectorate was valued by Europeans as a corridor to the fertile land around Lake Victoria, but the government's offer to lease land to British settlers was initially unpopular. Two factors, however, changed this negative attitude: a railway was constructed from the coast to Lake Victoria, and the western highlands were transferred from Uganda (where regulations made it impossible to lease land to Europeans) to the East Africa Protectorate in 1902. Work on the railway began at Mombasa in December 1895, and the first locomotive reached Kisumu on Lake Victoria in December 1901. The entire line was completed by 1903. The protectorate was responsible for making the railway profitable, and the export of cash crops seemed to provide the perfect solution for generating revenue. Sir Charles Eliot,

who became commissioner of the protectorate in 1901, invited South Africans to settle in the protectorate when European settlers were less than enthusiastic about the proposal, but they too were uninterested. At first only small areas of land in Kiambu district, which had formerly been occupied by Africans and which the Kikuyu regarded as part of their legitimate area of expansion, were allocated to European settlers, but by 1906 more than 1,550 square miles (4,000 square km) had been leased or sold. Some Africans, such as the Maasai, were confined to reserves. By 1911 the Maasai reserve extended south of the railway to the present-day border with Tanzania.

As more Africans were separated from their land and as more European settlers entered the region, the Europeans became concerned with maintaining an adequate supply of African labour. Because few Africans voluntarily chose whether or not to work for Europeans, the settlers wanted the government to institute a system that would compel Africans to offer their services to European farmers. Successive commissioners and governors responded in varying degrees to the settlers' demands, and it was not until immediately after World War I, and largely as a result of public outcry in Britain, that compulsory labour on either public or private projects was strictly forbidden.

Thousands of Indian labourers were brought in to the protectorate to construct the railway. Although most of these labourers returned to India after their contracts were completed, some remained. The opening of the railway encouraged Indian traders who had been living nearer the coast to penetrate farther into the interior, even ahead of the administration. Other Indians hoped to obtain land, but European settlers consistently opposed the Indians' claim to land and to political and economic equality.

Prior to the outbreak of World War I in 1914, European participation in political affairs was limited mainly to creating pressure groups. The most prominent of these was the Convention of Associations, which had developed in 1911 from earlier European settler organizations. An Executive Council was appointed in 1905, and the first Legislative Council convened in 1907. When the protectorate was transferred from the Foreign Office to the Colonial Office in April 1905 and the settlers did not gain the increased responsibility they had desired, they launched a campaign in 1913 to elect their own representatives to the Legislative Council. The outbreak of World War I temporarily limited the settlers' legislative prospects, but the War Council, which was concerned with the effects of the war on the protectorate and included settlers, satisfied some of their desire to have elected representation in the legislature.

## WORLD WAR I AND ITS AFTERMATH

Germany had hoped that no battles with Britain would be fought on African soil during World War I, but Britain was concerned with its communications with India and with the safety of the Ugandan railway. Britain initiated hostilities, to which Germany responded, with Britain ultimately prevailing in East Africa. The conflict caused great hardships for the African population. Thousands of Africans were forced to serve as porters and soldiers, often with disastrous results, and a large number of Africans died, mostly from disease. The entire East African economic structure was affected, as food production became geared solely to supplying the troops. The burden of providing this food fell largely on African women, who did most of the farming anyway. Women were forced to use the same plots of land repeatedly, thereby depleting the soil, because most able-bodied men, who were responsible for clearing new land, had been conscripted. Droughts and famines recurred.

Most European settlers quickly joined the armed forces, leaving their farms to be looked after by their wives or abandoning the farms altogether. An attempt was made immediately after the war to revive the settler sector by introducing a "soldier settler" scheme, but the hopes of prosperity encouraged by the postwar demand for agricultural produce received a severe setback in the early 1920s when a worldwide economic recession brought bankruptcy to many of those who had started out with inadequate capital or had relied on credit from the banks. Stability was further delayed by the replacement of the rupee currency with East African shillings. By the mid-1920s Kenya's economy had wholly revived, although the Great Depression of the 1930s brought further economic difficulties to East Africa.

Rail communications had been improved when branch lines were opened to Thika and to the soda deposits at Lake Magadi in 1913; during the war a link was made between the main line and the German railway system to the south. The most important postwar project was the building of a new extension of the main line across the Uasin Gishu Plateau to tap the agricultural wealth of the highlands and then to Uganda in order to provide an outlet for the cotton crops of that protectorate. The line was eventually completed from Nakuru to Jinja in January 1928 and was carried on to Kampala, which it reached in January 1931.

## KENYA COLONY

In 1920 the East Africa Protectorate was turned into a colony and renamed Kenya, for its highest mountain. The colonial government began to concern itself with the plight of African peoples. In 1923 the colonial secretary issued a white paper in which he indicated that African interests in the colony had to be paramount, although his declaration did not immediately result in any great improvement in conditions. One area that definitely needed improvement was education for Africans; up to that point nearly all African schooling had been provided by missionaries. Those Africans who did manage to receive a Western education, though, found no place in Kenya's legislature, their interests being represented officially by the members of the appointed council and by a European unofficial member, usually a missionary.

## POLITICAL MOVEMENTS

As more Africans worked on European farms and in urban areas such as Nairobi, they began to imitate political techniques used by European settlers as they attempted to gain more direct representation in colonial politics. At the outset, political pressure groups developed along ethnic lines, the first one being the Young Kikuyu Association (later the East African Association), established in 1921, with Harry Thuku as its first president. The group, which received most of its support from young men and was not supported by most of the older chiefs, demanded African representation in the legislature and won support among the Kikuyu when it complained about low wages, the prohibition of coffee growing by Africans, and the condemnation by Christian missionaries of such traditional practices as female genital cutting. At a protest in March 1922 Thuku was arrested, and eventually he was exiled for more than eight years. Although its attempts to win the support of other ethnic groups failed because of their unwillingness to accept Kikuyu leadership, the association was an important beginning in the African search for greater participation in the political process.

Throughout the 1920s and '30s European settlers continued to oppose

Indian demands for greater representation on the Legislative Council. Another concern among European settlers was the proposal, first made toward the end of World War I, to introduce some form of closer union with Uganda and Tanganyika (which had become a British possession after World War I). At first the European settlers of Kenya opposed closer union with the other territories because they feared African domination, but, in light of the British government's determination on this issue, they agreed by the late 1920s to a compromise that would protect their political status in Kenya. By the 1930s they actively supported a union with Tanganyika as a protection against Germany's claims to its former overseas dependencies.

## World War II to Independence

The outbreak of World War II forced the colony to focus on its borders. With the entry of Italy into the war, Kenya's northern border with Ethiopia and Somaliland was briefly threatened. The colonial government then turned its attention to African political representation, and in 1944 Kenya became the first East African territory to include an African on its Legislative Council. The number was increased to two in 1946, four in 1948, and eight in 1951, although all were appointed by the governor from a list of names submitted by local governments. However, this did not satisfy African demands for political equality. While

the East African Association had been banned after Thuku's arrest, a new organization, the Kikuyu Central Association, emerged with Jomo Kenyatta as its general secretary beginning in 1928. Kenyatta, who advocated a peaceful transition to African majority rule, traveled widely in Europe and returned in 1946 to become the president of the Kenya African Union (KAU; founded in 1944 as the Kenya African Study Union), which attempted to gain a mass African following. There were, however, Africans in the colony who felt that Kenyatta's tactics were not producing enough concrete results. One such group, which advocated a violent approach, became known as the Mau Mau. The actions attributed to the Mau Mau caused the colonial government to proclaim a state of emergency from October 1952 until 1960 and also resulted in a massive relocation of Africans, particularly Kikuyu. Kenyatta and other Africans were charged with directing the Mau Mau movement and sentenced in 1953 to seven years' imprisonment. After Kenyatta was released from prison in 1959, he was confined to his home.

Numerous economic and social changes resulted either directly or indirectly from the Mau Mau uprising. A land-consolidation program centralized the Kikuyu into large villages. This plan was also extended to the area near Lake Victoria in the Nyanza province, and many thousands of Africans in Nairobi were resettled in rural detention camps. At the same time, the Swynnerton Plan (a

## MAU MAU

*Mau Mau was the name of a militant African nationalist movement that originated in the 1950s among the Kikuyu people of Kenya. The Mau Mau (origin of the name is uncertain) advocated violent resistance to British domination in Kenya; the movement was especially associated with the ritual oaths employed by leaders of the Kikuyu Central Association to promote unity in the independence movement.*

*In 1950 the Mau Mau were banned by British authorities, and in October 1952, after a campaign of sabotage and assassination attributed to the Mau Mau, the British Kenya government declared a state of emergency and began four years of military operations against Kikuyu rebels. By the end of 1956, more than 11,000 rebels had been killed in the fighting, along with about 100 Europeans and 2,000 African loyalists. More than 20,000 other Kikuyu were put into detention camps, where intensive efforts were made to convert them to the political views of the government (i.e., to abandon their nationalist aspirations). Despite these government actions, Kikuyu resistance spearheaded the Kenya independence movement, and Jomo Kenyatta, who had been jailed as a Mau Mau leader in 1953, became prime minister of an independent Kenya 10 years later. In 2003 the ban on the Mau Mau was lifted by the Kenyan government.*

proposal to strengthen the development of African agriculture) provided Africans more opportunities to cultivate cash crops such as coffee. Throughout the 1950s, foreign investment in Kenya continued, and limited industrial development occurred along with agricultural expansion.

Although the leadership of the KAU had been arrested, the party was not immediately banned, because the government hoped that new party leadership might provide a more moderate approach. However, this was not forthcoming, and the party was banned by mid-1953; African political organizations were not allowed again until 1960. The Kenya African National Union (KANU), founded in May of that year and favouring a strong centralized government, was built around Kenyatta, who was still in detention. Nevertheless, in June two of KANU's founding members, Ronald Ngala and Daniel arap Moi, created their own organization, the Kenya African Democratic Union (KADU). KADU's position was that ethnic interests could best be addressed through a decentralized government. It was also concerned about Kikuyu domination. KANU won more seats than KADU in elections held in February 1961, but both parties called for the release of Kenyatta, who was finally freed from house detention in August. A coalition government of the two parties was formed in 1962, and after elections in May 1963 Kenyatta became prime minister under a constitution that gave Kenya self-government.

## THE REPUBLIC OF KENYA

After Kenya was granted self-government, further discussions were held in London, which resulted in Kenya becoming fully independent on Dec. 12, 1963. One year later, Kenya became a republic, with Kenyatta as its first president and Oginga Odinga as vice president. By that time most KADU members had transferred their allegiance to KANU, and KADU ceased to exist.

### KENYATTA'S RULE

In 1964, Kenyatta sought the help of British troops to suppress a mutiny by the army. The president then introduced better service conditions and promotion prospects to the army, although the proportion of Kenyatta's own Kikuyu people in the officer corps steadily increased. At the same time, to forestall any new opposition, Kenyatta tried consistently to appoint members of different ethnic groups to official posts, with all the patronage such appointments conferred. Ideological differences led to disagreements with Vice President Odinga, whom Kenyatta had appointed to satisfy the powerful Luo. Odinga believed that, by adopting a pro-Western, essentially capitalist economic policy, the government was neglecting the interests of poorer people. He broke with KANU to form a new opposition party, the Kenya People's Union (KPU), but his position was weakened by legislation that required elected officials who switched parties to resign their seats and run for reelection. By contrast, Kenyatta's authority was strengthened because greater powers had been given to the office of president.

Kenyatta responded to Odinga's claims about his neglect of the poor by redistributing hundreds of thousands of small landholdings to Africans. This was made possible by a satisfactory financial settlement with European farmers who were prepared to leave the country amicably. Not all the new landowners were successful, but living standards improved widely enough to ensure continued support for the government.

The assassination in July 1969 of Tom Mboya, a KANU founder who had been serving as minister of economic planning and development, widened still further the serious ethnic gap that had already emerged as a result of Odinga's fall from grace. Mboya, like Odinga, was a Luo, though neither had pursued ethnic goals. Their supporters among the Luo, however, believed there was a Kikuyu plot, centred on Kenyatta, that threatened Luo interests. The division grew greater after October 1969, when Odinga and some of his leading party members were arrested and the KPU was banned. The arrested men were subsequently released, and Odinga himself was freed in 1971 when the president endeavoured to achieve a measure of reconciliation and national unity. The transfer of more than 1,500,000 acres (600,000 hectares) of government land to a group of wealthy Kenyans, many of whom were

As the first president of Kenya, Jomo Kenyatta's rule was one of overall peace, with only occasional eruptions owing to ethnic contention or disparity over political principles. Keystone/ Hulton Archive/Getty Images

Kikuyu, proved to be less profitable than had been hoped, largely because the new owners were bad managers. This and similar actions only provided more fuel for those, like Odinga, who accused the government of self-interest and for those who believed there was an ethnic plot to benefit the Kikuyu at the expense of other ethnic groups.

Another coup attempt was defused in 1971, and in its wake Kenyatta once again responded by improving the pay and conditions of military service, but, at the same time, he made sure that the army remained small in size. Odinga and other former KPU leaders were prevented from running in the parliamentary elections of 1974 by new regulations that forbade the candidacy of anyone who had not been a member of KANU for the previous three years. The challenge to Kenyatta was then taken up in the National Assembly by Josiah Mwangi Kariuki, another former supporter of KANU. Kariuki was critical of growing corruption in the government, and he won considerable support when increasing oil prices and the consequent worldwide inflation caused hardship among the poorer members of the community. His murder in March 1975, which the government tried to cover up, aroused angry protests, particularly among younger members of the parliament, whose criticisms of the government came to have increasing significance.

The question of who should succeed the aging president exacerbated the disagreements already existing among the country's leaders. Kenyatta encouraged no one to claim the inheritance, but leading Kikuyu who had benefited greatly under his leadership plotted to secure a complaisant successor. The attorney general, Charles Njonjo, though himself a Kikuyu, opposed such a plan, as did another Kikuyu, the minister of finance, Mwai Kibaki. Together the two ensured that, upon Kenyatta's death in August 1978, he was succeeded by his deputy, Daniel arap Moi, a member of the minority Kalenjin people. Moi was elected president in October, while Kibaki became vice president.

## Moi's Rule

Misgivings about what would happen with the departure of such a dominant figure as Kenyatta were soon dispelled. The transfer of power took place smoothly, owing mainly to the skillful leadership of Njonjo and Kibaki, but the transition was also helped by a boom in coffee prices that eased the country's economic problems to a considerable extent. At first, Moi followed Kenyatta's policy of distributing offices among as many different ethnic groups as possible, but over the years members of his own Kalenjin group acquired a disproportionate number of appointments. Odinga was still critical of the government, and university students supported him on idealistic grounds— and also because they saw little prospect in the near future of being able to supplant those holding the limited number of lucrative offices.

Moi felt most threatened by Njonjo. Exercising his almost unassailable presidential powers, Moi began a campaign to discredit the former kingmaker, who traded his appointment as attorney general for the more vulnerable office of a cabinet minister in the newly created Ministry of Constitutional Affairs. Njonjo's responsibilities were cut, as were those of Kibaki, who was considered by Moi to have become too powerful because he commanded widespread Kikuyu support. Although Kenya had been a de facto one-party state since 1969 (when the KPU was banned), KANU's power—as well as Moi's—was reinforced in 1982 when the KANU-dominated National Assembly amended the constitution, officially designating KANU the only legal political party in the country. Moi's position was further bolstered when the army loyally rallied to suppress an attempted coup later that same year by some of the lower-ranking officers in the air force. A number of the leaders of the rebellion were Luo, and many university students took part in the disturbances. Ethnic, idealistic, and economic motives were thus joined together in unsuccessful opposition to the government. Eager to prevent the students from becoming effective leaders of discontented groups of ethnic or impoverished minorities, Moi closed the universities temporarily when opposition was voiced. Njonjo, meanwhile, was rendered ineffective when he was found guilty of involvement in treason or subversion, although he was pardoned because of his earlier services to the country. Odinga continued to be subjected to periodic restrictions.

Generous financial support that had come from the Western powers since independence was an important factor in ensuring that Kenya's precarious economy survived the traumas of inflation. Moi followed Kenyatta's example by continuing to align his country with the West. The enormous increase in landownership among Africans in the postindependence period also helped to create a modestly prosperous class that was anxious to avoid revolutionary change, while the powers vested in the presidency made successful opposition an unlikely prospect.

Increasingly, however, Western financial aid came to be tied to demands for political and economic reforms. It was for this reason that in December 1991 Moi finally accepted a constitutional amendment that reinstated multiparty elections. When elections were held the following December, however, Moi was reelected, and, with the opposition divided, KANU won a strong majority in the National Assembly. One opposition party, Forum for the Restoration of Democracy (FORD), had been founded in 1991 but by 1992 had split into two factions: FORD-Kenya, led by Odinga until his death in 1994, and FORD-Asili, headed by Kenneth Matiba.

Kibaki, who had left the government late in 1991, became the official leader of the opposition after elections in 1997. Many Kenyans had hoped that the various opposition parties would cooperate and field a single candidate who would oust Moi, but there were more than eight on the ballot. Moi, the incumbent, used the preexisting political network and won by a large margin. Kibaki challenged the results in court, but his case was dismissed. When appointing his cabinet, Moi selected KANU members and continued to ignore the opposition. However, in July 1999, in an apparent change of heart, Moi made Njonjo chairman of the Kenya Wildlife Services and Richard Leakey head of the civil service and permanent secretary to the cabinet. Leakey's popularity was cited as the main reason Moi appointed him to this post; the appointment was also seen as Moi's way of showing Kenya's commitment to tackling the issues of corruption and gross mismanagement in the government.

## Kenya in the 21st Century

Moi announced in 2002 that he would not run again for the presidency, and Uhuru Kenyatta, son of Jomo Kenyatta, was chosen to be KANU's presidential candidate. Kibaki, this time representing a coalition of opposition groups (the National Rainbow Coalition [NARC]), soundly defeated Kenyatta in the 2002 presidential elections, thus ending KANU's long period of uninterrupted rule.

Although Kibaki pledged to fight the corruption that had plagued Kenya under KANU's rule, it continued to affect the country's economic and political credibility in the 21st century. In 2005 his administration was embroiled in a corruption scandal, and later that year a draft of a new constitution championed by Kibaki was defeated in a national referendum. The defeat was largely perceived as protest against Kibaki's administration. The debate over the constitution spawned a powerful new coalition of political parties, the Orange Democratic Movement (ODM), which included KANU. In 2007 dissension caused a rift within ODM, resulting in the formation of an additional coalition group, the Orange Democratic Movement–Kenya (ODM-K).

Kibaki prepared for the December 2007 presidential and parliamentary elections by forming a new coalition, the Party of National Unity (PNU), which included some of the political parties that had previously formed his NARC coalition. Surprisingly, PNU also included KANU despite its position as an opposition party. There were several challengers to Kibaki for the presidency, including Raila Odinga of ODM and Kalonzo Musyoka of ODM-K. The election boasted a record-high voter turnout and was one of the closest in Kenya's history. The provisional results indicated that Odinga would be victorious, but, when the final election results were released after a delay, Kibaki was declared the winner by a narrow margin. Odinga immediately disputed the outcome, and international observers questioned the validity of the final results. Widespread protests ensued throughout the country and degenerated into horrific acts of violence involving some of Kenya's many ethnic groups, most notable of which were the Kikuyu (Kibaki's group) and the Luo (Odinga's group). Both groups were victims as well as perpetrators. More than 1,000 people were killed and more than 600,000 were displaced in the election's violent aftermath as efforts to resolve the political impasse between Kibaki and Odinga (including mediation attempts by former UN secretary-general Kofi Annan) were not immediately successful.

On Feb. 28, 2008, Kibaki and Odinga agreed to a power-sharing plan brokered by Annan and Jakaya Kikwete, the president of Tanzania and chairman of the African Union. The plan called for the formation of a coalition government between PNU and ODM and the creation of several new positions, with Kibaki to remain president and Odinga to hold the newly created post of prime minister. Despite the agreement, however, conflict persisted over the distribution of posts. After several weeks of talks, settlement on the allocation of cabinet positions between PNU and ODM members was reached, and on April 13, 2008, President Kibaki named the coalition government.

# CHAPTER 14

## SOMALIA

Somalia is an eastern African country located on the Horn of Africa, along the coasts of the Gulf of Aden and the Indian Ocean. The country was formed in 1960 by the federation of a former Italian colony and a British protectorate. The capital is Mogadishu.

### EARLY ACTIVITY ON THE COASTS

From their connection with the Ethiopian hinterland, their proximity to Arabia, and their export of precious gums, ostrich feathers, ghee (clarified butter), and other animal products as well as slaves from farther inland, the northern and eastern Somali coasts have for centuries been open to the outside world. This area probably formed part of Punt, "the land of aromatics and incense," mentioned in ancient Egyptian writings. Between the 7th and the 10th century, immigrant Muslim Arabs and Persians developed a series of trading posts along the Gulf of Aden and Indian Ocean coasts. Many of the early Arab geographers mentioned these trading posts and the sultanates that grew out of them, but they rarely described the interior of the country in detail.

Intensive exploration really began only after the occupation of Aden by the British in 1839 and the ensuing scramble for Somali possessions by Britain, France, and Italy. In 1854, while Richard Burton was exploring the country to the northwest in the course of his famous journey from Berbera to Hārer, his colleague John Hanning Speke was making his way along the Makhir coast in the northeast. This region had previously been visited by Charles Guillain, captain of the brig *Ducouedid*, between 1846 and 1848. Guillain also sailed down the Indian Ocean coast and went ashore at Mogadishu, Marca, and Baraawe, penetrating some distance inland and collecting valuable geographic and ethnographic information. In 1865 the German explorer Karl Klaus von der Decken sailed up the Jubba River as far as Baardheere in the small steamship *Welf*, which foundered in rapids above the town. Decken was killed by Somali, but much valuable information collected by his expedition survived.

## PENETRATION OF THE INTERIOR

In 1883 a party of Englishmen (F.L. and W.D. James, G.P.V. Aylmer, and E. Lort-Phillips) penetrated from Berbera as far as the Shabeelle River, and between 1886 and 1892 H.G.C. and E.J.E. Swayne surveyed the country between the coast and the Shabeelle and also reached farther east toward the Nugaaleed valley. During 1894–95, A. Donaldson-Smith explored the headwaters of the Shabeelle in Ethiopia, reached Lake Rudolf, and eventually descended the Tana River to the Kenyan coast. In 1891 the Italian Luigi Robecchi-Bricchetti trekked from Mogadishu to Hobyo and then crossed the Ogaden region to Berbera. About the same time, further explorations were

made by another Italian, Capt. Vittorio Bottego. In the 20th century several extensive surveys were made, especially in the British protectorate, by J.A. Hunt between 1944 and 1950, and much of the country was mapped by aerial survey.

## BEFORE PARTITION

Until recent times the history of the Horn of Africa was dominated by two great themes: the southward expansion of the Somali from the Gulf of Aden littoral and the development by Arab and Persian Muslim settlers of a ring of coastal trading towns dating from at least the 10th century CE. By this time, Islam was firmly established in the northern ports of Seylac (Zeila) and Berbera and at Marca, Baraawe, and Mogadishu on the Indian Ocean coast in the south. These centres were engaged in a lively trade, with connections as far as China. Initially the trend of expansion was from these coastal centres inland, especially in the north.

### PEOPLES OF THE COASTS AND HINTERLAND

Probably by the 10th century the country from the Gulf of Aden coast inland had been occupied first by Somali nomads and then, to their south and west, by various groups of pastoral Oromo who apparently had expanded from their traditional homelands in southwestern Ethiopia. To the south of these Cushitic-speaking Somali and

## THE SOMALI

*The Somali people of Africa occupy all of Somalia, a strip of Djibouti, the southern Ethiopian region of Ogaden, and part of northwestern Kenya. Except for the arid coastal area in the north, the Somalis occupy true nomad regions of plains, coarse grass, and streams. They speak a language of the Cushitic branch of the Afro-Asiatic (formerly Hamito-Semitic) family.*

*In the 14th century many Somalis, converted to Islam by Arabs from across the Red Sea, began their expansion southward from the arid steppes to their present borders, which overflow what was traditionally known as Somaliland. Although three great divisions of Somalis exist, roughly corresponding to the northern, central, and southern parts of the region, the Somalis demonstrate considerable cultural unity.*

*The basis of Somali society is the rēr, or large, self-contained kinship group or clan, consisting of a number of families claiming common descent from a male ancestor. A Somali has obligations both to his rēr and to the loosely defined social unit of which his rēr is a part. Government of the rēr is markedly patriarchal, although the chief is chosen by a group of elders who counsel him.*

*The Somalis are primarily nomadic herdsmen who, because of intense competition for scarce resources, have been extremely individualistic and frequently involved in blood feuds or wars with neighbouring tribes and peoples. Their conception of Islam is vague, and religious practices are dominated by the worship of ancestral saints.*

*A second category of Somalis are the townspeople and agriculturists of the urban centres, especially along the coast of the Horn of Africa, where intense and prolonged intimacy with the Islamic tradition has rendered the culture highly organized and religiously orthodox and where geographic position has turned the townspeople into commercial middlemen between the Arab world and the nomadic peoples of the interior.*

Oromo—the "Berberi" of classical times and of the Arab geographers—the fertile lands between the Shabeelle and Jubba rivers were occupied, partly at least, by sedentary Bantu groups of the Nyika confederacy, whose ancient capital was Shungwaya. Remnants of the Zanj, as these people were known to the Arab geographers, still survive in this region, but their strongest contemporary representatives are found among the coastal Bantu, of whom the Pokomo live along the Tana River in northern Kenya.

Another smaller allied population consisted of the ancestors of the scattered bands of hunters of northern Kenya and southern Somalia known as the Wa-Ribi, or the Wa-Boni, a people whose appearance and mode of existence recall those of the San of other areas of Africa.

## THE GREAT SOMALI MIGRATIONS

With this distribution of peoples in the 10th century, the stage was set for the great movements of expansion of the Somali toward the south and of the Oromo to the south and west. The first known major impetus to Somali migration was that of Sheikh Ismā'īl Jabartī, ancestor of the Daarood Somali, who apparently traveled from Arabia to settle in the northeastern corner of the Somali peninsula in the 11th century. This was followed, perhaps two centuries later, by the settlement of Sheikh Isaq, founder of the Isaaq Somali. As the Daarood and Isaaq clans grew in numbers and territory in the northeast, they began to vie with their Oromo neighbours, thus creating a general thrust toward the southwest. By the 16th century the movements that followed seem to have established much of the present distribution of Somali clans in northern Somalia. Other Somali pressed farther south, and some, according to the Arab geographer Ibn Sa'īd, had already reached the region of Marca by as early as the 13th century.

In the meantime, farther to the west a ring of militant Muslim sultanates had grown up around the Christian kingdom of Ethiopia, and the two sides were engaged in a protracted struggle for supremacy. Somali clansmen regularly formed part of the Muslim armies: the name "Somali" first occurs in an Ethiopian song of victory early in the 15th century. In the 16th century the Muslim state of Adal, whose port was Seylac, assumed the lead in the holy wars against the Christian Amhara. The turning point in the struggle between Christians and Muslims was reached with the Ethiopian victory in 1542, with Portuguese support, over the remarkable Muslim leader Aḥmad ibn Ibrāhīm al-Ghāzī (known to the Ethiopians as Aḥmad Grāñ). With his Somali armies, Aḥmad had harried Ethiopia almost to the point of collapse. This victory, which saved Ethiopia, also closed the door to Somali expansion westward and increased the pressure of the Somali and Oromo thrust southward. With this stimulus the main mass of the Oromo swept into Ethiopia from the south and southwest and streamed in conquering hordes as far north as the ancient city of Hārer.

This massive invasion left something of a political vacuum in the south of the Horn, which new Somali settlers were quick to fill. By the 17th century the influx of new migrants, competing and jostling with each other, had become considerable. The old Ajuran Somali sultanate, linked with the port of Mogadishu, was overthrown, and Mogadishu itself was invaded and split into two rival quarters. Some of the earlier Somali groups found refuge in northern Kenya. The continuing Somali thrust south—largely at the expense of Oromo and Zanj predecessors—was ultimately effectively halted at the Tana River only by the establishment of administrative posts in about 1912.

## SOMALI CLANS AND FOREIGN TRADERS

Thus, by the latter part of the 19th century, the coastal and hinterland traditions had merged, and the centre of pressure had swung from the coast to the interior. In the north the ancient ports of Berbera and Seylac, much reduced in prosperity and importance, were now controlled by Somali nomads, and the position of the old ports of Marca, Baraawe, and Mogadishu was very similar. These towns had all been penetrated by various Somali clans, and the dominant political influence became that exercised by the Geledi clan ruling the lower reaches of the Shabeelle. Commercial and political links that provided an opening for European infiltration had, however, also been forged between these two coasts and the outside world. Part of the northern Somali coast, including Seylac, was then nominally under Turkish suzerainty (the Turkish claim going back to the 16th century, when Turkish forces had aided Aḥmad Grāñ in his campaigns against Ethiopia). The southern coastal towns, on the other hand, acknowledged the overlordship of the sultan of Zanzibar, although the latter's authority was slight in comparison with that exercised locally by the Geledi Somali.

## THE IMPERIAL PARTITION

About the middle of the 19th century, the Somali peninsula became a theatre of competition among Great Britain, Italy, and France. On the African continent itself Egypt also was involved, and later Ethiopia, expanding and consolidating its realm under the guiding leadership of the emperors Tewodros II, Yohannes IV, and Menilek II.

## COMPETITION BETWEEN THE EUROPEAN POWERS AND ETHIOPIA

Britain's interest in the northern Somali coast followed the establishment in 1839 of the British coaling station at Aden on the short route to India. The Aden garrison relied on the importation of meat from the adjacent Somali coast. France sought its own coaling station and obtained Obock on the Afar coast in 1862, later thrusting eastward and developing the Somali port of Djibouti. Farther north, Italy opened a station in 1869 at Aseb, which, with later acquisitions, became the colony of Eritrea. Stimulated by these European maneuvers, Egypt revived Turkey's ancient claims to the Red Sea coast. In 1870 the Egyptian flag was raised at Bullaxaar (Bulhar) and at Berbera.

Britain at first protested these Egyptian moves but by 1877 had come to regard the Egyptian occupation as a convenient bulwark against the encroachments of European rivals. With the disorganization caused by the revolt in the Sudan during this period, however, Egypt was obliged to curtail its colonial responsibilities, evacuating Hārer and its Somali possessions in 1885. In these circumstances the British government reluctantly decided to fill the gap left by Egypt. Between 1884 and 1886, accordingly, treaties of protection were drawn up with the main northern Somali clans guaranteeing them their "independence." Somali territory was not fully ceded to

Britain, but a British protectorate was proclaimed and vice-consuls appointed to maintain order and control trade at Seylac, Berbera, and Bullaxaar. The interior of the country was left undisturbed, only the coast being affected.

Meanwhile, France had been assiduously extending its colony from Obock, and a clash with Britain was only narrowly averted when an Anglo-French agreement on the boundaries of the two powers' Somali possessions was signed in 1888. In the same period, the Italians were also actively extending their Eritrean colony and encroaching upon Ethiopian territory. Not to be outdone, Menilek took the opportunity of seizing the Muslim city of Hārer, left independent after the Egyptian withdrawal. In 1889 Ethiopia and Italy concluded the Treaty of Wichale, which in the Italian view established an Italian protectorate over Ethiopia. Arms and capital were poured into the country, and Menilek was able to apply these new resources to bring pressure to bear on the Somali clansmen around Hārer. In 1889 Italy also acquired two protectorates in the northeastern corner of Somalia, and by the end of the year the southern part of the Somali coast leased by the British East Africa Company from the sultan of Zanzibar was sublet to an Italian company.

Italy had thus acquired a Somali colony. From 1892 the lease was held directly from Zanzibar for an annual rent of 160,000 rupees, and, after the failure of two Italian companies by 1905, the Italian government assumed direct responsibility for its colony of Italian Somaliland. To the south of the Jubba River the British East Africa Company held Jubaland until 1895, when this became part of Britain's East Africa protectorate. Britain and Italy had reached agreement in 1884 on the extent of their respective Somali territories, but the Battle of Adwa (1896), at which the infiltrating Italian armies were crushed by Ethiopian forces, radically changed the position. Ethiopia, then independent of Italy, was plainly master of the hinterland, and in 1896–97 Italy, France, and Britain all signed treaties with Emperor Menilek, curtailing their Somali possessions. Italy gave up the Somali Ogaden, and Britain excised much of the western Hawd from its protectorate. Although the land and the Somali clansmen (who were not consulted), so abandoned, were not recognized as belonging to Ethiopia, there was nothing then to stop their gradual acquisition by Ethiopia.

## REVOLT IN BRITISH SOMALILAND

These arrangements had scarcely been completed when the British Somaliland protectorate administration found its modest rule threatened by a religious rebellion led by Maxamed Cabdulle Xasan. This Somali sheikh (known to the British as the Mad Mullah) of the Ogaadeen clan, living with his mother's people in the east of the protectorate, was an adherent of the Ṣaliḥiyyah religious order, whose reformist message he preached with messianic zeal. He quickly achieved wide recognition for his learning, piety, and skill as a mediator and initially cooperated with the authorities. In 1899, however, Sheikh Maxamed came into conflict with the recently established Christian mission and also was involved in a petty dispute with the administration. With the current European and Ethiopian encroachment and with the example of the Sudanese mahdi (in Islamic eschatology, a messianic deliverer), these two incidents provided the seeds that rapidly developed into a major Somali insurrection.

Maxamed did not appropriate the title of mahdi but assumed the title of sayyid (a descendant of the Prophet), and his followers were known as the dervishes. He displayed great skill in employing all the traditional tactics of Somali clan politics in building up his following, strengthening these with the call to national Muslim solidarity against the infidel colonizers. Arms and ammunition, denied to Somali in the past, became easily available through the ports of Djibouti and the northeastern coast, and the dervishes, although opposed by many Somali, who were branded as traitors to Islam, successfully weathered four major British, Italian, and Ethiopian campaigns between 1900 and 1904. The cumbersome British armies, hampered by their supply and water requirements, found the dervish guerrilla tactics hard to combat effectively, and, when in 1910 the British government decided to abandon its inconclusive, extremely expensive operations and withdrew to the coast, leaving chaos in the interior, Sayyid Maxamed seemed to have emerged victorious. A new policy was subsequently adopted, however, and, with the aid of an increasingly effective camel constabulary (whose founder, Richard Corfield, was killed at the Battle of Dulmadoobe in 1913), the dervishes were kept at bay until 1920, when a combined air, sea, and land operation finally routed them. The formidable dervish stronghold at Taleex, or Taleh, was bombed, but the sayyid escaped, as so often before, only to die of influenza a few months later while desperately seeking to rally his scattered followers.

## ITALIAN SOMALILAND

After 1920, administrative control (under the colonial office since 1905) was gradually restored in the protectorate. In Italian Somaliland, where the Italians had been gradually extending their hold on the country, the sayyid's rebellion had caused less disruption, and the appointment in 1923 of the first fascist governor marked a new active phase in the life of the colony. Two years later Britain ceded Jubaland with the port of Kismaayo, and in 1926, after a bitter military campaign, the two northern Italian protectorates were firmly incorporated. Italian settlement was encouraged, and fruit plantations were developed along the Shabeelle and Jubba valleys. Although agreements of 1897 and 1908 had defined the border with Ethiopia, this had not been demarcated, except for a stretch of about 18 miles (29 km) delimited in 1910, and remained in dispute, thus facilitating the gradual Italian infiltration into Ethiopia. In late 1934 the celebrated Welwel incident, in which an Ethiopian patrol clashed with an Italian garrison, occurred at the Welwel oasis in the eastern part of the Ogaden claimed by both Italy and Ethiopia. The Italian conquest of Ethiopia that followed in 1935–36 brought the Ethiopian and Italian Somali territories together within the framework of Italy's short-lived East African empire. Italian Somaliland became the province of Somalia.

## THE SOMALI REPUBLIC

During World War II the British protectorate was evacuated (1940) but was recaptured with Italian Somalia in 1941, when Ethiopia also was liberated. With the exception of French Somaliland, all the Somali territories were then united under British military administration. In 1948 the protectorate reverted to the Colonial Office; the Ogaden and the Hawd were gradually surrendered to Ethiopia; and in 1950 the Italians returned to southern Somalia with 10 years to prepare the country for independence under a United Nations trusteeship.

Taking advantage of the modest progress that the British military administration had effected, the Italians rapidly pursued social and political advancement,

although economic development proved much more difficult. The British protectorate, in the event, became independent on June 26, 1960. On July 1, Italian Somalia followed suit, and the two territories joined as the Somali Republic.

The politics of the new republic were conditioned by clan allegiances, but the first major problems arose from the last-minute marriage between the former Italian trust territory and the former British protectorate. Urgent improvements in communication between the two areas were necessary, as were readjustments in their legal and judicial systems. The first independent government was formed by a coalition of the southern-based Somali Youth League (SYL) and the northern-based Somali National League (SNL).

### PAN-SOMALISM

While modest developments were pursued internally with the help of mainly Western aid, foreign policy was dominated by the Somali unification issue and by the campaign for self-determination of adjoining Somali communities in the Ogaden, French Somaliland, and northern Kenya. The Somalian government strongly supported the Kenyan Somali community's aim of self-determination (and union with Somalia). When this failed in the spring of 1963, after a commission of inquiry endorsed Somali aspirations, Somalia broke off diplomatic relations with Britain, and a Somali guerrilla war broke out in northern Kenya, paralyzing the region until 1967. By the end of 1963 a Somali uprising in the Ogaden had led to a brief confrontation between Ethiopian and Somalian forces. Because the United States and the West provided military support to Ethiopia and Kenya, Somalia turned to the Soviet Union for military aid. Nevertheless, the republic maintained a generally neutral but pro-Western stance, and, indeed, a new government formed in June 1967 under the premiership of Maxamed Xaaji Ibrahiim Cigaal (Muhammad Haji Ibrahim Egal) embarked on a policy of détente with Kenya and Ethiopia, muting the Pan-Somali campaign.

## The Era of "Scientific Socialism"

In March 1969 more than 1,000 candidates representing 64 parties (mostly clan-based) contested the 123 seats in the National Assembly. After these chaotic elections, all the deputies (with one exception) joined the SYL, which became increasingly authoritarian. The assassination of Pres. Cabdirashiid Cali Sherma'arke (Abdirashid Ali Shermarke) on Oct. 15, 1969, provoked a government crisis, of which the military took advantage to stage a coup on October 21.

The overthrow of Cigaal brought to power as head of state and president of a new Supreme Revolutionary Council the commander of the army, Maj. Gen. Mohamed Siad Barre (Maxamed

Siyaad Barre). At first the new regime concentrated on consolidating its power internally. Siad quickly adopted "Scientific Socialism," which, he claimed, was fully compatible with his country-men's traditional devotion to Islam. Leading a predominantly military administration, Siad declared a campaign to liberate the country from poverty, disease, and ignorance. The president was soon hailed as the "Father" of the people (their "Mother" was the "Revolution," as the coup was titled). Relations with socialist countries (especially the Soviet Union and China) were so greatly strengthened at the expense of Western connections that, at the height of Soviet influence, slogans proclaiming a trinity of "Comrade Marx, Comrade Lenin, and Comrade Siad" decorated official Orientation Centres throughout the land. Siad's authoritarian rule was reinforced by a national network of vigilantes called Victory Pioneers, by a National Security Service headed by his son-in-law, and by National Security Courts notorious for ruthless sentencing. Rural society was integrated into this totalitarian structure through regional committees on which clan elders (now renamed "peace-seekers") were placed under the authority of a chairman, who was invariably an official of the state apparatus. Clan loyalties were officially outlawed, and clan-inspired behaviour became a criminal offense. Of the government's many crash programs designed to transform society, the most successful were mass literacy campaigns

*A bloodless coup established Mohamed Siad Barre (Maxamed Siyaad Barre) as dictator over Somalia for more than 20 years, until he was ousted in an ensanguined civil war.* Mike Nelson/ AFP/Getty Images

in 1973 and 1974, which made Somali a written language (in Latin characters) for the first time.

After 1974 Siad turned his attention to external affairs. Somalia joined the Arab League, gaining much-needed petrodollar aid and access to political support from those Persian Gulf states to which Somali labour and livestock were exported at a growing rate. Following Haile Selassie's overthrow in September 1974, Ethiopia began to fall apart, and

guerrilla fighters of the Western Somali Liberation Front (WSLF) in the Ogaden pressed Siad (whose mother was an Ogaadeen) for support. When in June 1977 France granted independence to Djibouti (under a Somali president), the WSLF, backed by Somalia, immediately launched a series of fierce attacks on Ethiopian garrisons. By September 1977 Somalia had largely conquered the Ogaden region, and the war was at the gates of Hārer. Then the Soviet Union turned to fill the superpower vacuum left in Ethiopia by the gradual withdrawal of the United States. In the spring of 1978, with the support of Soviet matériel and Cuban soldiers, Ethiopia reconquered the Ogaden, and hundreds of thousands of Somali refugees poured into Somalia.

## CIVIL WAR

Somalia's defeat in the Ogaden War strained the stability of the Siad regime as the country faced a surge of clan pressures. An abortive military coup in April 1978 paved the way for the formation of two opposition groups: the Somali Salvation Democratic Front (SSDF), drawing its main support from the Majeerteen clan of the Mudug region in central Somalia, and the Somali National Movement (SNM), based on the Isaaq clan of the northern regions. Formed in 1982, both organizations undertook guerrilla operations from bases in Ethiopia. These pressures, in addition to pressure from Somalia's Western backers, encouraged Siad to improve relations with Kenya and Ethiopia. But a peace accord (1988) signed with the Ethiopian leader, Mengistu Haile Mariam, obliging each side to cease supporting Somali antigovernment guerrillas, had the ironic effect of precipitating civil war in Somalia.

Threatened with the closure of their bases in Ethiopia, the SNM attacked government forces in their home region, provoking a bitter conflict that left ghost towns in the hands of government forces. Ogaadeen Somali, who had been progressively absorbed into the army and militia, felt betrayed by the peace agreement with Ethiopia and began to desert, attacking Siad's clansmen. Siad became preoccupied with daily survival and consolidated his hold on Mogadishu. Clan-based guerrilla opposition groups multiplied rapidly, following the example of the SSDF and SNM. In January 1991 forces of the Hawiye-based United Somali Congress (USC) led a popular uprising that overthrew Siad and drove him to seek asylum among his own clansmen. Outside Mogadishu, all the main clans with access to the vast stores of military equipment in the country set up their own spheres of influence. Government in the south had largely disintegrated and existed only at the local level in the SSDF-controlled northeast region. In May 1991 the SNM, having secured control of the former British Somaliland northern region, declared that the 1960 federation was null and void and that henceforth the northern region would be independent and known as the Republic of Somaliland.

In Mogadishu the precipitate appointment of a USC interim government triggered a bitter feud between rival Hawiye clan factions. The forces of the two rival warlords, Gen. Maxamed Farax Caydiid (Muhammad Farah Aydid) of the Somali National Alliance (SNA) and Cali Mahdi Maxamed (Ali Mahdi Muhammad) of the Somali Salvation Alliance (SSA), tore the capital apart and battled with Siad's regrouped clan militia, the Somali National Front, for control of the southern coast and hinterland. This brought war and devastation to the grain-producing region between the rivers, spreading famine throughout southern Somalia. Attempts to distribute relief food were undermined by systematic looting and rake-offs by militias. In December 1992 the United States led an intervention by a multinational force of more than 35,000 troops, which imposed an uneasy peace on the principal warring clans and pushed supplies into the famine-stricken areas. The military operation provided support for a unique effort at peacemaking by the United Nations.

In January and March 1993 representatives of 15 Somali factions signed peace and disarmament treaties in Addis Ababa, but by June the security situation had deteriorated. American and European forces, suffering an unacceptable number of casualties, were withdrawn by March 1994. The UN force was reduced to military units mainly from less-developed countries, and the clan-based tensions that had precipitated the civil war remained unresolved. The remaining UN troops were evacuated a year later. Over the next few years there were several failed attempts at peace as fighting persisted between the various clans. The SSA and the SNA continued to be two of the primary warring factions.

In 1998 another portion of the war-torn country—the SSDF-controlled area in the northeast, identified as Puntland— announced its intentions to self-govern. Unlike the self-declared Republic of Somaliland, Puntland did not claim complete independence from Somalia— it instead sought to remain a part of the country as an autonomous region, with the goal of reuniting the country as a federal republic.

## ATTEMPTS AT PEACE

During the 1990s more than 10 peace conferences were held to address the warfare in Somalia, but they were largely unsuccessful. A 2000 peace conference held in Djibouti, however, sparked international optimism when it yielded a three-year plan for governing Somalia. A Transitional National Assembly, comprising representatives of the many clans, was established and later that year formed a Transitional National Government (TNG). But the TNG's authority was not widely accepted within the country: the new government faced constant opposition and was never able to rule effectively.

Another series of peace talks began in 2002. These talks, sponsored by the Intergovernmental Authority on Development (IGAD) and based in Kenya, eventually produced a new transitional government, known as the Transitional Federal Government (TFG). A transitional parliament was inaugurated in 2004, and in October of that year the parliament elected Abdullah Yusuf Ahmed interim president for a five-year period. Somalia's new government remained based in Kenya, however, as much of Somalia, especially Mogadishu, was unsafe. Also in 2004, a tsunami struck the Somali coast, killing several hundred people, displacing many thousands more, and destroying the livelihood of Somalia's fishing communities.

In February 2006 the transitional parliament met in Baydhabo (Baidoa)—the first time it had met on Somali soil since its formation in 2004. Although not the Somali capital, Baydhabo had been selected as the meeting place because it was deemed safer than Mogadishu, where clan-based violence continued to escalate. Matters were further complicated when in June 2006 an Islamic group, the Islamic Courts Union (ICU), took control of Mogadishu and southern regions of Somalia after defeating the militias of clan warlords. The ICU then challenged the authority of the TFG, and further hostilities ensued. In response, Ethiopia sent troops to Somalia to defend the beleaguered TFG. This action was generally supported by the international community, since the TFG was internationally recognized as the legitimate government of Somalia and there were concerns that the ICU had ties to al-Qaeda. Peace talks were held in an attempt to reach a compromise between the TFG and the ICU, but tensions remained. In December 2006 Ethiopian and Somali troops engaged in a coordinated air and ground war in defense of the TFG, and they were able to push the ICU out of Mogadishu in January 2007. (Ethiopian troops did not pull out of Somalia until January 2009, however, and ICU guerilla attacks continued.)

The Ethiopian intervention in the Somali crisis additionally affected regional affairs, as it heightened existing tensions with Eritrea, which had lent support to the ICU. However, fears that Ethiopia and Eritrea would use the Somali conflict as the arena for a proxy war began to subside as the initial crisis between the ICU and the TFG faded. In February 2007 the United Nations Security Council authorized a small African Union peacekeeping mission in Somalia, which, unfortunately, was extremely limited in what it was able to do. Unrelenting violence and warfare—as well as drought, flooding, and famine—continued to devastate Somalia.

In December 2008 Yusuf, who faced growing criticism for his handling of the peace efforts, resigned as president. A moderate Islamist, Sheikh Sharif Ahmed, was elected president in January 2009. Also that month, the transitional parliament extended the TFG's mandate for another two years. In April, the transitional parliament agreed to adopt Sharī'ah (Islamic law) for use throughout the country, a move viewed by many as an attempt to attract some of the support enjoyed by the ICU. A faction of the ICU, al-Shabaab, soon emerged as one of the biggest threats to Sheikh Sharif's government as the group increased the number and intensity of its attacks in Somalia and enforced its own particularly strict interpretation of Sharī'ah in areas of the country under its control. Incidents of piracy off the Somali coast—a problem for many years—greatly increased in the first decade of the 21st century and aroused international concern.

# CHAPTER 15

## TANZANIA

Tanzania is an eastern African country situated just south of the Equator along the coast of the Indian Ocean. It was formed as a sovereign state in 1964 through the union of the theretofore separate states of Tanganyika and Zanzibar. Dodoma is the country's designated capital, but Dar es Salaam remains the seat of most government administration.

### TANGANYIKA

Tanganyika was a historical state in eastern Africa. It is coterminous with the mainland portion of the modern Tanzania.

### EARLY EXPLORATION

Most of the known history of Tanganyika before the 19th century concerns the coastal area, although the interior has a number of important prehistoric sites. The most significant of these is the Olduvai Gorge, situated in the northwestern corner of Tanzania near the Ngorongoro crater. In 1959, following years of excavations in the gorge with her husband, Louis Leakey, Mary Leakey discovered the near-perfect skull of the "Eastern Man" (*Zinjanthropus boisei*; now regarded as *Paranthropus boisei*, a type of australopith), who inhabited the area between 2.3 and 1.2 million years ago. Available evidence from other archaeological sites and historical records attests to the existence of numerous major waves of in-migration onto the Tanzanian littoral over the millennia. The earliest of these likely included traders from such locales as Greece, Rome, Phoenicia, Arabia, Persia, and India, possibly beginning as early as the 5th century BCE and continuing into the next millennium.

The trading contacts between Arabia and the East African coast resulted in the establishment of numerous Asian and Arab trade settlements along the coast and in the interior of what is now the Tanzania mainland. The coastal trading centres were mainly Arab-controlled, and relations between the Arabs and their African neighbours appear to have been fairly friendly. After the arrival of the Portuguese in the late 15th century, the position of the Arabs was gradually undermined, but the Portuguese made little attempt to penetrate into the interior. They lost their foothold north of the Ruvuma River early in the 18th century as a result of an alliance between the coastal Arabs and the ruler of Muscat on the Arabian Peninsula. This alliance remained extremely tenuous, however, until French interest in the slave trade from the Tanganyikan coastal town of Kilwa revived the trade in 1776. This attention by the French aroused the sultan of Muscat's interest in the economic possibilities of the East African coast, and a new Omani governor was appointed at Kilwa. For some time most of the slaves came from the Kilwa hinterland, and until the 19th century any contact between the coast and the interior was due mainly to African caravans from the interior.

In their constant search for slaves, Arab traders began to penetrate farther into the interior, particularly in the southeast toward Lake Nyasa. Farther north two merchants from India followed the trade routes to reach the country of the Nyamwezi about 1825. Along this route ivory appears to have been as great an attraction as slaves, and Saʿīd ibn Sulṭān himself, after the transfer of his capital from Muscat to Zanzibar, gave every encouragement to the Arabs to pursue these trading possibilities. From the Nyamwezi country the Arabs pressed on to Lake Tanganyika in the early 1840s. Tabora (or Kazé, as it was then called) and Ujiji, on Lake Tanganyika, became important trading centres, and a number of Arabs made their homes there. They did not annex these territories but occasionally ejected hostile chieftains. Mirambo, an African chief who built for himself a temporary empire to the west of Tabora in the 1860s and '70s, effectively blocked the Arab trade routes when they refused to pay him tribute. His empire was purely a personal one, however, and collapsed on his death in 1884.

The first Europeans to show an interest in Tanganyika in the 19th century were missionaries of the Church Missionary Society, Johann Ludwig Krapf and Johannes Rebmann, who in the late 1840s reached Kilimanjaro. It was a fellow missionary, Jakob Erhardt, whose famous "slug" map (showing, on Arab information, a vast shapeless inland lake) helped stimulate the interest of the British explorers Richard Burton and John Hanning Speke. They traveled from Bagamoyo to Lake Tanganyika in 1857–58, and Speke also saw Lake Victoria.

*Summit of Kilimanjaro, northeastern Tanzania.* © Shawn McCullars

This expedition was followed by Speke's second journey, in 1860, in the company of J.A. Grant, to justify the former's claim that the Nile River rose in Lake Victoria. These primarily geographic explorations were followed by the activities of David Livingstone, who in 1866 set out on his last journey for Lake Nyasa. Livingstone's object was to expose the horrors of the slave trade and, by opening up legitimate trade with the interior, to destroy the slave trade at its roots. Livingstone's journey led to the later expeditions of H.M. Stanley and V.L. Cameron. Spurred on by

Livingstone's work and example, a number of missionary societies began to take an interest in East Africa after 1860.

## GERMAN EAST AFRICA

It was left to Germany, with its newly awakened interest in colonial expansion, to open up the country to European influences. The first agent of German imperialism was Carl Peters, who, with Count Joachim von Pfeil and Karl Juhlke, evaded the sultan of Zanzibar late in 1884 to land on the mainland and made a number of "contracts" in the Usambara area by which several chiefs were said to have surrendered their territory to him. Peters's activities were confirmed by Otto von Bismarck, chancellor of the German Empire. By the Anglo-German Agreement of 1886, the sultan of Zanzibar's vaguely substantiated claims to dominion on the mainland were limited to a 10-mile- (16-km-) wide coastal strip, and Britain and Germany divided the hinterland between them as spheres of influence, the region to the south becoming known as German East Africa. Following the example of the British to the north, the Germans obtained a lease on the coastal strip from the sultan in 1888, but their tactlessness and fear of commercial competition led to a Muslim uprising in August 1888. The rebellion was put down only after the intervention of the imperial German government and with the assistance of the British navy.

Recognizing the administrative inability of the German East Africa Company, which had theretofore ruled the country, the German government in 1891 declared a protectorate over its sphere of influence and over the coastal strip, where the company had bought out the sultan's rights. Germany was eager to exploit the resources of its new dependency, but lack of communications at first restricted development to the coastal area. The German agronomist Richard Hindorff's introduction of sisal from Florida in 1892 marked the beginning of the territory's most valuable industry, which was encouraged by the development of a railway from the new capital of Dar es Salaam to Lake Tanganyika. In 1896 work began on the construction of a railway running northeastward from Tanga to Moshi, which it reached in 1912. This successfully encouraged the pioneer coffee-growing activities on the slopes of Kilimanjaro. Wild rubber tapped by Africans, together with plantation-grown rubber, contributed to the economic development of the colony. The government also supplied good-quality cottonseed free to African growers and sold it cheaply to European planters. The administration tried to rectify the lack of clerks and minor craftsmen by encouraging the development of schools, an activity in which various missionary societies were already engaged.

The enforcement of German overlordship was strongly resisted, but control was established by the beginning of the 20th century. Almost at once came a reaction to German methods of administration, the outbreak of the Maji Maji uprising in 1905. Although there was little organization behind it, the uprising spread over a considerable portion of southeastern Tanganyika and was not finally suppressed until 1907. It led to a reappraisal of German policy in East Africa. The imperial government had attempted to protect African land rights in 1895 but had failed in its objective in the Kilimanjaro area. Similarly, liberal labour legislation had not been properly implemented. The German government set up a separate Colonial Department in 1907, and more money was invested in East Africa. A more liberal form of administration rapidly replaced the previous semimilitary system.

World War I put an end to all German experiments. Blockaded by the British navy, the country could neither export produce nor get help from Germany. The British advance into German territory continued steadily from 1916 until the whole country was eventually occupied. The effects of the war upon Germany's achievements in East Africa were disastrous, completely disrupting the administration and economy. In these circumstances the Africans reverted to their old social systems and their old form of subsistence farming. Under the Treaty of Versailles (signed June 1919; enacted January 1920), Britain received a League of Nations mandate to administer the territory except for Ruanda-Urundi, which came under Belgian administration, and the Kionga triangle, which went to Portugal.

## TANGANYIKA TERRITORY

Sir Horace Byatt, administrator of the captured territory and, from 1920 to 1924, the first British governor and commander in chief of Tanganyika Territory (as it was then renamed), enforced a period of recuperation before new development plans were set in motion. A Land Ordinance (1923) ensured that African land rights were secure. Sir Donald Cameron, governor from 1925 to 1931, infused a new vigour into the country. He reorganized the system of native administration by the Native Authority Ordinance (1926) and the Native Courts Ordinance (1929). His object was to build up local government on the basis of traditional authorities, an aim that he pursued with doctrinaire enthusiasm and success. He attempted to silence the criticisms by Europeans that had been leveled against his predecessor by urging the creation of a Legislative Council in 1926 with a reasonable number of nonofficial members, both European and Asian. In his campaign to develop the country's economy, Cameron won a victory over opposition from Kenya by gaining the British government's approval for an extension of the Central Railway Line from Tabora to Mwanza (1928). His attitude toward European settlers was determined by their potential contribution to the country's economy. He therefore was surprised by the British government's reluctance to permit settlement in Tanganyika. The economic depression after 1929 resulted in the curtailment of many of Cameron's development proposals. In the 1930s, there were persistent fears that Tanganyika might be handed back to Germany in response to demands by Adolf Hitler—then chancellor of Germany—for overseas possessions.

At the outbreak of World War II, Tanganyika's main task was to make itself as independent as possible of imported goods. Inevitably the retrenchment evident in the 1930s became still more severe, and, while prices for primary products soared, the value of money depreciated proportionately.

# JULIUS NYERERE

(b. March 1922, Butiama, Tanganyika—d. Oct. 14, 1999, London, Eng.)

*Julius Kambarage Nyerere was the first prime minister of independent Tanganyika (1961), and later became the first president of the new state of Tanzania (1964). Nyerere was also the major force behind the Organization of African Unity (OAU; now the African Union).*

*Nyerere was a son of the chief of the small Zanaki ethnic group. He was educated at Tabora Secondary School and Makerere College in Kampala, Uganda. A convert to Roman Catholicism, he taught in several Roman Catholic schools before going to Edinburgh University. He was the first Tanganyikan to study at a British university. He graduated with an M.A. in history and economics in 1952 and returned to Tanganyika to teach. Nyerere soon joined the Tanganyika African Association, a social organization, and quickly became its president in 1953. In 1954 he converted the organization into the politically oriented Tanganyika African National Union (TANU). Under Nyerere's leadership the organization espoused peaceful change, social equality, and racial harmony.*

*The British administration overseeing the Tanganyika territory nominated him a member of the Tanganyikan Legislative Council, but he resigned in 1957 in protest against the slowness of progress toward independence. When Tanganyika became independent on Dec. 9, 1961, Nyerere was its first prime minister. The next month, however, he resigned from this position to devote his time to writing and the issues of government and of African unity. When Tanganyika became a republic in 1962, he was elected president, and in 1964 he became president of the United Republic of Tanzania (Tanganyika and Zanzibar).*

*Nyerere was reelected president of Tanzania in 1965 and was returned to serve three more successive five-year terms. Committed to the creation of an egalitarian socialist society based on cooperative agriculture, he collectivized village farmlands, carried out mass literacy campaigns, and instituted free and universal education. He also emphasized Tanzania's need to become economically self-sufficient rather than remain dependent on foreign aid and foreign investment. Nyerere termed his socialist experimentation ujamaa (Swahili: "familyhood").*

*Though enthusiastically adopted by his countrymen and steadfastly supported by sympathetic western European nations, Nyerere's socialist policies failed to spur economic development in Tanzania. At the time of his resignation in 1985, Tanzania was still one of the world's poorest countries. Tanzania had one of the highest literacy rates in Africa, however, and the society was both politically stable and notably free of economic inequalities. Nyerere remained committed to socialist policies throughout his political career.*

*As a major force behind the modern Pan-African movement and one of the founders in 1963 of the OAU, Nyerere was a key figure in African events in the 1970s. From independence until 1990, Nyerere also headed Tanzania's only political party, Chama Cha Mapinduzi. Thereafter he assumed the role of elder statesman and was regularly called upon to act as arbiter in international crises.*

*Julius Nyerere was widely credited with impressive oratorical skills and unusual powers of political perception. His thoughts, essays, and speeches are collected in his books,* Uhuru na Umoja *(1967; Freedom and Unity),* Uhuru na Ujamaa *(1968; Freedom and Socialism),* **and** Uhuru na Maendeleo *(1973; Freedom and Development).* **He also translated two plays by William Shakespeare,** The Merchant of Venice **and** Julius Caesar, **into Swahili.**

Tanganyika's main objective after the war was to ensure that its program for economic recovery and development went ahead. The continuing demand for primary produce strengthened the country's financial position. The chief item in the development program was a plan to devote 3 million acres (1.2 million hectares) of land to the production of peanuts (the Groundnuts Scheme). The plan, which was to be financed by the British government, was to cost £25 million, and, in addition, a further £4.5 million would be required for the construction of a railway in southern Tanganyika. It failed because of the lack of adequate preliminary investigations and was subsequently carried out on a greatly reduced scale.

Constitutionally, the most important immediate postwar development was the British government's decision to place Tanganyika under United Nations trusteeship (1947). Under the terms of the trusteeship agreement, Britain was called upon to develop the political life of the territory, which, however, only gradually began to take shape in the 1950s. In 1953 Julius Nyerere was elected president of the Tanganyika African Association (TAA), an organization made up mainly of African civil servants, which had been formed in Dar es Salaam in 1929. In early 1954 Nyerere and his associates transformed the TAA from a social organization to a political one, and later the same year the TAA became the Tanganyika African National Union (TANU), with the stated aims of self-government and independence.

The first two African members had been nominated to the Legislative Council in December 1945. This number was subsequently increased to four, with three Asian nonofficial members and four Europeans. An official majority was retained. In an important advance in 1955, the three groups were given parity of representation on the unofficial side of the council with 10 nominated members each, and for a time it seemed as if this basis would persist. The first elections to the unofficial side of the council (in 1958 and 1959), however, enabled TANU to show its strength, for even among the European and Asian candidates, only those supported by TANU were elected.

## INDEPENDENCE

A constitutional committee in 1959 unanimously recommended that after the elections in 1960 a large majority of the members of both sides of the council be Africans and that elected members form the basis of the government. In the 1960 Legislative Council elections, TANU and its allies were again overwhelmingly victorious, and when Tanganyika became independent on Dec. 9, 1961, Nyerere became its first prime minister. The next month, however, he resigned from this position to devote his time to writing and to synthesizing his views of government and of African unity. He was succeeded by Rashidi Kawawa. One of Nyerere's more important works was a paper called "Ujamaa—the Basis for African Socialism," which later served as the philosophical basis for the Arusha Declaration of 1967.

On Dec. 9, 1962, Tanganyika adopted a republican constitution, and Nyerere became executive president of the country. The next month, he announced that in the interest of national unity and economic development, TANU had decided that Tanganyika would now be a one-party state. Nyerere's administration was challenged in 1964, and an army mutiny was suppressed in January only after the president reluctantly sought the assistance of British marines.

Although TANU was the only legal party, voters in each constituency were often offered a choice between more than one TANU candidate in parliamentary elections. That this arrangement amounted to something more than lip service to the idea of democracy was demonstrated in 1965 and in subsequent elections when, although Nyerere was

reelected again and again as the sole candidate for president, a considerable number of legislators, including cabinet ministers, lost their seats.

## ZANZIBAR

The history of Zanzibar has been to a large extent shaped by the monsoons (prevailing trade winds) and by the island's proximity to the African continent. The regular annual recurrence of the monsoons has made possible Zanzibar's close connection with India and the countries bordering the Red Sea and the Persian Gulf. Its proximity to the continent has made it a suitable jumping-off point for trading and exploring ventures not only along the coast but also into the interior.

### Portuguese and Omani Domination

Though the first references to Zanzibar occur only after the rise of Islam, there appears to be little doubt that its close connection with southern Arabia and the countries bordering the Persian Gulf began before the Common Era. At the beginning of the 13th century, the Arab geographer Yāqūt recorded that the people of Langujah (namely, Unguja, the Swahili name for Zanzibar) had taken refuge from their enemies on the nearby island of Tumbatu, the inhabitants of which were Muslim.

In 1498 Vasco da Gama visited Malindi, and in 1503 Zanzibar Island was attacked and made tributary by the Portuguese.

It appears to have remained in that condition for about a quarter of a century. Thereafter the relations between the rulers of Zanzibar and the Portuguese seem to have been those of allies, the people of Zanzibar more than once cooperating with the Portuguese in attacks upon Mombasa. In 1571 the "king" of Zanzibar, in gratitude for Portuguese assistance in expelling certain African invaders, donated the island to his allies, but the donation was never implemented. A Portuguese trading factory and an Augustinian mission were established on the site of the modern city of Zanzibar, and a few Portuguese appear also to have settled as farmers in different parts of the island. The first English ship to visit Zanzibar (1591–92) was the *Edward Bonaventure*, captained by Sir James Lancaster.

When the Arabs captured Mombasa in 1698, all these settlements were abandoned, and (except for a brief Portuguese reoccupation in 1728) Zanzibar and Pemba came under the domination of the Arab rulers of Oman. For more than a century those rulers left the government of Zanzibar to local hakims (governors). The first sultan to take up residence in Zanzibar was Sayyid Saʿīd ibn Sulṭān, who after several short visits settled there soon after 1830 and subsequently greatly extended his influence along the East African coast. On Saʿīd's death in 1856, his son Majīd succeeded to his African dominions, while another son, Thuwayn, succeeded to Oman.

As a result of an award made in 1860 by Lord Canning, governor general of India, the former African dominions of Saʿīd were declared to be independent of Oman. Majīd died in 1870 and was succeeded by his brother Barghash. Toward the end of the latter's reign, his claims to dominion on the mainland were restricted by Britain, France, and Germany to a 10-mile- (16-km-) wide coastal strip, the administration of which was subsequently shared by Germany and Britain. Barghash died in 1888. Both he and Majīd had acted largely under the influence of Sir John Kirk, who was British consular representative at Zanzibar from 1866 to 1887. It was by Kirk's efforts that Barghash consented in 1873 to a treaty for the suppression of the slave trade.

## BRITISH PROTECTORATE

In 1890 what was left of the sultanate was proclaimed a British protectorate, and in 1891 a constitutional government was instituted under British auspices, with Sir Lloyd Mathews as first minister. In August 1896, on the death of the ruling sultan, Ḥamad ibn Thuwayn, the royal palace at Zanzibar was seized by Khālid, a son of Sultan Barghash, who proclaimed himself sultan. The British government disapproved, and, as he refused to submit, British warships bombarded the palace. Khālid escaped and took refuge at the German consulate, whence he was conveyed to German East Africa. Ḥamud ibn Moḥammed was then installed as sultan (Aug. 27, 1896). In 1897 the legal status of slavery was finally abolished. In 1913 the control of the protectorate passed from the Foreign Office to the Colonial Office, when the posts of consul general and first minister were merged into that of British resident. At the same time, a Protectorate Council was constituted as an advisory body. In 1926 the advisory council was replaced by nominated executive and legislative councils.

Khalīfa ibn Harūb became sultan in 1911. He was the leading Muslim prince in East Africa, and his moderating influence did much to steady Muslim opinion in that part of Africa at times of political crisis, especially during the two world wars. He died on Oct. 9, 1960, and was succeeded by his eldest son, Sir Abdullah ibn Khalīfa.

In November 1960 the British Parliament approved a new constitution for Zanzibar. The first elections to the Legislative Council then established were held in January 1961 and ended in a deadlock. Further elections, held in June, were marked by serious rioting and heavy casualties. Ten seats were won by the Afro-Shirazi Party (ASP), representing mainly the African population; 10 by the Zanzibar Nationalist Party (ZNP), representing mainly the Zanzibari Arabs; and 3 by the Zanzibar and Pemba People's Party (ZPPP), an offshoot of the ZNP. The ZNP and the ZPPP combined to form a government with Mohammed Shamte Hamadi as chief minister.

Because of failure to agree on franchise qualifications, the number of elected seats in the legislature, and the timing of the elections, a constitutional conference held in London in 1962 was unable to fix a date for the introduction of internal self-government or for independence. An independent commission, however, subsequently delimited new constituencies and recommended an increase in the numbers of the Legislative Council, which the council accepted, also agreeing to the introduction of universal adult suffrage. Internal self-government was established in June 1963, and elections held the following month resulted in a victory for the ZNP-ZPPP coalition, which won 18 seats, the ASP winning the remaining 13. Final arrangements for independence were made at a conference in London in September. In October it was agreed that the Kenya coastal strip—a territory that extended 10 miles (16 km) inland along the Kenya coast from the Tanganyika frontier to Kipini and that had long been administered by Kenya although nominally under the sovereignty of Zanzibar—would become an integral part of Kenya on that country's attainment of independence.

## INDEPENDENCE

On Dec. 10, 1963, Zanzibar achieved independence as a member of the Commonwealth. In January 1964 the Zanzibar government was overthrown by an internal revolution, Sayyid Jamshid ibn Abdullah (who had succeeded to the sultanate in July 1963 on his father's death) was deposed, and a republic was proclaimed.

Although the revolution was carried out by only about 600 armed men under the leadership of the communist-trained "field marshal" John Okello, it won considerable support from the African population. Thousands of Arabs were massacred in riots, and thousands more fled the island. Sheikh Abeid Amani Karume, leader of the ASP, was installed as president of the People's Republic of Zanzibar and Pemba. Sheikh Abdulla Kassim Hanga was appointed prime minister, and Abdul Raḥman Mohammed ("Babu"), leader of the new left-wing Umma (The Masses) Party (formed by defectors from the ZNP), became minister for defense and external affairs. Pending the establishment of a new constitution, the cabinet and all government departments were placed under the control of a Revolutionary Council of 30 members, which was also vested with temporary legislative powers. Zanzibar was proclaimed a one-party state. Measures taken by the new government included the nationalization of all land, with further powers to confiscate any immovable property without compensation except in cases of undue hardship.

## THE UNITED REPUBLIC

Zanzibar and the mainland have had a close relationship that dates back to several centuries before the Common Era. Although both were administered separately during colonial rule, Africans from the mainland traveled to Zanzibar for employment, and many who did so settled in the islands permanently. At times during the struggles for national independence, TANU in Tanganyika and the ASP in Zanzibar worked together. The decision of the two countries to amalgamate was a natural outcome of many years of close relationship between the people of Zanzibar and the mainland.

On April 26, 1964, the two countries merged to form the United Republic of Tanganyika and Zanzibar, with Nyerere as president and Karume as first vice president. The nascent country was renamed the United Republic of Tanzania in October 1964. Despite unification, for years Zanzibar continued to pursue its own policies, paying little attention to mainland practices.

## TANZANIA UNDER NYERERE

Nyerere's chief external task was to convince the international community, particularly the Western powers, that Tanzania's foreign policy was to be one of nonalignment. But the overt involvement of the Eastern bloc in Zanzibar, as well as Nyerere's own insistence that, to rectify the imbalance created in the colonial era, Tanzania had to turn more to the East for aid, did little to make the task easier. The high moral tone taken by the president over Britain's role in Rhodesia and over the supply of British arms to South Africa also strained the bonds of friendship between the two countries, with Tanzania severing diplomatic relations with Britain from 1965 to 1968. The consequent loss of aid from Britain was more than compensated for by help from Eastern countries, notably from China, whose aid culminated in 1970 in the offer of an interest-free Chinese loan to finance the construction of a railway line linking Dar es Salaam with Zambia.

Though Nyerere fully appreciated the generous assistance his country was receiving, he was eager to impress upon his countrymen the need for maximum self-reliance. Political freedom, he insisted, was useless if the country was to be enslaved by foreign investors. His views were formulated in the Arusha Declaration of Feb. 5, 1967, which put forth the policy of *ujamaa* (familyhood) and called for socialism and self-reliance. The resources of the country, Nyerere said, were owned by the whole people and were held in trust for their descendants. The leaders had to set an example by rejecting the perquisites of a capitalist system and should draw only one salary. Banks had to be nationalized, though compensation would be given to shareholders. The same would apply to the more important commercial companies. Agriculture, however, was the key to development, and only greater productivity could hold at bay the spectre of poverty. To give a fillip to his argument, people were to be moved into cooperative villages where they could work together for their mutual benefit.

Nyerere's exhortations did not arouse the enthusiasm for which he had hoped. Individuals resisted his plans for collectivization, and not even the majority of his supporters wholeheartedly adopted his moral stand. The cooperative village scheme failed, bringing additional pressure to bear upon an already desperately weak economy. The sisal industry, one of those nationalized, was badly run down by the mid-1970s because of inefficient management.

Nyerere's criticisms were not reserved for his own people—or yet for the wealthy countries of the world. In 1968 he challenged the rules of the Organization of African Unity (OAU) by recognizing the secession of Biafra from Nigeria, and in 1975 he attacked the OAU for planning to hold its summit meeting in Uganda, where Pres. Idi Amin was acting with extreme cruelty. Deteriorating relations with both Uganda and Kenya contributed to the collapse of the East African Community in 1977, which had been established 10 years earlier to foster economic development between the three countries.

Tense relations between Tanzania and Uganda in the early 1970s—caused primarily by Nyerere's continued support of Milton Obote, the former Ugandan president deposed by Amin in 1971—led to occasional border clashes between the two countries. Despite an agreement to cease their hostilities, a new round of conflict was initiated in 1978 when Amin's forces entered northwestern Tanzania and occupied territory north of the Kagera River. Tanzanian forces counterattacked and regained the region. The clashes continued in the months that followed, and in April 1979, Tanzanian-led forces proceeded to capture the Ugandan capital of Kampala. Amin's rule ended when he fled the country just before the city was captured. The retention of Tanzanian troops in Uganda for several years after Amin's overthrow also contributed to strained relations with some of Uganda's leaders as well as arousing suspicions in Kenya. Elsewhere in Africa, however, Nyerere was able to play an authoritative role, notably in the negotiations leading to the independence of Zimbabwe and in the formation of an organization of African states to try to resist economic domination by South Africa.

Events in Zanzibar caused continuing concern for the mainland leadership. The arbitrary arrest and punishment of anyone believed to oppose the state gave rise to regret that the constitution of the joint republic prevented the mainland authorities from intervening in the island's affairs where questions of law and justice were involved. The failure to hold elections in Zanzibar also contrasted unfavourably with developments on the mainland. In April 1972 Karume was assassinated by members of the military. His successor, Aboud Jumbe, had been a leading member of Karume's government, and, while his policies did not differ markedly from those of Karume, they appeared to be moving gradually closer into line with mainland practices. The amalgamation of TANU and the ASP under the title of Revolutionary Party (Chama cha Mapinduzi; CCM) early in 1977 was a hopeful sign but was followed by demands for greater autonomy for Zanzibar. This trend was checked for a short while when Ali Hassan Mwinyi

succeeded Jumbe in 1984 and became president of the joint republic after Nyerere resigned in November 1985.

## POLITICAL AND ECONOMIC CHANGE

Mwinyi inherited an economy suffering from the country's lack of resources, the fall in world prices for Tanzanian produce, the rise in petroleum prices, and inefficient management. An acute shortage of food added still further to his problems. Though he promised to follow Nyerere's policy of self-reliance, Mwinyi soon concluded that his predecessor's resistance to foreign aid could no longer be sustained. In accepting an offer of assistance from the International Monetary Fund (IMF) in 1986, Mwinyi adopted some structural reforms and furthered the devaluation of the currency begun in 1984 by Nyerere, who also had denationalized the state-run sector of the sisal industry in 1985. Moreover, private enterprise had been allowed to take over other areas of business.

In the late 1980s dissent again resurfaced in Zanzibar, culminating in the revelation in January 1993 that Zanzibar had joined the Organization of the Islamic Conference. Criticism on the mainland forced its withdrawal later that year.

In May 1992 the country's constitution was amended to provide for a multiparty political system, and in 1995 the first national elections under this system were held; Benjamin Mkapa of the CCM was elected president. Mkapa

*Pres. Jakaya Kikwete, 2009.* Photograph by Pete Souza/The White House

continued the economic reforms pursued by his predecessors.

## CHALLENGES INTO THE 21ST CENTURY

Beginning in the mid-1990s and continuing into the 2000s, Tanzania's already-tenuous economy and food supply were strained by the number of refugees arriving from the neighbouring countries of Rwanda, Burundi, and Zaire (now the Democratic Republic of the Congo); the country eventually requested international aid to assist with the care of the refugees. Meanwhile, Tanzania was

the site of a terrorist act in 1998 when the U.S. embassy in Dar es Salaam was bombed, killing 11 people and injuring many more.

Mkapa was reelected in late 2000 amid allegations of electoral fraud in Zanzibar. Several violent demonstrations followed, including one in January 2001 in which police intervention resulted in at least 40 people dead and 100 people injured. Zanzibar also experienced an escalation in Islamic militancy. Several demonstrations, violent attacks, and bombings in the 2000s were attributed to a few radical organizations protesting the government's refusal to comply with their extremist views. In late 2004, when 10 people were killed in Dar es Salaam by the Indian Ocean tsunami, the government was criticized for not doing enough to warn the public about the impending threat.

After more than a decade of preparation, Tanzania, Uganda, and Kenya launched the East African Community Customs Union in 2005 in an effort to stimulate economic activity in the region. In Tanzania's concurrent presidential and legislative elections held later that year, former foreign minister Jakaya Mrisho Kikwete, the CCM candidate, was elected president. The CCM itself won a strong majority in the National Assembly. In 2009 Tanzania signed an agreement providing for the free movement of people and goods across the East African Community, which by this time also included Burundi and Rwanda.

# CHAPTER 16

# UGANDA

Uganda is a landlocked country in east-central Africa. The former British protectorate became independent in 1962. The capital is Kampala.

## EARLY HISTORY

The early history of Uganda, like much of sub-Saharan Africa, is a saga of movements of small groups of cultivators and herders over centuries. Cultures and languages changed continuously as peoples slowly migrated to other regions and intermingled. By the mid-19th century, when the first non-African visitors entered the region later to become the Uganda Protectorate, there were a number of distinct languages and cultures within the territory. The northern areas were occupied generally by peoples speaking Nilotic and Sudanic languages, while the central, western, and southern portions of the territory were predominantly occupied by Bantu-speaking peoples.

## BUNYORO AND BUGANDA

The organization of the peoples who came to inhabit the area north of the Nile River was mainly based on their clan structures. In this respect the northerners differed markedly from the peoples to the southwest of the Nile. There, peoples were organized into states—or "kingdoms," as they were labeled by the earliest European visitors. The dominant state was Bunyoro-Kitara, which originated at the end of the 15th century and, under able rulers, extended its influence eastward and southward over a considerable area. To the south there were a number of lesser states, each with a chief who, like the ruler of Bunyoro-Kitara, combined priestly functions with those of a secular leader. To the southeast of Bunyoro-Kitara, the smaller state of Buganda grew as an offshoot of its larger neighbour. By the end of the 18th century, however, the boundaries of Bunyoro-Kitara had been stretched so far that the authority of the ruler began to weaken, and a succession of pacific chiefs accelerated this decline. Simultaneously the smaller, more compact state of Buganda enjoyed a succession of able and aggressive *kabaka*s (rulers), who began to expand at the expense of Bunyoro-Kitara.

It was during the period of Buganda's rise that the first Swahili-speaking traders from the east coast of Africa reached the country in the 1840s. Their object was to trade in ivory and slaves. Kabaka Mutesa I, who took office about 1856, admitted the first European explorer, the Briton John Hanning Speke, who crossed into the *kabaka*'s territory in 1862.

Henry Morton Stanley, the British-American explorer who reached Buganda in 1875, met Mutesa I. Although Buganda had not been attacked, Achoiland, to the north, had been ravaged by slavers from Egypt and the Sudan since the early 1860s, and, on the death of Kamrasi, the ruler of Bunyoro, his successor, Kabarega, had defeated his rivals only with the aid of the slavers' guns. Moreover, an emissary from the Egyptian government, Linant de Bellefonds, had reached Mutesa's palace before Stanley, so the *kabaka* was anxious to obtain allies. He readily agreed to Stanley's proposal to invite Christian missionaries to Uganda, but he was disappointed, after the first agents of the Church Missionary Society arrived in 1877, to find that they had no interest in military matters. In 1879 representatives of the Roman Catholic White Fathers Mission also reached Buganda. Although Mutesa I attempted to limit their movements, their influence rapidly spread through their contact with the chiefs whom the *kabaka* kept around him, and inevitably the missionaries became drawn into the politics of the country. Mutesa I was not concerned about these new influences, however, and, when Egyptian expansion was checked by the Mahdist rising in the Sudan, he was able to deal brusquely with the handful of missionaries in his country. His successor, Mwanga, who became *kabaka* in 1884, was less successful: he was deposed in 1888 while attempting to drive the missionaries and their supporters from the country.

## THE UGANDA PROTECTORATE

Mwanga, who was restored to his throne with the assistance of the Christian (both Roman Catholic and Protestant) Ganda, soon faced European imperialism. Carl Peters, the German adventurer, made a treaty of protection with Mwanga in 1889, but this was revoked when the Anglo-German agreement of 1890 declared all the country north of latitude 1° S to be in the British sphere of influence. The Imperial British East Africa Company agreed to administer the region on behalf of the British government, and in 1890 Capt. F.D. Lugard, the company's agent, signed another treaty with Mwanga, whose kingdom of Buganda was now placed under the company's protection. Lugard also made treaties of protection with two other chiefs, the rulers of the western states of Ankole and Toro. However, when the company did not have the funds to continue its administrative position, the British government, for strategic reasons and partly through pressure from missionary sympathizers in Britain, declared Buganda its protectorate in 1894.

Britain inherited a country that was divided into politico-religious factions, which had erupted into civil war in 1892. Buganda was also threatened by Kabarega, the ruler of Bunyoro, but a military expedition in 1894 deprived him of his headquarters and made him a refugee for the rest of his career in Uganda. Two years later the protectorate included Bunyoro, Toro, Ankole, and Busoga, and treaties were also made with chiefs to the north of the Nile. Mwanga, who revolted against British overlordship in 1897, was overthrown again and replaced by his infant son.

A mutiny in 1897 of the Sudanese troops used by the colonial government led Britain to take a more active interest in the Uganda Protectorate, and in 1899 Sir Harry Johnston was commissioned to visit the country and to make recommendations on its future administration. The main outcome of his mission was the Buganda Agreement of 1900, which formed the basis of British relations with Buganda for more than 50 years. Under its terms the *kabaka* was recognized as ruler of Buganda as long as he remained faithful to the protecting authority. His council of chiefs, the *lukiko*, was given statutory recognition. The leading chiefs benefited most from the agreement, because, in addition to acquiring greater authority, they were also granted land in freehold to ensure their support for the negotiations. Johnston made another agreement of a less-detailed nature with the ruler of Toro (1900), and subsequently a third agreement was made with the ruler of Ankole (1901).

Meanwhile, British administration was being gradually extended north and east of the Nile. However, in these areas, where a centralized authority was unknown, no agreements were made, and British officers, frequently assisted by agents of Buganda, administered the country directly. By 1914 Uganda's boundaries had been fixed, and British control had reached most areas.

## GROWTH OF A PEASANT ECONOMY

Early in the 20th century Sir James Hayes Sadler, who succeeded Johnston as commissioner, concluded that the country was unlikely to prove attractive to European settlers. Sadler's own successor, Sir Hesketh Bell, announced that he wished to develop Uganda as an African state. In this he was opposed by a number of his more senior officials and in particular by the chief justice, William Morris Carter. Carter was chairman of a land commission whose activities continued until after World War I. Again and again the commission urged that provision be made for European planters, but their efforts were unsuccessful. Bell himself had laid the foundations for a peasant economy by encouraging the Africans to cultivate cotton, which had been introduced into the protectorate as a cash crop in 1904. It was mainly because of the wealth derived from cotton that Uganda became independent of a grant-in-aid from the British Treasury in 1914.

In 1914, at the outset of World War I, there were a few skirmishes between the British and Germans on the southwestern frontier, but Uganda was never in danger of invasion. The war, however, did retard the country's development. Soon after the war it was decided that the protectorate authorities should concentrate, as Bell had suggested, on expanding African agriculture, and Africans were encouraged to grow coffee in addition to cotton. The British government's decision to forbid the alienation of land in freehold, and the economic depression of the early 1920s, dealt a further blow to the hopes of European planters. The part to be played by Europeans, as well as Asians, was now mainly on the commercial and processing side of the protectorate's agricultural industry.

As the output of primary produce increased, it became necessary to extend and improve communications. Just before World War I a railway had been built running northward from Jinja, on Lake Victoria, to Namasagali, the intent being to open up the Eastern Province. In the 1920s a railway from Mombasa, on the Kenyan coast, was extended to Soroti, and in 1931 a rail link was also completed between Kampala, the industrial capital of Uganda, and the coast.

The depression of the early 1930s interrupted Uganda's economic progress, but the protectorate's recovery was more rapid than that of its neighbours, so that the later years of the decade were a period of steady expansion.

## POLITICAL AND ADMINISTRATIVE DEVELOPMENT

In 1921 a Legislative Council was instituted, but its membership was so small (four official and two nonofficial members) that it made little impact on the protectorate. The Indian community, which played an important part in the commercial life of the region, resented the fact that it was not to have equal representation with Europeans on the unofficial side of the council and so refused to participate until 1926. There was no evidence of a desire on the part of the Africans to sit in the council, since the most politically advanced group in the community, the Ganda, regarded its own *lukiko* as the most important council in the country.

In light of the Africans' indifference toward the protectorate legislature, it is not surprising that they opposed the suggestion, made in the later 1920s, that there should be some form of closer union between the East African territories. An interest in preserving the traditions of the various ethnic groups was one source of this opposition, but there was also fear, among Africans as well as Asians, that they would be dominated by Kenya's European settlers.

An important development was the beginning of government interest in education. The protectorate administration set up an education department in 1925, and, while aid was given to the missionary societies, which had already opened a number of good schools in Buganda, the government also established schools. This led to the gradual replacement of older chiefs (men of strong personality who usually lacked a Western-style education) by younger, Western-educated men who were more capable of carrying out government policy and more amenable to British control. In Buganda, too, the government began to interfere more actively in the kingdom's affairs in order to increase efficiency. The main result was that the people showed less respect to non-Bugandan chiefs, which caused some of the chiefs to resent the curtailment of their powers.

# WORLD WAR II AND ITS AFTERMATH

During World War II the protectorate faced the task of becoming as self-sufficient as it could. More important for Uganda was the attempt by the governor, Sir Charles Dundas, to reverse his predecessors' policy and to give more freedom to the factions striving for power in Buganda. The old policy was revived, however, after an outbreak of rioting in 1945. Also in that year the first Africans were nominated to the Legislative Council, and in succeeding years African representation steadily increased. An important step was taken in 1954 when the African council membership increased to 14 out of a total of 28 nonofficial members; the 14 were selected from districts thought to be more natural units of representation than the provinces that had previously existed. In 1955 a ministerial system was introduced, with 5 nonofficial African ministers out of a total of 11. The success of the council was undermined, however, by the erratic participation of Buganda, which viewed a central legislature as a threat to its autonomy. This feeling reinforced the resentment Bugandans harboured after Mutesa II had been deported in 1953 for refusing to cooperate with the protectorate government. He returned two years later as a constitutional ruler, but the rapprochement between Buganda and the protectorate government was lukewarm.

In the immediate postwar years the protectorate administration placed greater emphasis on economic and social development than on political advance. From 1952 the government rapidly expanded secondary education, while legislation was enacted and a loan fund established to encourage Africans to participate in trade. A relatively ambitious development program was greatly assisted by the high prices realized for cotton and coffee, and coffee overtook cotton as Uganda's most valuable export in 1957. In 1954 a large hydroelectric project was inaugurated at Owen Falls on the Nile near Jinja, and in 1962 a five-year development plan was announced.

## THE REPUBLIC OF UGANDA

In the late 1950s, as a few political parties emerged, the African population concentrated its attention on achieving self-government, with focus on the Legislative Council. The kingdom of Buganda intermittently pressed for independence from Uganda, which raised the question of the protectorate's future status. Discussions in London in 1961 led to full internal self-government in March 1962. Benedicto Kiwanuka, a Roman Catholic Ganda who was formerly chief minister, became the first prime minister, but in the elections in April 1962 he was displaced by Milton Obote, a Lango (Langi) who headed the Uganda Peoples Congress (UPC) party. At further discussions in London in June 1962, it was agreed that Buganda should receive a wide degree of autonomy within a federal relationship. Faced with the emergence of Obote's UPC, which claimed support throughout the country apart from Buganda, and of the Democratic Party (DP), which was based in Buganda and led by Kiwanuka, conservative Ganda leaders set up their own rival organization, Kabaka Yekka (KY), "King Alone."

## OBOTE'S FIRST PRESIDENCY

Uganda became independent on Oct. 9, 1962, although it was divided politically on a geographic as well as an ethnic basis. By accepting a constitution that conceded what amounted to federal status to Buganda, Obote contrived an unlikely alliance with the Ganda establishment. Together the UPC and KY were able to form a government with Obote as prime minister and with the DP in opposition. Obote agreed to replace the British governor-general by appointing Mutesa II as the country's first president in an attempt to unify the alliance further, but this move was unsuccessful. Although Obote was able to win over some of the members of the KY and even of the DP so that they joined the UPC, tension grew steadily between the *kabaka* on the one hand and the UPC on the other. The Ganda leaders particularly resented their inability to dominate a government composed mainly of members of other ethnic groups. There were also divisions within the UPC, because each member of parliament owed his election to local ethnic supporters rather than to his membership in a political party. Those supporters frequently put pressure on their representatives to redress what they saw as an imbalance in the distribution of the material benefits of independence.

Faced with this dissatisfaction among some of his followers and with increasingly overt hostility in Buganda, Obote arrested five of his ministers and suspended the constitution in 1966. Outraged, the Ganda leaders ordered him to remove his government from the kingdom. Obote responded by sending troops under the leadership of Col. Idi Amin to arrest the *kabaka*, who escaped to England, where he died in 1969. When Obote imposed a new republican constitution—appointing himself executive president, abolishing all the kingdoms, and dividing Buganda into administrative districts—he also lost the support of the peoples of southwestern Uganda. Internal friction subsequently grew in intensity, fostered by mutual suspicion between the rival groups, by assassination attempts against the president, and by the increasingly oppressive methods employed by the government to silence its critics.

At independence the export economy was flourishing without adversely affecting subsistence agriculture, and the economy continued to improve, largely because of the high demand and high prices for coffee. To answer accusations that the profits from exports did not benefit the producers enough, Obote attempted in 1969 to distribute the benefits from the prospering economy more

widely. To this end he published a "common man's charter," which focused on removing the last vestiges of feudalism by having the government take a majority holding in the shares of the larger, mainly foreign-owned companies. In order to unite the country more firmly, he also produced a plan for a new electoral system in 1970 that would require successful candidates for parliament to secure votes in constituencies outside their home districts.

These proposals met with a cynical response in some quarters, but the government was overthrown before they could be put into effect. Obote had relied heavily on the loyalty of Idi Amin, but Amin had been building support for himself within the army by recruiting from his own Kakwa ethnic group in the northwest. The army, which had previously been composed of Acholi and their neighbours, Obote's own Lango people, now became sharply divided. Simultaneously, a rift developed between Obote and Amin, and in January 1971 Amin took advantage of the president's absence from the country to seize power.

## TYRANNY UNDER AMIN

Idi Amin's coup was widely welcomed, as there was hope that the country would finally be unified. Several Western nations, including Britain, who feared the spread of communism, were also relieved at Obote's overthrow: they had become suspicious that his policies were moving to the left. Amin promised a return

## IDI AMIN

(b. 1924/25, Koboko, Uganda—d. Aug. 16, 2003, Jiddah, Saudi Arabia)

*Idi Amin Dada Oumee was a military officer and president (1971–79) of Uganda. His regime was noted for its brutality.*

*A member of the small Kakwa ethnic group of northwestern Uganda, Amin had little formal education and joined the King's African Rifles of the British colonial army in 1946 as an assistant cook. He quickly rose through the ranks, serving in the Allied forces' Burma (Myanmar) campaign during World War II and in the British action against the Mau Mau revolt in Kenya (1952–56). Amin was one of the few Ugandan soldiers elevated to officer rank before Ugandan independence in 1962, and he became closely associated with the new nation's prime minister and president, Milton Obote. He was made chief of the army and air force (1966–70). Conflict with Obote arose, however, and on Jan. 25, 1971, Amin staged a successful military coup. He became president and chief of the armed forces in 1971, field marshal in 1975, and life president in 1976.*

*Amin ruled directly, shunning the delegation of power. He was noted for his abrupt changes of mood, from buffoonery to shrewdness, from gentleness to tyranny. He came to be known as the "Butcher of Uganda" for his brutality, and it is believed that some 300,000 people were killed and countless others tortured during his presidency.*

*Amin's downfall was initiated in October 1978, when he ordered an attack on Tanzania. Aided by Ugandan nationalists, Tanzanian troops eventually overpowered the Ugandan army. As the Tanzanian-led forces neared Kampala, on April 13, 1979, Amin fled the city. Escaping first to Libya, he finally settled in Saudi Arabia.*

to civilian government in five years, but problems with his leadership were soon apparent. Amin had little Western-style education and virtually no officer training, so he often resorted to arbitrary violence in order to maintain his position. In one incident, he destroyed the one potential centre of effective opposition by a wholesale slaughter of senior army officers loyal to Obote.

To win more general support among the Ugandan population, Amin ordered all Asians who had not taken Ugandan nationality to leave the country in 1972. His move won considerable approval in the country because many Africans believed that they had been exploited by the Asians, who controlled the middle and some of the higher levels of the economy, but the action isolated Uganda from the rest of the world community. Although a few wealthy Ugandans profited from Amin's actions, the majority of the commercial enterprises formerly owned by Asians were given to senior army officers who rapidly squandered

*Idi Amin's coup was welcomed with high hopes for unification, but his rule is infamous for its cruelty.* Hulton Archive/Getty Images

the proceeds and then allowed the businesses to collapse.

Most people in the countryside were able to survive the total breakdown of the economy that followed in the mid- and late 1970s because the fertility of Uganda's soil allowed them to continue growing food. In the towns an all-pervading black market developed, and dishonesty became the only means of survival. This economic and moral collapse stirred up criticism of the government, and during this period the country experienced several serious coup attempts.

In an attempt to divert attention from Uganda's internal problems, Amin launched an attack on Tanzania in October 1978. Tanzanian troops, assisted by armed Ugandan exiles, quickly put Amin's demoralized army to flight and invaded Uganda. With these troops closing in, Amin escaped the capital. A coalition government of former exiles, calling itself the Uganda National Liberation Front (UNLF), with a former leading figure in the DP, Yusufu Lule, as president, took office in April 1979. Because of disagreement over economic strategy and the fear that Lule was promoting the interests of his own Ganda people, he was replaced in June by Godfrey Binaisa, but Binaisa's term of office was also short-lived. Supporters of Obote plotted Binaisa's overthrow, and Obote returned to Uganda in May 1980.

## OBOTE'S SECOND PRESIDENCY

In December 1980 Obote's party, the UPC, won a majority in the highly controversial elections for parliament. The DP leadership reluctantly agreed to act as a constitutional opposition, but Yoweri Museveni, who had played a significant part in the military overthrow of Amin, refused to accept the UPC victory. He formed a guerrilla group in the bush near Kampala and waged an increasingly effective campaign against the government.

With the support of the International Monetary Fund and other external donors, Obote tried hard to rebuild the economy. Initially his efforts seemed successful, but the extraordinary inflation rate resulting from an entrenched black market system worked against him. It was impossible for urban wage earners to keep pace with rising prices, and salaried civil servants grew frustrated at the government's inability to increase their pay in line with their needs. In addition, the guerrilla war drew strength from the fact that it was based in Buganda, among people already suspicious of Obote. That strength grew as an ill-paid, ill-disciplined, and vengeful army, consisting largely of Acholi and Lango, ravaged the countryside for loot and took vengeance on their longtime Ganda enemies.

## MUSEVENI IN OFFICE

A split within the army itself—in particular, between its Acholi and Lango members—led to Obote's overthrow and exile in 1985 and to the seizure of power by an Acholi general, Tito Okello. This, however, could not prevent a victory for

Museveni's force of southern fighters, who now called themselves the National Resistance Army (NRA), and Museveni became president on Jan. 29, 1986. While a new constitution was being drafted, an indirectly elected National Resistance Council, dominated by the National Resistance Movement, acted as the national legislature.

Faced with the same problems that had confronted the UNLF in 1979 and Obote in 1980, Museveni announced a policy of moral as well as economic reconstruction, although it was not easy to enforce. Sporadic military resistance to the new government continued, particularly in the north and east. Arms were plentiful, and dissatisfied persons were willing to use them to promote their ends. The NRA, despite the president's injunctions, sometimes proved as heavy-handed in dealing with opponents as Obote's forces had been.

Security did improve, however, at least in most of central, southern, and western Uganda, and observers claimed that human rights were more widely protected. A constitutional amendment in 1993 led to the restoration of the monarchies, and the Ganda, Toro, Bunyoro, and Soga crowned their traditional rulers. The new constitution was promulgated in 1995, and presidential elections were held in May 1996. Museveni easily won the majority of votes. He was reelected in 2001 and 2006, although the 2006 contest was clouded by allegations that Kizza Besigye, the leader of the opposition group Forum for Democratic Change, was imprisoned in the months leading up to the presidential election to stop him from participating. Besigye was ultimately released in January 2006 and able to stand for election in February. Although he lost, he garnered almost two-fifths of the vote. Meanwhile, in the late 1990s Uganda faced international criticism over its involvement in the Democratic Republic of the Congo's civil war. After many attempts at resolution, the last of the Ugandan troops withdrew from the Democratic Republic of the Congo in 2003. In December 2005 the International Court of Justice determined that Uganda was guilty of unlawful military intervention in the Democratic Republic of the Congo and that Uganda's military violated international human rights law and international humanitarian law and exploited the country's natural resources. The court ruled that Uganda owed reparations to the country.

During the 1990s and continuing into the 2000s, Uganda was faced with an increase in rebel activity, particularly from the Lord's Resistance Army (LRA). Established in the late 1980s, the LRA abducted tens of thousands of children to serve as slaves or soldiers in its fight against Museveni's government. Its vicious attacks on civilians in the northern part of the country—including rape, murder, and acts of mutilation, such as cutting off the ears, noses, lips, and limbs of their victims—terrorized and displaced more than one million Ugandans, creating a humanitarian crisis in the early 2000s. After years of refusal, the LRA agreed to meet with government officials for peace talks in late December 2004. However, the talks broke down in early 2005, and the LRA resumed their brutal attacks on civilians. Peace talks resumed in July 2006, and although a cease-fire agreement was reached in late August, talks again broke down, and negotiations to end the decades-old conflict continued intermittently. In late 2007 there was some concern that the quest for peace might be hindered by a rift between Joseph Kony, the leader of the LRA, and some of the group's high-ranking leadership. Another concern was that some of the northern communities that had been terrorized by the LRA would refuse to accept any type of reconciliation agreement with the group.

Although the country's continued economic growth was praised by the West, inflation and unemployment continued to be problems, especially given Uganda's dependence on fluctuating markets for its agricultural produce. In an effort to enhance economic activity in the region, Uganda, Tanzania, and Kenya launched the East African Community Customs Union on Jan. 1, 2005. In 2009 Uganda signed an agreement providing for the free movement of people and goods across the East African Community, which by this time also included Burundi and Rwanda.

# CONCLUSION

Evidence indicates that Central and eastern Africa have been inhabited since prehistoric time. Therefore, it is not surprising that the histories of both regions have seen much change and development.

The oldest population of Central Africa is known almost exclusively from the evidence of its tools, while the populations of the last 10,000 years or so are known for spurring the development of the societies that are familiar in modern times. These societies arose from a blend of old populations well suited to surviving in their environment and new immigrants with different sets of skills to share. Prior to the beginning of European colonial intrusion, Central Africa was home to several strong states, such as the Luba empire and the kingdoms of Kongo and Kuba. Eventually, the Central African states fell to each other or collapsed under the pressure from colonial powers.

Human history in East Africa dates back millions of years, evident in the fossilized remains of hominids that have been discovered in the region. Since that time, humans developed and evolved. The history of the Horn of Africa has largely been dominated by Ethiopia—one of the world's oldest countries, its territorial extent having varied over the millennia of its existence—and has been characterized by struggles between Muslim and other herdsmen and Christian farmers for resources and living space. East Africa has seen centuries of interaction among indigenous African groups, Arabs, and Europeans. Arab influence was most prevalent along the East African coast and on the island of Zanzibar and is still evident today in the Swahili culture prominent in the region. African kingdoms such as Bunyoro and Buganda flourished prior to being absorbed into European colonial administration in the late 19th century.

Eastern and Central Africa are home to hundreds of various ethnic groups. As with other regions in Africa, most of the modern countries in Central and eastern Africa were not determined by logical ethnic groupings but were a reflection of arbitrary administrative divisions developed during the colonial era. Notable exceptions include Ethiopia, Burundi, and Rwanda. These factors have contributed to both the conflict that has occurred within individual countries and that which has spilled across borders.

In the postcolonial era, both regions have had their share of economic troubles and conflict across ethnic, religious, and political lines, much of which continues today. Nonetheless, several of the countries in Central and eastern Africa have demonstrated their ability to emerge from conflict and crisis to move forward, providing hope for the future.

# GLOSSARY

**accord** A formal reaching of agreement.

**alluvial** Relating to soil or sediments that are deposited by running water.

**authoritarian** Of, relating to, or favouring a concentration of power in a leader not constitutionally responsible to the people.

**Bantu languages** Group of some 500 languages belonging to the Bantoid subgroup of the Benue-Congo branch of the Niger-Congo language family.

**cassava** Also known as manioc, a tuberous edible perennial plant (Manihot esculenta) of the spurge family, from the New World tropics.

**copal** A recent or fossil resin from various tropical trees.

**coup (in full, coup d'état)** Sudden overthrow, often violent, of an existing government by a group of conspirators.

**democracy** Form of government in which supreme power is vested in the people and exercised by them directly or indirectly through a system of representation usually involving periodic free elections.

**entrepôt** An intermediary centre of trade and transshipment.

**exile** A state or period of forced or voluntary absence from one's country or home.

**feudalism** Any of various political or social systems similar to medieval feudalism, that is, having as its basis the relationship between a dominant power over subordinates.

**genocide** Deliberate and systematic destruction of a religious, political, or ethnic group.

**haven** A place of safety; refuge.

**hegemony** Dominance of one group over another.

**holy war** Any war fought by divine command or for a primarily religious purpose.

**hominin** Any member of the zoological "tribe" Hominini (family Hominidae, order Primates), of which only one species exists today—Homo sapiens, or human beings.

**ingot** Mass of metal cast into a size and shape such as a bar, plate, or sheet convenient to store, transport, and work into a semifinished or finished product.

**lingua franca** Language used for communication between two or more groups that have different native languages.

**littoral** A coastal region.

**monsoon** Major wind system that seasonally reverses its direction (e.g., one that blows for six months from the northeast and six months from the southwest).

**pagan** Traditional designation of a practitioner of classical polytheisms.

**pandemic** Occurring over a wide geographic area and affecting an exceptionally high proportion of the population.

**promulgate** To declare; to set forth publicly.

**proxy** An authorized substitute.

**referendum** The practice of submitting to popular vote a measure passed on or proposed by a legislative body or by popular initiative.

**refugee** Person involuntarily displaced from his or her homeland.

**sack** To plunder (as a town), especially after capture, or to strip of valuables.

**secede** To withdraw from an organization (as a religious communion or political party or federation).

**sisal** Plant (Agave sisalana) of the agave family and the fibre from its leaves.

**vegeculture** Plant cultivation replicated by vegetative reproduction; largely tropical roots.

# BIBLIOGRAPHY

## CENTRAL AFRICA

David Birmingham and Phyllis M. Martin, *History of Central Africa* (1983, reprinted 1994), provide a comprehensive overview of the region's history from prehistoric time into the colonial era. Sidney Langford Hinde, *The Fall of the Congo Arabs* (1897, reprinted 2008), offers an eyewitness account of the colonial conquest of eastern Democratic Republic of the Congo in the 1890s. Adam Hochschild, *King Leopold's Ghost: A Story of Greed, Terror, and Heroism in Colonial Africa* (1998), discusses the exploitation of African labour in what became the Belgian Congo. Thomas Pakenham, *The Scramble for Africa: White Man's Conquest of the Dark Continent from 1876 to 1912* (2003), examines European expansion on the continent of Africa. Patrick Manning, *Francophone Sub-Saharan Africa, 1880–1995* 2nd ed (1998), discusses the colonization and then decolonization of parts of Central Africa. David Birmingham and Phyllis M. Martin (eds.), *History of Central Africa: The Contemporary Years Since 1960* (1998), examines countries in the region to elucidate their postcolonial experience. Tamara Giles-Vernick, *Cutting the Vines of the Past: Environmental Histories of the Central African Rain Forest* (2002), focuses on the differing views that Africans and Europeans have of Africa's environment. Of the many books on the genocide in Rwanda and Burundi, two of the best are Gérard Prunier, *The Rwanda Crisis: History of a Genocide*, expanded (1998); and René Lemarchand, *Burundi: Ethnic Conflict and Genocide* (1996). Europa Regional Surveys of the World, *Africa South of the Sahara* (annual), is a useful source that contains historical overviews of each Central African country and updated essays on political, social, and economic developments.

## EASTERN AFRICA

A useful single-volume survey of the history of East Africa is Robert M. Maxon, *East Africa: An Introductory History*, 3rd ed. (2009). Roland A. Oliver et al. (eds.), *History of East Africa*, 3 vol. (1963–76), still constitutes the most ambitious account so far. Mark Horton and John Middleton, *The Swahili: The Social Landscape of a Mercantile Society* (2000) is a very full study on that topic. Frederick Cooper, *Plantation Slavery on the East Coast of Africa* (1977, reprinted 2002), provides an excellent socioeconomic study of Zanzibar and Kenya in the 19th century.

One of the first books to deal with the history of the Horn of Africa is John Markakis, *National and Class Conflict in the Horn of Africa* (1987). Also useful is Leenco Lata, *The Horn of Africa as Common Homeland: The*

State and Self-Determination in the Era of Heightened Globalization (2004). With a limited historiography, the history of the entire Horn must also be examined through such works devoted to Somalia and Ethiopia as Harold G. Marcus, A History of Ethiopia, rev. ed. (2002), a general history of Ethiopia from Australopithecus afarensis to 21st century; and I.M. Lewis, A Modern History of the Somali: Nation and State in the Horn of Africa, 4th ed. (2002), a comprehensive treatment of the political history of affairs in all the Somali territories.

Historical overviews of each eastern African country and updated essays on political, social, and economic developments can be found in Europa Regional Surveys of the World, Africa South of the Sahara (annual).

# INDEX